Dervla Murphy was born in Ireland in 1931, to a family involved in the Irish Republican movement. She was educated at the Ursuline Convent in Waterford until she was fourteen, when she left to keep house for her father and to nurse her mother who had been invalided by arthritis. Dervla did this for sixteen years with occasional breaks bicycling across Europe. Her mother's death left her free to go farther afield and in 1963 she cycled to India. Here she worked with Tibetan refugee children before returning home after a year to write her first two books. Dervla's first book, *Full Tilt: Ireland to India with a Bicycle*, was published in 1965. Over twenty other titles have followed. Dervla has won worldwide praise for her writing and has been described as a 'travel legend' and 'the first lady of Irish cycling'. Now in her eighties, she continues to travel around the world and remains passionate about politics, conservation, bicycling and beer.

Praise for *Full Tilt*

'She avoided wolves (animal and human), floods, robbery, had three ribs broken in a brawl in an Afghan bus; waded across an ice torrent, hugging a cow...suffered extremes of heat and cold, ate everything, liked almost everybody.'

—*Homes and Gardens*

'This vivid journal...would have delighted Cervantes with its almost incredible surprises: a valley full of birds the size of butterflies and butterflies as big as robins; a village where the cattle eat apricots and the villagers eat clover... Somewhere between Kabul and Jalalabad, she thought she was dreaming when she awoke from a roadside nap to find that nomads had raised a tent over her to shield her from the sun.'

—*The New Yorker*

'I don't know when I've enjoyed the account of a journey more. A great part of the enchantment of her book is that it is so good humoured and so funny. I laughed...and learned a good deal...one follows her with pleasure...a brave, intelligent, rare and amusing human being.'

—Margaret Lane

'A journey fraught with incalculable hardships and perils. It is unexpected, but then everything Dervla Murphy does is unexpected...an enchantment that holds the reader as engrossed as would an exciting thriller.'

—*Irish Independent*

'Warmly described, and with a lack of self-regard that immediately endears her to the reader.'

—*Sunday Times*

'Punctures, broken ribs, hornets and scorpions notwithstanding, it was a high old time between Miss Murphy and her Islamic hosts... her book is sensible, warm-hearted, unfinicky.'

—*The Observer*

Full Tilt

Ireland to India with a Bicycle

DERVLA MURPHY

SPEAKING TIGER

SPEAKING TIGER BOOKS LLP
4281/4 Ansari Road, Daryaganj,
New Delhi - 110002, India

First published in England by John Murray (Publishers) Ltd 1965
Published by Eland Publishing Limited 2010

First published in India in paperback by Speaking Tiger 2018

ISBN: 978-93-87693-16-6
eISBN: 978-93-87693-17-3

For sale in South Asia only

10 9 8 7 6 5 4 3

To the peoples of
Afghanistan and Pakistan,
with gratitude for their hospitality,
with admiration for their principles
and with affection for those who befriended me

Contents

Foreword

On my tenth birthday a bicycle and an atlas coincided as presents and a few days later I decided to cycle to India. I've never forgotten the exact spot on a hill near my home at Lismore, County Waterford, where the decision was made and it seemed to me then, as it still seems to me now, a logical decision, based on the discoveries that cycling was a most satisfactory method of transport and that (excluding the USSR for political reasons) the way to India offered fewer watery obstacles than any other destination at a similar distance.

However, I was a cunning child so I kept my ambition to myself, thus avoiding the tolerant amusement it would have provoked among my elders. I did not want to be soothingly assured that this was a passing whim because I was quite confident that one day I *would* cycle to India.

That was at the beginning of December 1941, and on 14 January 1963, I started to cycle from Dunkirk towards Delhi.

The preparations had been simple; one of the advantages of cycling is that it automatically prevents a journey from becoming an Expedition. I already possessed an admirable Armstrong Cadet man's bicycle named Rozinante, but always known as 'Roz'. By a coincidence I had bought her on 14 January 1961, so our journey started on her second birthday. This was ideal; we were by then a happy team, having already covered thousands of miles together, yet she was young enough to be dependable. The only preparation Roz needed was the removal of her three-speed derailleur gear, which I reckoned would be too sensitive to survive Asian roads. Apart from the normal accessories – saddle-bag, bell, lamp and pump – she carried only pannier-bag holders on either side of the back wheel. Unloaded she weighs thirty-seven pounds and at the start of the journey she was taking twenty-eight pounds of kit while I carried another six pounds in a small knapsack. (A list of kit is given on page 231.) Before leaving Ireland, four spare tyres had been posted ahead to various British Embassies, Consulates and High Commissions en route; Roz takes 27½" x 1¼" tyres, which are not a standard measurement abroad.

In London, at the end of November 1962, I obtained without difficulty visas for Yugoslavia and Bulgaria; I planned to get my visas for Persia in Istanbul and for Afghanistan in Teheran. During the same visit to London I endured vaccinations and inoculations for smallpox, cholera, typhoid and yellow-fever – the latter in case I decided to return from India via Africa.

Most of the following month was spent bending over maps bought through the AA in Dublin, working out the distances between towns which had intoxicatingly improbable names. I calculated that it was 4,445 miles from Dunkirk to Peshawar, and by New Year's Eve I could have told you without hesitation where I planned to be on any given date between 14 January and 14 May, when I hoped to arrive in Peshawar. The object of this exercise was to ensure that my mail – sent care of the British Council offices en route – would not miss me; nor did it, despite many inevitable changes in my original plans.

In the intervals between mapping I took myself off to remote areas in the mountains around Lismore and practised firing and reloading my ·25, the purchase of which had recently been achieved with the full and rather awe-struck co-operation of the local police. My friends regarded this purchase as so much adolescent melodrama on my part but fortunately I ignored their criticisms and stuck to my gun, though its presence in the right-hand pocket of my slacks – where I habitually carried it to accustom myself to the presence of a loaded weapon – frightened me considerably more than it did anyone else. Yet within a month of leaving home the seemingly childish game of whipping it out of my pocket and flicking up the safety catch was fully justified.

I arrived in Delhi on 18 July 1963, almost six months after leaving Ireland. People with mathematical brains are always anxious to know exactly how many miles I had cycled by then and what my daily average was. Unfortunately gadgets for measuring mileage do not function on Asian roads, so I can only estimate vaguely that Roz and I covered about three thousand miles, including our detours to Murree and Gilgit. From this the mathematically inclined can easily calculate our average daily mileage, but their findings would be slightly misleading, because there were so many days when we did not cover even a mile together. Our shortest run was, I think, nineteen miles, and our longest 118 miles, but I reckon that our average on a normal cycling day was between seventy and eighty miles.

This is perhaps the moment to contradict the popular fallacy that a solitary woman who undertakes this sort of journey must be 'very courageous'. Epictetus put it in a nutshell when he said, 'For it is not death or hardship that is a fearful thing, but the fear of death and hardship.' And because in general the possibility of physical danger does not frighten me, courage is not required; when a man tries to rob or assault me or when I find myself, as darkness is falling, utterly exhausted and waist-deep in snow halfway up a mountain pass, then I *am* afraid – but in such circumstances it is the instinct of self-preservation, rather than courage, that takes over.

For the first two months of the trip I struggled hard to keep my four closest friends informed of my progress through letters but the effort was too much; so from Teheran onwards I adopted the diary-keeping method used by most travellers and sent instalments home whenever a reliable-looking post office appeared en route. My friends circulated these instalments amongst themselves, the last on the circuit line storing the manuscript away for future reference. This book is the 'Future Reference'.

Apart from burnishing the spelling and syntax, which are apt to suffer when one makes nightly entries whether half asleep or not, I have left the diary virtually unchanged. A few very personal or very topical comments or allusions have been excised, but the temptation to make myself sound more learned than I am, by gleaning facts and figures from an encyclopaedia and inserting them in appropriate places, has been resisted. For this reason the narrative which follows will be seen to suffer from statistic-deficiency; it only contains such information as any traveller might happen to pick up from day to day along my route.

After arriving in Delhi I worked for six months with the Tibetan refugees in northern India and then enjoyed a few more treks with Roz in the Himalayas and in south-west Nepal, before submitting to the degradation of flying home on 23 February 1964, with a dismantled Roz by my side as 'personal effects'.

My thanks go in many directions: to the British and American consular officials in those countries where Ireland is not diplomatically represented, who adopted and cared for me as though I were their own; to the scores of individuals and families in every country on my route whose boundless hospitality taught me that for all the horrible chaos of the contemporary political scene this world is full of kindness; to the chance friends I made in odd places, whose names I never knew or have forgotten but whose companionship made a sometimes lonely journey much more pleasant; and last, but certainly not least, to Daphne Pearce, who suggested the title and gave invaluable help in editing the manuscript; to Patricia Truell, who compiled the index and guided me through the ordeal of correcting my first proofs; and to my other friends in Ireland, who loyally and patiently read over 200,000 words in an execrable hand and whose interest in my experiences was both the inspiration and the reward of keeping this diary.

For my part I travel not to go anywhere, but to go. I travel for travel's sake. The great affair is to move, to feel the needs and hitches of our life more nearly, to come down off the feather-bed of civilization and find the globe granite underfoot and strewn with cutting flints.

ROBERT LOUIS STEVENSON

FRO
OSLO
DUBLIN
Lismore
LONDON
Dunkirk
BERLIN
WARSAW
MOSCOW
PARIS
PRAGUE
VIENNA
Budapest
Grenoble
Turin
Venice
Ljubljana
Nova Gorizia
Zagreb
BUCHAREST
BELGRADE
Cuprija
Pirot
SOFIA
LISBON
ROME
CAIRO
SCALE
0
250
500
750
1000 Miles
0
400
800
1200
1600 Kilometres

IRELAND TO INDIA
Gilgit
Rawalpindi
Peshawar
Lahore
Sirhind
DELHI
Bulola
KABUL
Ghazni
Meshed
Nishapur
Herat
Kalat-i-Gilzai
Sabzevar
Ghurion
Khandahar
Shahrud
Dogubayzit
Tabriz
Ardebil
TEHERAN
Deh-Namak
BAGHDAD
DAMASCUS
AMMAN

Scale
0 50 100 150 Miles
0 50 100 150 200 Kilometres
International boundaries
Roads
Mazar-i-Sharif
Pul-i-Khumri
Doshi
Doab
Bamian
Bulola
Herat
AFGHANISTAN
Ghazni
Mukur
Kalat-i-Ghilzai
Khandahar

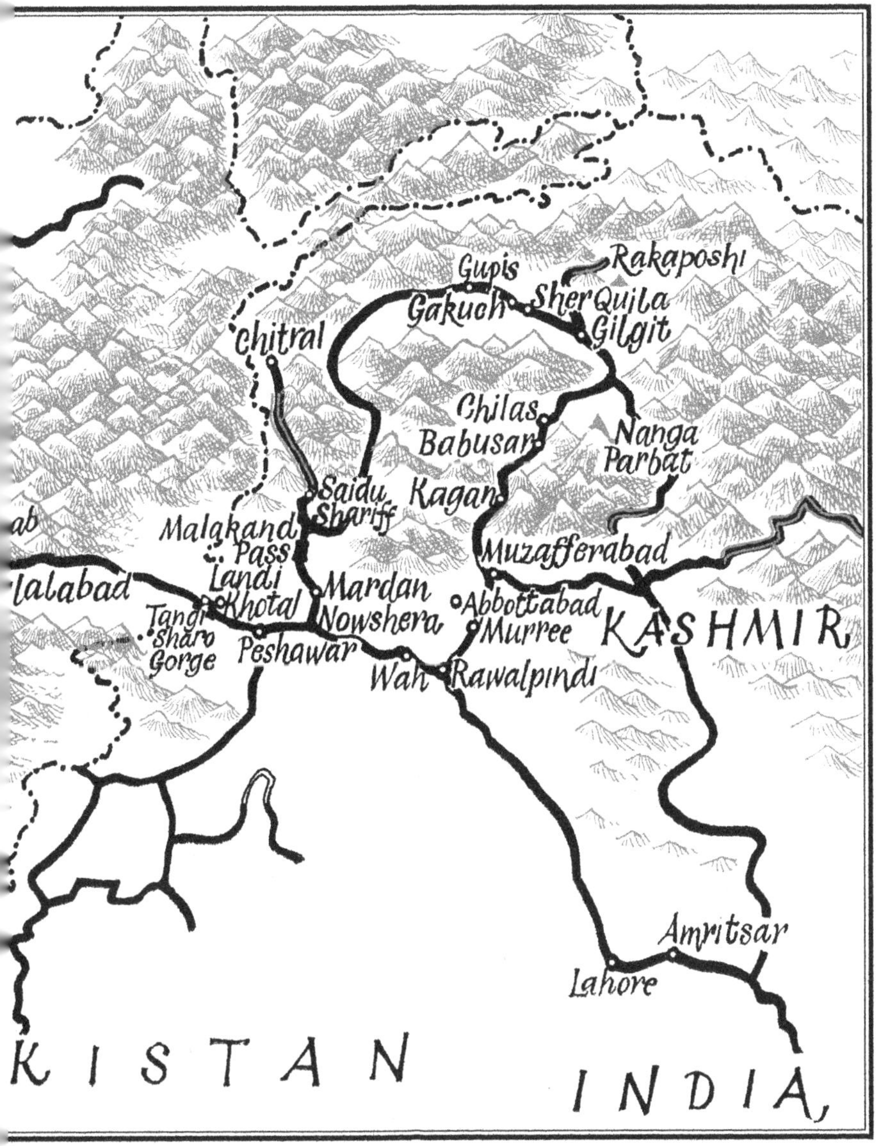
Rakaposhi
Gupis
Gakuch
Sher Quila
Gilgit
Chitral
Chilas
Babusar
Nanga Parbat
Saidu Shariff
Kagan
Malakand Pass
Muzaffarabad
Landi Khotal
Mardan
Nowshera
Abbottabad
Murree
KASHMIR
Tangi Sharo Gorge
Peshawar
Wah
Rawalpindi
Amritsar
Lahore
KISTAN
INDIA

Introduction to the Journey

DUNKIRK TO TEHERAN

I had planned a route to India through France, Italy, Yugoslavia, Bulgaria, Turkey, Persia, Afghanistan and Pakistan. Departure Day was to have been 7 January 1963, but by then the freak weather of that year had reached even Ireland and I postponed 'D-Day' for a week, innocently supposing that these conditions 'could not go on'. But of course they did go on, and in my impatience to be off I decided that to postpone departure from week to week would not be practical – though in retrospect I realised that it would have been a lot more practical than heading for Central Europe during the coldest winter in eighty years.

I shall never forget that dark ice-bound morning when I began to cycle east from Dunkirk; to have the fulfilment of a twenty-one-year-old ambition apparently within one's grasp can be quite disconcerting. This was a moment I had thought about so often that when I actually found myself living through it I felt as though some favourite scene from a novel had come, incredibly, to life. However, within a few weeks my journey had degenerated from a happy-go-lucky cycle trek to a grim struggle for progress by *any* means along roads long lost beneath snow and ice.

At first my disappointment was acute, but I had set out to enjoy myself by seeing the world, not to make or break any record, so I soon became adjusted to these conditions, which led to quite a few interesting adventures. Also, I was aware of 'seeing the world' in circumstances unique to my generation. Should I survive to the end of this century it will be impressive to recall that I crossed the breadth of Europe in the winter of 1963, when every humdrum detail of daily life was made tensely dramatic by the weather and going shopping became a scaled-down Expedition to the Antarctic. It was neat hell at the time – I cycled up to the Rouen Youth Hostel with a quarter-inch icicle firmly attached to my nose and more than once the agony of frozen fingers made me weep rather uncharacteristically – yet it seemed a reasonably good exchange for the satisfaction of cycling all the way to India.

I give full marks to Italy for the superb efficiency with which her main northern roads were kept clear during that January. Having been compelled to take a train from Grenoble to Turin, across the Alps, I found myself able to cycle, and enjoy it, almost all the way to Nova Gorizia, through a deserted and impeccably beautiful Venice.

At this bisected frontier town of Nova Gorizia the formalities for being admitted into Yugoslavia seemed diabolically complicated. Repeatedly I was shuttled back and forth through the darkness from Police to Customs Officers; then, while innumerable forms were being completed in triplicate, I stood shivering outside warm offices, trying to explain why I was so improbably entering Yugoslavia with a bicycle on 28 January. And every time I took off a glove to sign yet another document the bitter wind seared my hand like caustic acid.

Suddenly a policeman shouted to someone in another room and a tall, rugged-featured woman, wearing Customs Officer's uniform, appeared beside me. I stared at her in horror, only then remembering that my automatic lay in the right-hand pocket of my slacks, where the most casual search would at once detect a sinister hard object. In the stress and strain of searching Gorizia for the open frontier post (there were four in all, but three were closed to tourists) I had quite forgotten my ingenious scheme for concealing the weapon. So now I foresaw myself being hurled into the nearest dungeon, from which I would eventually emerge, emaciated and broken in spirit, after years of negotiations between two governments who are not, diplomatically, on speaking terms. But alarm was unnecessary. The formidable female took one quick look at my intricately laden bicycle, my knapsack with its protruding loaf of bread and my scruffy self. Then she burst into good-humoured laughter – of which one would not have believed her capable – slapped me on the back and waved me towards the frontier. It was 6.15 p.m. when I passed under the railway bridge with 'Jugoslavija' painted across it in huge letters.

Two miles from the frontier, having cycled along an unlighted road that leads away from Italy and then curves back, I came to Nova Gorica, the Yugoslav half of the town. Here, beneath the weak glow of a street lamp, a solitary figure was walking ahead of me. Overtaking it I saw a good-looking girl who, in reply to my questions, said, 'Yes' she spoke German, but 'No' there wasn't a cheap inn available, only the Tourist Hotel, which was very expensive. Even in the dim light my look of dismay must have been apparent, because she immediately added an invitation to come home with her for the night. As this was within my first hour of entering Slovenia I was astonished; but soon I learnt that such kindness is common form in that region.

While we walked between high blocks of workers' flats, Romana told me that she shared a room with two other typists employed in a local factory at £3 per week, but as one was away in hospital there would be plenty of space for me.

The little room, at the top of three flights of stairs, was clean and adequately furnished, though the only means of cooking was an electric ring, and the bathroom and lavatory were shared with three families living, in one room each, on the same floor. Arita, Romana's room-mate, gave me a most enthusiastic welcome and we settled down to a meal of very curious soup, concocted out of some anaemic meat broth, in which lightly whipped eggs were cooked, followed by my bread and cheese (imported from Italy) and coffee (imported from Ireland).

I found these youngsters delightful company – vivacious, perfectly mannered and intelligent. They were simply dressed and it was pleasant to see their clear-skinned faces, innocent of any make-up, and their well-groomed heads of unpermed sanely-cut hair. I noted too the impressive row of books in the little shelf by the stove – among them translations of *Dubliners, The Heart of the Matter, The Coiners, Black and Red* and *The Leopard.*

Anticipating a tough mountain ride on the following day I was relieved to find that 9.30 p.m. was bedtime, as these girls rise at 5.30 a.m. to catch the factory bus and be at work by seven o'clock.

It was a deceptively fine morning when I left Nova Gorica. The second-class but well-kept road to Ljubljana wound through a range of fissured mountains, whose lower slopes were studded with tiny villages of brown-roofed, ramshackle farmhouses, and whose upper slopes, of perpendicular bare rock, gave the valley an odd appearance, as though it had been artificially walled in from the rest of the world. Then, towards midday, as I was revelling in the still, crisp air and brilliant sunshine, a violent wind arose. Whether because of the peculiar configuration of the mountains here, or because it was one more manifestation of freakish weather, this wind blew with a force such as I had never previously encountered. Before I could adjust myself on the saddle to do battle with my new enemy it had lifted me right off Roz and deposited me on a heap of gravel by the wayside. None the worse, I remounted, but ten minutes later, despite my efforts to hold Roz on the road and myself on Roz, we were again separated, and this time I went rolling down a fifteen-foot sloping ditch, unable to get a grip on the icy bank to check my fall. I ended up on a stream which happily was frozen so solid that my impact produced not a crack in the ice. After crawling cautiously along the stream for some twenty yards, to find a way up to the road and Roz, I decided that from now on walking was the only logical means of progress.

At the valley's end my road started to climb the mountains, sweeping up and up and again up, in a series of hairpin bends that each revealed a view more wild and splendid than the last. At one such bend I was actually frightened by the power of the gale; I couldn't walk against it, and for some four or five minutes I simply stood, bent over Roz, my body braced with all its strength in the effort to hold us both on the road.

Near the top of the pass, seven miles from the valley floor, things were further complicated by the reappearance of my old enemies – packed snow and black ice underfoot. On the west side of this mountain range there had been strangely little snow (although everything that could freeze had frozen) but now, going over the pass, I was abruptly back to the too-familiar vision of a landscape completely white, each contour and angle rounded and disguised. Then yet another blizzard started, the flakes whirling round me like a host of malicious little white demons.

By now I was exhausted from the struggle uphill against the gale and the agony of frost-bitten hands and feet. My hands were too numb for me to consult the map, which in any case would probably have been ripped away by the wind or rendered illegible by the snow. Crawling along over the ice, I told myself that this was an advantage, because if no village was marked I would probably curl up by the wayside in despair.

In fact there was a tiny village, called Hrusevje, less than two miles ahead, and on arriving there I thanked my guardian angel, as I blundered about among piles of snow stacked four and five feet high on either side of the road, searching for something that looked like an inn. At last I saw two old men emerging from a doorway, wiping their moustaches with the backs of their hands. This looked hopeful, so I dragged Roz over a pile of snow, propped her against the wall, and entered the two-storeyed stone house.

Obviously the primary need was brandy, yet my face was so numb that I couldn't articulate one word. I merely pointed to the relevant bottle, and stood by the stove to thaw out, while a group of card-playing men stared at me with a trace of that hostility shown by all peasants in remote places to unexpected strangers. Then an old man came rushing in to inform the company that I had arrived with a bicycle – and, as I soon recovered the power of speech, friendly relations were easily established.

I now broached the subject of accommodation for the night and the landlady at once broke into excited discussions with her customers. In the middle of this the door opened again and a young woman entered. She was hailed with great relief all round, and turning to me introduced herself in English as a local social worker. She explained that tourists are not allowed to stay in any but Tourist Hotels – which meant yet another disruption of my plans, for I had intended, on crossing the frontier from expensive Italy, to settle down in some village such as Hrusevje and wait there, living cheaply, until weather conditions again permitted cycling.

However, *pace* Government regulations, it was obvious that this particular tourist could not now be accommodated anywhere but at the village inn. The next step was to contact the local policeman, so that he might give his blessing to the irregularity. This formality completed, I was shown up to my large room, which contained one small bed in a corner and nothing else whatever.

When I came down to eat some bread and cheese by the stove in the pub I found a young girl waiting for me – one who was to prove a true friend and who provided me with the most congenial companionship during the following days. A daughter of the local postman and postwoman, Irena was a student of psychology at Ljubljana University, and was now home for the winter vacation, that is to say, the month of January. She was due to return to Ljubljana on 31 January, and she advised me to wait at Hřusevje until then, as the road down to the plain would be impassable after such a blizzard. She added that she would smuggle me into her room at the University Students' Hostel, where one of the five beds was vacant, thus saving me the expense of the Tourist Hotel.

For the next two days my landlady mothered me so successfully that I settled down to write as happily as though I were in my own home. Indeed, I was enthusiastically adopted by the whole locality; the men reported my arrival to their womenfolk who paid a special call at the inn to shake me by the hand, slap me on the back, tell me that I was welcome to Slovenia, and, as often as not, invite me to come and stay in their homes indefinitely.

On the 31st Roz and I left for Ljubljana in a snow-chained truck and that drive was one of the worst frustrations of the expedition. The road swept down for thirty miles through magnificent mountains and valleys and pine forests, all glittering in the sunshine as though covered in diamond-dust, yet here was I being ignominiously transported by truck. However, I could not complain of having no time to admire my surroundings, for the ice was so treacherous that it took us three hours to cover forty-five miles.

The university hostel, converted from an old convent, was such a vast building that there was little difficulty in smuggling me to Irena's room. Personally I was of the opinion that the Authorities, who had given me a warm welcome when I arrived in search of Irena, were perfectly well aware of the situation and quite happy about it, but my room-mates were obviously enjoying the conspiracy so I entered into the spirit of the thing with as much enthusiasm as my more advanced years allowed.

On the following morning Roz and I left Irena and her companions in Ljubljana, equipped with a bundle of introductions from them to Slovenes living all along our route, but after cycling about twenty miles we were again forced to get a lift by truck to Zagreb.

After a stay of four days in Zagreb I arrived in Belgrade, following a nightmarish journey by truck over the 250 miles of frozen plain which stretched with relentless white anonymity from Zagreb to the capital. During our thirty-nine hours on the road we saw not one other vehicle – fortunately for me this truck was carrying some vital, mysterious military load – and the only traffic was an occasional pony-sleigh travelling between villages. Three times the engine broke down and once, in the middle of the night, repairs took so long that by the time we were ready to start again an impassable snowdrift had formed in front of us. But the two drivers and I agreed afterwards that this was a blessing, because by the time we had dug ourselves out with spades carried for the purpose we were almost warm.

Apart from these breakdowns we never stopped, so our average speed over the ridged surface of rock-hard snow was about eight miles per hour. I remember these two Serbs with a special affection, so gruelling were the hardships which we shared and so brave was the gaiety with which they faced them.

By now I felt that I had lost my rôle of 'traveller' and become no more than a demoralised fugitive from the weather and I retain only confused, unreal impressions of Zagreb and Belgrade.

However, on the morning of my third day in Belgrade, there came a rise in temperature that not merely eased the body but relaxed the nerves. Never shall I forget the joy of standing bareheaded in my host's front garden, watching tenuous, milky clouds drifting across the blue sky; only then did I appreciate the peculiar tension imposed by the savageness of the past weeks. Yet the thaw held its own dangers. That day thick, six-foot icicles came crashing from eaves to pavements, killing at least two pedestrians in Belgrade; the streets became uncontrollable torrents, as the ten-foot walls of dirty snow which lined them gradually dwindled.

On the following morning, with the optimism of impatience, I started to cycle towards Nîs; but it had frozen again during the night and though the cold was no longer intolerable I had to admit defeat by black ice once more.

Before midday a Montenegrin driver had taken Roz and me up ten miles outside Belgrade, but at dusk we were still trying, by one road or another, to reach Nîs. In despair my companion finally decided to try a détour via a third-class mountain road of which he knew nothing. So, as darkness gathered in the deep valleys, and spread upwards to cover the wooded mountains, we slowly ascended a twisting track, its ridged surface made all the more dangerous by the beginnings of the thaw. My companion had been driving all through the night from Zagreb, his mate having been taken ill there, so I felt the greatest sympathy for him, and I attribute our next misfortune to his extreme fatigue.

At one of the bends, before I could realise what was happening, the truck had skidded off the road and was leaning at a slight angle against a sturdy and very fortunately placed tree, which probably saved us from death at the foot of the precipice.

Having reassured each other that we had received no more than minor injuries, we got out the map, which told us that a village lay about two miles away through the forest on our left. It seemed unlikely that any other traffic would appear and my companion was obviously too exhausted, and too shaken by the crash, to undertake the walk himself, so I suggested that he should write a note for me to deliver to the village policeman, explaining the situation.

It was soon after 6 p.m. when, leaving Roz on the truck, I set off along a convenient cart-track through the trees, where the snow had been packed down by sleighs collecting fire-wood. It was some fifteen minutes later when a heavy weight hurled itself at me without warning.

I stumbled, dropping the torch that I had been carrying, then recovered my balance, and found one animal hanging by its teeth from the left shoulder of my wind-cheater, another worrying at the trousers around my right ankle, and a third standing about two yards away, looking on, only its eyes visible in the starlight.

Ironically enough, I had always thought that there was something faintly comical in the idea of being devoured by wolves. It had seemed to me the sort of thing that doesn't *really* happen . . . So now, as I braced my body against the hanging weight, slipped off my glove, pulled my ·25 out of my pocket, flicked up the safety-catch and shot the first animal through the skull, I was possessed by the curious conviction that none of this was true, while at the same time all my actions were governed by sheer panic.

At the sound of the report, and as the first animal dropped to the ground, the second one released my ankle and was about to make off when I fired at him. Meanwhile the third member of the pack (if three can be said to constitute a pack) had tactfully disappeared. Retrieving the torch, I found that one bullet had got the second animal in the ribs – a fantastic fluke shot. Both animals (some authorities think they may have been wild dogs) were males, hardly as big as the average Irish sheep-dog, with dreadfully emaciated bodies.

It was when I had left the scene that the reaction set in. Also, forgetting that there was another mile and a half between me and the village, I had lavishly, and quite unnecessarily, emptied my gun, so that every real or imaginary sound made me tremble with apprehension. Walking rapidly, I dwelt with morbid fascination on the part that luck had played in my escape, and the longer I thought about this the more terrified I became, until at last the conviction that I must have gone astray prompted me to take out my compass to confirm the fact that I was still going towards the village.

When I arrived there, the policeman and his wife were having their supper of cold garlic sausage and pickled cucumbers. While the policeman was driving by sleigh to the truck his wife bathed the scalp-wound I had suffered in the crash and gave me hot rum. I slept soundly that night; only during the following week did I start having nightmares about wolves . . .

The next morning was overcast and very much milder so, reunited with Roz, I set off at 8 a.m. to walk the twelve miles to the low-lying main road, where the thaw might be sufficiently advanced to permit cycling.

There was a strange feeling in the air that day. It was warm enough for me to leave my wind-cheater open as I pushed Roz uphill, yet there were no visible signs of the thaw at this height. All around me the mountains, valleys and forests lay white and lifeless under a low, grey sky, in the profound stillness of a landscape where no breeze stirred, there was neither house nor bird to be seen and the streams were silent under their covering of ice. I stopped often to look around me, and savour the uncanny sensation of being the only living, moving thing in the midst of this hushed desolation, where my own breathing sounded loud.

Then, on the other side of the pass, the spell was broken. Villages appeared, huddled improbably on the steep mountain-sides, and I joined a group of friendly peasants, sitting on their sleigh behind two ambling, cream-coloured oxen. One of the men spoke German, and told me that down on the plains flooding was already extensive.

At midday I reached the main road, but found the icy patches still too frequent for cycling, though the surface was streaming with water. So I thumbed the next truck, and was taken twenty-five miles to Svetozarevo.

Here, at last, I saw a road completely free of ice and snow. After weeks of using Roz as a hand-cart for pushing luggage my exhilaration at being able to cycle again made up for my lack of training and I sped joyously towards Nîs, too pleased with myself to heed the ominous fact that in every direction flood-waters covered the flat fields.

I did not speed for long. After five or six miles the road dipped slightly, and now the floods were right across it, some twelve inches deep, so that at each revolution of the pedals my feet were alternately submerged. As it would not have helped to dismount, I cycled slowly on, passing anxious-looking groups of people in bullock- and pony-carts, watching men in little boats punting over the fields to rescue families from farmhouses which had been suddenly isolated by the rapidly rising waters.

Leaving these scenes behind me I saw that the Morava River was now flowing on my left, parallel to and level with the road. From the near distance came a dull, booming sound, as soldiers blew up the gigantic accumulations of rock-hard snow which, unless artificially loosened, would have dammed the river and sent its overflow rushing through the nearby town of Cuprija.

It was awe-inspiring to see the wide, angry Morava swiftly sweeping its tremendous burden of ice and snow-chunks through the vast wilderness of sullen, brown flood-waters, and my awe was soon justified when a massive wave came crashing across the road, swept me off Roz and rolled me over and over, choking as I swallowed the muddy water and gasping as its iciness penetrated my clothes. Next a branch of a little roadside tree appeared above me and pulling myself up by it I found that the water, though still flowing strongly, was now no more than three feet deep. I looked for Roz and, during one appalling moment, thought that she had disappeared. Then I saw a yellow handlebar grip in a ditch, and hurried to rescue her. Fortunately my kit had been wrapped in waterproof coverings, to avoid the danger of melting snow seeping through the bags when we entered warm buildings at night, so most of it remained undamaged.

Cuprija was less than half a mile away, but as I was semi-paralysed by my sodden clothes, had to half-carry Roz to keep the pannier-bags clear of the water, and was in constant danger of being again swept off-balance by the strength of the current, this half-mile seemed one of the longest that I have ever travelled.

Reaching the safety of the bridge outside Cuprija I saw hundreds of people standing watching the threatening river in an atmosphere of tense excitement. My appearance proved almost too much for them in their already overwrought state and I was accorded a singularly undeserved Hero's Welcome, when I should have been presented with a Dunce's Cap.

At Pirot, fifteen miles north of Bulgaria, the mutual antagonism of Yugoslavia and her southern neighbour becomes irritatingly obvious. So contemptuous are the Yugoslavs of their Communist cousins that they simply ignore Sofia's existence, thereby failing to maintain the high standard of sign-posting found throughout the rest of the country. They have also, with what can only be malice aforethought, so efficiently neglected the road to the frontier town of Dimitrovgrad that its surface would deter any sane traveller from attempting to enter Bulgaria.

This road, part of one of the world's most important intercontinental highways, was marked first-class on my map. As I stood outside Pirot, looking from the map to the unglorified goat-track ahead of me, which I had been repeatedly assured by the locals really was the road to Sofia, I felt a sense of betrayal. However illustrious it might have been in past history, or might still be in theory, it should now be described by map-makers, in realistic terms, as a tenth-class track, negotiable only by those with no respect either for their persons or their mode of conveyance. Admittedly I cycled along it under very trying conditions, but in summer it would be just as bad.

All through the previous night it had been snowing – a fall of quickly melting snow, typical of this thawing period – and now the track was covered in slush, between deep broad craters brimful of yellow-brown water. At first I attempted to weave acrobatically around these miniature lakes, through the slush, but as they occupied at least seventy per cent of the surface area I soon decided to pedal on regardless, plunging and bouncing in and out of the water. It was 'cycling with a difference', as one never knew just how deep the next crater would be, and there was always the stimulating possibility that it would be deep enough to unseat one . . .

Pirot and Dimitrovgrad lie at opposite ends of an oval shaped, level valley some eight miles wide, and completely enclosed by low mountains with a sparse covering of trees on their stony slopes. Through the centre of this valley, which was now a dismal expanse of mud and water, runs the 'road' and the railway line connecting Europe and Asia. Apart from trains, of which there were a prodigious number, both passenger and goods (though the carriages and wagons were almost always empty), I saw no traffic whatever, a fact which could have been explained by the general wisdom of mankind, or by the flood which had swept away the wooden bridge over the Nisava about five miles from Dimitrovgrad.

At first I was appalled by this catastrophe. It had taken me two hours to cycle the ten miles from Pirot and there was nothing I wanted to do less than return there. Then I saw the concrete and steel railway bridge on my left and waded towards it through a flooded field. First I made sure that there were no trains coming (a precaution easily taken, as Yugoslav trains emit volcanic clouds of smoke, and are constantly whistling excited variations on an unidentifiable theme) before climbing with Roz on to the line, and crossing the bridge, to join the road again through a field three feet deep in water. By this time worrying about pneumonia seemed futile; for days I had been living in a state of permanent saturation from the waist down, so that the only sensible reaction was lots of rum and no fuss.

While cycling the two miles from Dimitrovgrad to the Bulgarian frontier my attention was equally divided between the odd things that craters in the road can do to one's lunch and the excitement of approaching for the first time the sinister Iron Curtain. At each bend I looked eagerly for tangled masses of barbed wire, watch-towers manned by vigilant soldiers armed with machine-guns and binoculars, and alert policemen keenly observing every movement for miles around. But not one of these thrilling phenomena appeared and it was only when I saw a locked, five-foot high gate across the road that I realised I had arrived at the significant point.

Looking around, I saw a neat little bungalow beside the road which, though it didn't actually say so, was obviously the Police-cum-Customs post. I knocked loudly on the open hall-door, got no reply, entered and knocked on each of the doors leading out of the hall, with no more success, and finally opened one of them, yelling and whistling hopefully; stamps on my passport are the only souvenirs that I can afford to collect, and I didn't want to be cheated of this one. Still nothing happened, and I stood in the doorway viewing the desk and reflecting that if I wanted to enter the spy business here was my chance to make away with a fine collection of vitally important seals. Finally I left the building, to investigate the possibilities of getting into Bulgaria unaided.

If one looked hard enough, a half-hearted barbed-wire fence was visible stretching away from the road in either direction, marking the frontier. It was so like the kind of ineffectual barrier that some Irish farmers put up to prevent their sheep from straying that I felt quite home-sick. I had no difficulty in dragging Roz through one of the many gaps made by the local peasants and then, returning to the main road, I entered the insignificant little house which is Bulgaria's Northern Frontier Fortress. Again my knock remained unanswered, but this time, when I opened a door leading out of the hall, I found a policeman happily dozing by the stove, with a cat and two kittens on his lap. I immediately diagnosed that he was a *nice* policeman, and when I had gently roused him, and he had recovered from the shock of being required to function officially, I had my diagnosis confirmed.

In December, the Bulgarian Embassy in London had issued me with a visa valid for only four days. Now this genial policeman, who spoke fluent English, took one look at the card, said that it was ridiculous, and issued me with a new visa entitling me to stay in Bulgaria as long as I wished! After which we sat by the stove and amiably discussed our two countries over glasses of brandy.

On leaving the Bulgarian frontier-post, I propped Roz against a tree and returned to Yugoslavia, in another attempt to obtain my souvenir passport-stamp. By now a pathetically bored-looking young man was sitting at the desk, listlessly attempting to solve a crossword puzzle. I explained how it was that my passport had received a Bulgarian entry stamp before it had had a Yugoslav exit one, and he said wearily that he had gone into Dimitrovgrad for a hot lunch. Obviously, at both frontier-posts, the attitude was that not even spies, much less tourists, would operate in the prevailing weather.

I had entered my first orthodox Communist country as a 'neutral' equally suspicious of both pro- and anti-Communist propaganda, but after a week in Bulgaria I left it as an admirer of the limited good that Communism can achieve within less than two decades.

Everywhere I was received with spontaneous friendliness and if any Secret Police had me under surveillance they were very discreet indeed. My movements remained completely unrestricted and I spent two nights as a guest in the households of a factory-worker and a collective farmer, where the standard of living was comparable with that of present-day Irish workers. On my last night I stayed at the home of a regional Party leader and was interested to observe that his standard of living was almost on a par with that of the ordinary workers. Nowhere did I see any evidence of extreme poverty and the average citizen – a cheerful, singularly unoppressed-looking individual – appeared to be adequately clothed, housed and fed.

Admittedly, this spectacular improvement in Bulgaria's standard of living has been gained at the cost of religious and intellectual freedom, though judging by some conversations I had with the younger generation it will not be long before the phoenix of the individual human spirit rises again from its ashes.

Personally I recoil at once from regimentation and I am far too reactionary to regard 'backward peasants' as being *ipso facto* in need of modernisation; yet in fairness I must give my personal impression of that side of the Communist coin which is not popular among Western propagandists.

I was able to cycle almost all the way from Cuprija to Istanbul, through Bulgaria and Turkey-in-Europe, but the Turkish highlands were still under snow so here again we became dependent on buses and trucks – when such vehicles could operate between blizzards. Mercifully the temperature was not quite as low as it had been in Europe, but the quantity of snow was far in excess of anything I had yet experienced; it was common to see fifty-foot high drifts, shaped so exquisitely by the wind that I still catch my breath at the memory.

En route to Erzurum our bus barely escaped being entombed in snow. We were stuck in a drift on a narrow mountain road and the gallant snowplough which had come to rescue us skidded over a precipice, killing both men on board. Another snowplough then set out from the opposite direction but its progress was understandably slow and meanwhile the blizzard began again. As we waited the snow piled higher and higher around us, its silent softness contrasting eerily with the whine of the gale through the pass.

It is on occasions such as these that I thank God for my sanguine temperament, which refuses to allow me to believe in disaster until it is finally manifest, and I noticed that my comrades in distress were equally well fortified against panic by their fatalistic acceptance of Allah's Will. Yet perhaps we were all more apprehensive than we had allowed ourselves to recognise, for we cheered very loudly when the second snowplough eventually appeared.

An ancient Jewish legend says that the Kurds are descended from four hundred virgins who were deflowered by devils while on their way to King Solomon's court and my own experiences in both Turkish and Persian Azerbaijan prompt me to accept this genealogy as an historic fact.

At Dogubayzit, the last little town en route to the Persian frontier-post, I stayed in the local doss-house, where my bedroom was a tiny box leading off the wide loft which accommodated the majority of the 'Otel's' patrons. This room had a flimsy door, without any fastening, and there was no movable piece of furniture which could have been placed against it as a security measure. The squalid bedding was inhabited by a host of energetic fleas, but their attentions were wasted on me and within minutes of retiring I was sound asleep.

Some hours later I awoke to find myself bereft of bedding and to see a six-foot, scantily-clad Kurd bending over me in the moonlight. My gun was beneath the pillow and one shot fired at the ceiling concluded the matter. I felt afterwards that my suitor had showed up rather badly; a more ardent admirer, of his physique, could probably have disarmed me without much difficulty.

As a result of the loud report and my visitor's rapid retreat there was a stirring of many bodies on the floor outside my room and a few sleepy mutterings – then quiet. Obviously gunshots in the small hours are not regarded locally as signs of an emergency.

By now I had finally escaped from snow and ice and on the following morning came one of the most glorious experiences of the entire journey – a fifteen-mile cycle-run in perfect weather around the base of Mount Ararat. This extraordinary mountain, which inspires the most complex emotions in the least imaginative traveller, affected me so deeply that I have thought of it ever since as a personality encountered, rather than a landscape observed.

Then came the Persian frontier – the most closely guarded we had yet crossed – and now Roz and I were really in our stride, cycling day after day beneath a sky of intense blue, through wild mountains whose solitude and beauty surpassed anything I had been able to imagine during my day-dreams about this journey. Particularly I remember the unique purity of the light, which gave to every variation of every colour an individual vitality and which lucidly emphasised every line, curve and angle. Here, for the first time, I became fully aware of light as something positive, rather than as a taken-for-granted aid to perceiving objects.

Between Tabriz and the Caspian coast the terrain becomes fiercely wild and the few inhabitants match it. One midday when I was sitting eating my lunch at the edge of the track, near a hairpin bend overlooking a deep valley, three elderly men came round the bend, carrying spades on their shoulders. As a little farming village lay some two miles back this seemed to me a most natural sight, but then, as I was about to salute the group, two of them seized Roz, who was leaning against the cliff a few yards away, and made off down the track with her, while the third advanced towards me, his spade raised threateningly. I fired over his head and quickly backed along the edge of the track, ready to fire again, but the amateur bandits had had enough and bolted like rabbits, mercifully abandoning Roz.

Many experienced travellers have since advised me that it is wiser to go unarmed in such areas, where a gun can provoke more trouble than it averts. Obviously, this would be true if one became involved with genuine armed bandits – yet a ·25 does have its uses.

However, my next misadventure was such that I judged it best not to produce the pistol. Passing through Adabile at lunchtime on a cold day (we had now risen to a considerable altitude) I paused to treat myself to a hot meal in an eating-house. As usual Roz and I attracted a curious crowd and soon a young police officer, gorgeously uniformed and braided, approached me to say that as this was a Restricted Area, because of Russia's proximity, I must accompany him to the police-barracks to fill in some forms. My inbred trust in police had not yet been undermined so, having finished my lunch, I innocently followed him through a maze of alleyways between mud houses. At last he turned into a little compound with a well in the centre, ushered me through a doorway, locked the door and put the key in his trouser pocket. Only then did I realise that we were alone in an obviously empty private house.

At first my captor was ingratiatingly amiable. But soon, having discovered that European women are not as obliging as he had supposed them to be, he lost all control, and the ensuing scene was too sordid for repetition. As my adversary was armed with a revolver I kept my gun in my pocket and used unprintable tactics to reduce him to a state of temporary agony. During this respite I grabbed his trousers, which by then were lying on the floor, fled to the hallway, found the key, unlocked the door just as my victim appeared behind me, and raced back through the alleyways to the centre of the town.

It is perhaps understandable that, of all the regions I travelled through, Azerbaijan is the only one I would not wish to revisit alone.

Roz and I arrived in Teheran on 20 March, the eve of the Shiah Muslims' New Year of 1342, and the Now Ruz Festival involved me in a delay of five days. Before continuing my journey I had to get a visa for Afghanistan, collect a spare tyre from the Customs and change a travellers' cheque into Afghan currency – none of which transactions would be possible until the conclusion of the Now Ruz celebrations.

1

The Elusive Visa

TEHERAN

TEHERAN, 26 MARCH

Today a deep depression has moved over Dervla; I presented myself to the Afghan Embassy at 9 a.m. this morning, only to be told that under no circumstances whatever would they grant a visa to a woman who intended cycling alone through Afghanistan. But if this is true, why wasn't I told of the ruling at the Afghan Embassy in London? Apparently about six years ago a lone Swedish woman motorist was carved up into small pieces, since when solitary female travellers have been banned – or so they say here. Probably I could easily get a visa in New Delhi, as official decisions rarely confirm each other in this part of the world: but that's not much consolation at the moment. Of course everyone at the Embassy was very sorry to frustrate me thus and they offered to provide free transport from here to Kabul and looked bewildered when I patiently pointed out that I wanted to cycle because I liked cycling, not because of economic distress. I also pointed out that women get murdered in Europe with monotonous regularity and that the hazards of travelling alone through their country were probably no greater than the hazards of doing likewise in Britain or France. But they refused to be swayed by my eloquence, so this evening it looks as though I'm beaten. However, since leaving the Embassy I've incubated a few nefarious schemes to be tried out tomorrow.

This afternoon, having expensively cut through interminable lengths of red tape, I extricated my tyre from the Customs. Those who know assure me that I'm very lucky to have received a parcel posted from Dublin on only 8 January. Yesterday one of my hosts received a letter sent from Brussels by airmail on 18 November, and letters posted in Teheran to Teheran addresses often spend a week en route.

The temperature has been around 72° F. for the past few days but this evening a cool wind rose suddenly and we've had a heavy, homelike shower.

TEHERAN, 27 MARCH

The Afghans have the most kindly way of trying to thwart one. On arrival at the Embassy this morning, I was received like an old friend and informed that all arrangements had been made for my safe transport to Kabul. Two German motorists – a writer and a painter – were enlisted for the purpose and had very kindly agreed to take on Roz and myself, without even seeing how presentable or otherwise either of us might be. The idea was that I'd be entered like a camera or a radio on their passports, so that they'd have to produce me to the police in Kabul and I couldn't get away on Roz once we're over the frontier without *them* being involved in trouble. Being thus reduced to the status of a piece of luggage naturally did no good to my *amour propre*, but with everyone being so pleasantly insistent on my reaching India alive I couldn't decently lose my temper. This lightning move – as it was by local standards – kiboshed one of my nefarious schemes, so having profusely thanked all concerned, I said that I had an important appointment in half an hour and that I would be back later to fill in and sign the countless relevant documents. Then I sped off by taxi to the Embassy of a 'Friendly Power' where I set about implementing the second nefarious scheme.

Having pleaded my way into the office of a sufficiently senior man, I outlined my miserable predicament and begged for a letter written on his government's behalf requesting the Afghan Government to grant bearer a visa for a month's travelling by cycle through Afghanistan at her own risk. I added that no one need worry about the consequences if I vanished, as none of my relatives are close enough to 'create'. Fortunately, the victim of my machinations was an upholder of Free Enterprise and the Liberty of the Individual. He looked at me in silence for a moment, then said, 'Well, I suppose if visas had been required in

1492, the New World would not have been discovered. All right – I'll play ball. But remember that all this is very unofficial and unbecoming to my position and I'm depending on you to come out alive at the other end, for my sake – which I somehow think you will do.' Then he proceeded to devise a most impressive document, all red ribbons and massive seals and flourishing signatures, in which concoction he took a fatherly pride. So now I simply *cannot* allow myself to be murdered in Afghanistan!

Half an hour later I was back in the Afghan Embassy, waving the Ruritanian-looking scroll with ill-concealed triumph. Not surprisingly, it worked. No one was happy at the thought of me being granted a visa, but since another state had nobly elected to hold the baby they gloomily agreed – against their better judgement, underlined – to give the lunatic her head. However, Kabul has to be contacted so I won't have everything signed, sealed and delivered until the 30th; but I'm too elated tonight to fuss about another few days' delay.

TEHERAN, 28 MARCH

At a party yesterday evening I met three Pakistani officers – a general, a brigadier and a colonel – who are here on a three-months' military mission and who immediately took me under their collective wing. They are all Pathans and are the first people I've met who do *not* expect me to be murdered in Afghanistan. For this, among other reasons, I find their company singularly congenial; being generally regarded as something next door to a corpse becomes tedious after a while. Acting on their cheerfully original assumption that I will eventually cross the Khyber Pass in one piece, they have advised me on which parts of Pakistan are most worth seeing and have given me a list of addresses of their friends and relatives all along my route. Colonel Jahan Zeb went to enormous trouble to plan an itinerary for me, which included a detour to the Tribal Territory of Gilgit, so now all is set fair for Pakistan and I'm assured I'll have the Army behind me there – which is quite something in a country now run by the Army!

TEHERAN, 29 MARCH

On leaving Constantinople, where one spends a small fortune on beggars, I had resolved to give nothing to anyone during the rest of the journey lest I end up with a begging-bowl myself. But of course Persia has undermined that resolution: the pathetic wretches seen here simply can't be ignored. (Many of them in the towns and villages are lepers diagnosed too late for treatment – even if treatment were available in their area, which it often isn't – and left to die slowly at home.) So now I've got the problem worked out systematically. I reckon that by being a guest at my friend's house I'm saving £1 a day, which I distribute as baksheesh. This obviously is an oblique form of selfishness; one couldn't come home after a walk through Teheran and settle down to enjoy the luxuries of Capitalism if one hadn't done something, however trivial, to alleviate the surrounding misery. Yet it's well to remember that this misery is not as total or as neglected as it appears to be. One of the religious duties of Muslims – as of Christians – is to give alms to the needy and the vast majority of Muslims of every sect regularly fulfil this duty in proportion to their means. In effect the citizens of these countries provide for their deprived brothers as generously as do the tax-paying citizens of a Welfare State and the disparity between the circumstances of the disabled of Persia and the disabled of Britain is no greater than that between the circumstances of the working men of the two countries: in fact it may well be less, though the distribution of funds is more haphazard. Also the Muslim method of providing 'Social Services' has the important virtue of maintaining a natural and humane link between individuals. It is obviously more desirable to have citizens giving to beggars voluntarily, out of compassion, rather than to have them grumblingly paying taxes to an impersonal government which dispenses what is left, after its civil servants have been paid, to unknown sufferers who are mere names in a filing cabinet.

Similarly, the bribery which is so rife here, is another, though much less desirable form of indirect taxation; everyone is paid so inadequately that they simply augment their official income as best they can from day to day – a situation accepted by all with much the same brand of resentful resignation as we show towards tax-paying. House-owners pay the local police a regular monthly sum to ensure that their homes and cars will be properly guarded – and if some newcomer refuses to pay on principle his home will be the inevitable target for the next burglary. I've asked several responsible Persians why an orthodox tax isn't imposed and their answer was that you can't do that sort of thing with a mainly illiterate population and that the people who can afford property which needs protection can also afford to subsidise the police. But of course this is only one example and bribery is the determining factor in every sphere of activity from the university professor's correction of exam papers down to the dustman's collection of garbage. I must admit that it's difficult to get adjusted to such a fetid atmosphere, in which one is always conscious of the power of money over integrity.

TEHERAN, 30 MARCH

Today I've been receiving Good Advice in bulk from various Responsible Persons. H.I.M. the Shah was to have gone to Meshed this morning but the papers announced that his trip has been cancelled because of 'bad weather'; as the weather at the moment is perfection (74°F. and cloudless sky) everyone thinks the government a bit dim for not inventing a better excuse. The fact is that the Mullahs are now stirring up serious trouble there about Land Redistribution and Women's Emancipation and as they still have a very strong grip in that area, and are capable of working certain sections of the people into an anti-Shah frenzy, it was judged wiser for H.I.M. to avoid the Holy City just now. (Since I left Tabriz, two women have been killed there in Mullah-provoked anti-Women's Emancipation riots.) As Meshed is the next – and last – Persian city on my route I am being warned repeatedly that I must do my best to look like a man in that area. Also I'm to be very careful about using my camera between here and there as, if I were accidentally to include even a distant mosque in a picture and the crowd happened to be in the mood, I could be stoned and possibly seriously injured, as recently happened to two over-keen French photographers.

I've also been advised that hotel bedrooms without locks call for empty bottles balanced on top of the door to ensure that one is not taken altogether by surprise should wandering lechers have designs on one's virtue. (As creating empty bottles is one of the few things I'm good at, this is an appropriate suggestion.) However, I intend staying as often as possible in gendarmerie barracks between here and Afghanistan, as the Persian gendarmerie is a force existing primarily to protect travellers and is reputedly more dependable than other branches of the national police – how much more dependable remains to be seen.

Tonight I enjoyed a farewell hooley with my Pakistani friends – though hooley is hardly the *mot juste* as they drink only water. I suppose, if one will mix with good Muslims, it's only to be expected that they'll open for themselves another bottle of Pure Water (guaranteed) every time they refill your glass. And certainly Colonel Zeb needs no alcohol to stimulate his brain or improve his masterly skill in the use of the English language: quite apart from the considerable interest of what he has to say on an incredibly wide variety of topics, it's a joy to merely hear him *saying* it. I haven't enjoyed such a good evening's discussion for a long time: the five of us started talking at 6 p.m. and got so involved on so many fascinating points that no one wanted to break it up and we didn't have dinner till 10.40 p.m.! It's now 2.10 a.m. so, as I'm planning an early start, some sleep might not be a bad idea.

2

Hospitality of the Police

TEHERAN TO THE AFGHAN FRONTIER

DEH-NAMAK, 31 MARCH

Roz and I left Teheran at 6.30 a.m. and arrived here soon after 6 p.m. having covered 108 miles because of a strong following wind.

The road remained reasonable by Persian standards, though if I had met it at home I would have taken one horrified look and gone the other way round; it's amazing how quickly one becomes conditioned. It was such glorious cycling weather that I seemed to have boundless energy and did the last ten miles feeling positively fresh.

This really is a beautiful country and every mile from Teheran was pure joy – as much the joy of space and silence as of visual loveliness. These extravagantly sweeping lines of plain and mountain are intoxicating to an islander and the blending of shades on the barren hillsides is a symphony of colour. Yet that's only one aspect of the region; as a background to daily life it's cruel and contemptuous country where cultivation is a fight all the way, with victory not worth much.

The main crop is wheat and to come on a few little fields of it, looking so fresh and green, is a physical rest for the eyes after twenty or thirty miles of harsh, grey-brown desert, shuddering in the midday heat-haze. The mud villages of this area are much better designed than those of western Persia, where the houses are as primitive as you could find anywhere. Here they are most attractive, with domed roofs and miniature 'Gothic' windows and endless variations between one house and another. I longed to take a few photographs but Muslims being so sensitive on the subject it seemed wiser not to risk spoiling the good relations I'd achieved with the locals.

Twice I left the road to explore villages formerly belonging to the Shah and now handed over to the peasants. These people are totally different to the Azerbaijan toughs: I found them friendly and polite and there were no 'hands-out-for-baksheesh' though they went to endless trouble showing me round the farms. It may sound silly, but I maintain that I know instinctively the temper of a place, after being five minutes with the inhabitants. So today I hadn't the slightest qualm about abandoning Roz and my kit in the centre of the villages, and though on my return I found her surrounded by at least a hundred filthy, ragged children, nothing had been touched. In my experience this is the prevailing standard of honesty in Turkey and Persia at least towards guests and Azerbaijan was the unhappy exception.

On one of these farms I saw my very first tractor since entering Persia – it was the common property of a village. Elsewhere oxen are still pulling the most primitive form of all-wooden plough. There are very few camels in this area, oddly enough, nor are there many horses or cattle. Hundreds of sturdy little donkeys provide transportation for both people and goods and a few herds of sheep and goats are grazed by each village.

It was a most moving experience to see the pride and joy of those men and boys at *owning* their land. Some of the youths spoke a little English and repeatedly I heard the phrases 'This is *our* land', '*We* own this', 'This belongs to *us*', as they all beamed with fond pride at their pathetic few fertile acres in the midst of hundreds of square miles of desert. Obviously they can't quite believe it yet. Many of them carry photographs of the Shah in their pockets (I had to admire about thirty-five of these individually) and pictures of His Imperial Majesty and the Empress and the Crown Prince are in almost every home. They genuinely love their Shah – and would you blame them! Political commentators may question the motives behind his Land Reform but the effect for the peasants remains wholly good. When I think of those wretched Mullahs who try to persuade the villagers that it's immoral and against the Koran for the masses to *own* land – just because they themselves own so much of it . . . ! I suppose the nearest analogy in Christendom is the Spanish Church, even if its tactics were slightly more subtle. It's disconcerting how the men in the religious saddle repeatedly abuse their spiritual authority for personal gain.

Eighty per cent of the land here is useless for anything, yet when you observe how the irrigated patches flourish it becomes clear that a few hundred more dams are the answer, as the cultivated land is basically the same as the rest. When I first saw the whitened surface of the plain today I thought it had been snowing a little, even though that seemed wildly unlikely. Then I stopped and tasted the concentrated salt which forms a light film over everything; we're now just north of the Great Salt Desert.

On arriving at this little village I went straight to the gendarmerie barracks, left Roz there and walked beyond the sun-gold huddle of mud houses to attempt to get some pictures of the goat and sheep herds being penned for the night. I was followed by scores of children, all obviously regarding me as a sort of circus; they didn't beg but just wanted to be with me. I had to tell the gendarmerie to let them come as their tendency was literally to beat the infants back lest the visitor be annoyed. Actually it did me good to be able to provide so much innocent amusement by merely arriving in the village and soon my photography expedition degenerated into games for all, with me pretending to be a sheep-dog and the children convulsed by giggles and then me being a donkey (not difficult!) crawling around the sand on all fours, braying loudly, with two or three toddlers on my back.

This barrack where I'm staying the night is a huge old fort, built entirely of mud but very impressively proportioned. I'm half-blind now from writing by a feeble oil-lamp – you'd think they'd have enough oil here in Persia!

GOOSHEH, 1 APRIL

It's very funny – around here the idea of a woman travelling alone is so completely outside the experience and beyond the imagination of everyone that it's universally assumed I'm a man. This convenient illusion is fostered by the very short haircut I deliberately got in Teheran, and by a contour-obliterating shirt presented to me at Adabile by the US Army in the Middle East, who also donated a wonderful pair of boots – the most comfortable footwear I've ever had and ideal for tramping these stony roads. The result of the locals' little error of judgement is that last night and tonight I was shown to my bed in the gendarmerie dormitory. These beds consist of wooden planks with padded sleeping-bags laid on them and I have the bed of one of those on night-patrol. There are no problems involved as 'getting ready for bed' consists of removing boots, gun and belt and sliding into a flea-bag so I simply do likewise and that's that! Incidentally, these barracks are kept spotlessly clean: as much as an accidental crumb or cigarette ash isn't allowed on the mud floor and everything is neat and tidy. I bring in my own food and get hot water for coffee from the lads. I'm now sitting on the edge of my bed writing by a little oil-lamp while six gendarmes sleep soundly around me.

We left Deh-Namak at 5.30 a.m. when the sun was just up and the air pleasantly cool. Though the road was much worse than yesterday we covered eighty-two miles, arriving here at 6.40 p.m. I stopped for lunch at 12.30 p.m. and slept for an hour in blazing sun; apart from sunburn (there was no shade available) this is perfectly safe, as in the wide open spaces between villages there are no men, beasts, insects or reptiles to molest one, but I suspect I'm in for trouble with sunburnt arms as I was using my wind-cheater to cover Roz's tyres while I slept. Actually it is only when stationary that one is aware of the sun's power, whilst moving there's no sensation of it being 'too hot'. I believe it'll be the same in Afghanistan, before becoming intolerably hot in Pakistan and India. (I feel I've earned a few months of perfect weather!)

Soon after lunch I abandoned the road for over ten miles and cycled along a dried-up river-bed where the baked mud was firm and smooth and the boulders en route seemed a mere triviality as compared with the excruciating, sharp-edged gravel on a road with an inexorably corrugated surface. When I found the river-bed veering too much to the south I reluctantly left it and walked over a mile or so of desert back to the road. The last thirty miles were through another magnificent mountain range with a very stiff climb up to this village. I passed the scene of a ghastly smash-up reported a few days ago in the

English-language Teheran paper. A truck and bus were in a head-on collision on a V-bend – both went into a ravine and fifty-one were killed. Something similar happens almost every day somewhere in Persia and the drivers are always blamed. Watching Persian buses on mountain roads makes me feel quite ill; when I see the dust-cloud that heralds one I dismount and remove myself to a safe distance. During ten days in Teheran I witnessed seven bad traffic accidents, four of them involving the deaths of nine people.

This is a tiny village of some twenty domed mud huts, a tea-house and the barracks. There should be a level road tomorrow as the map shows no passes – but probably we'll have a worse surface each day.

SHAHRUD, 2 APRIL

How right can you be! We only covered sixty-six miles today (5.45 a.m.–6.50 p.m.) and I had to walk over twenty-five of them, not because of hills, but because no one with any regard for their cycle would ride it over this sort of infernal track. I haven't seen one private car or one lorry since leaving Teheran, though many buses pass, packed with people and overloaded on the roofs with rolls of carpet, bicycles, crates of hens, lambs and kids (alive and kicking – literally!) and diverse bundles containing God knows what. These buses unload for lunch (between 12 and 3) at village eating-houses, which have streams running beside them and a few green trees shading the carpet-covered 'tables' on which everyone sits cross-legged eating their bread and chives and hard-boiled eggs and minced-meat balls and *mast* (the Persian yoghourt). Before the meal all babies present have their napkins changed and these are washed in the stream (as are the chives and everybody's teeth after eating) and spread out to dry before the resumption of the journey. Today I joined one of these parties (obviously a pilgrimage returning from Meshed) and though I was addressed as 'Monsieur' the mere fact that I was from a Christian country provoked hostility. I didn't dare use the camera, though I would have valued a few shots of those fanatical-looking chaps in filthy rags and tatters. Many of them were adolescents, so it's going to take H.I.M. a long, long time to tame this lot. The children were terrified of me and wouldn't come for the sweets I offered and the whole atmosphere was so unpleasant that I removed myself sooner than I would have otherwise and took my siesta in the safety of the desert a few miles away.

A phenomenon that intrigues me is the number of Catholic religious oleographs in all these eating-houses and tea-houses – Christ as a baby in the manger or working in the carpenter's shop, the Immaculate Heart of Mary picture, highly coloured, Our Lady of Perpetual Succour, Our Lady of Good Counsel, cheap prints of the Raphael Madonna, and St Joseph. These are in addition, of course, to the Shah, the Empress and baby Prince in various stages of growth, not to mention luscious semi-nude females advertising Pepsi-Cola and aspirin. But how all these Christian pictures got here baffles me; granted the Muslims are devoted to Christ as a Prophet and to Our Lady, but I wouldn't have thought their devotion would go so far.

When I arrived on the outskirts of this town a car overtook me and the driver (manager of a local sugar factory and reader of the daily paper) stopped and said, 'Dervla going to India, yes?' I blushed with becoming modesty at this proof of fame and replied that I was indeed Dervla going to India, so he invited me to spend the night at his home, where I now am, having had a shower and a huge supper. It's quite impossible to retain one's youthful curves in these countries: to refuse food is an insult so one merely unbuttons one's slacks in a surreptitious way and goes on and on eating. Before the meal everyone consumes a vast amount of biscuits, oranges, pastries, figs stuffed with almonds, toffees and bon-bons of all descriptions, pistachio nuts and endless glasses of tea. Then you're expected to welcome with a glad smile a mound of rice you can hardly see over and masses of meat and vegetables.

This is a big town (8,000 population) with electricity, no less! My host's house is full of mod cons, including a telephone, fridge and washing-machine. But inevitably there's no bath because of the Islamic law about washing in running water – the bathroom is a marble-floored outfit with a shower. (In fact every room in every Persian house is marble- or mud-floored because of the shortage of wood.) My host's wife is away in Teheran on a Now Ruz visit to her family and will be home tomorrow. This is the last day of the Now Ruz festival but my route today was so gloriously desolate that I saw little evidence of the traditional picnicking in the open. The four children here are delightful – two boys, two girls – and are tickled to bits by my arrival, having read about me in the Teheran paper. We were joined for supper by a twenty-year-old nephew of my host, with his sixteen-year-old wife – a made match that was clearly not working very well.

I'm in for torture with sunburn on my right arm – not, I now realise, the result of lying in the sun, but the result of cycling every day due east so that this arm is continuously exposed; and though I don't feel it when cycling it is a fierce sun. There's nothing like carrying six tubes of sunburn lotion across two continents and then forgetting to use it in time!

ABBAS-ABAD, 3 APRIL

We covered eighty-three miles today, but that meant breaking my 'not-after-dark' rule and cycling till 9.30 p.m. However, in such uninhabited country I don't think there's any danger and bright moonlight showed the way; it was indescribably beautiful on the huge sand-dunes, which look like mountains. I'm at last getting used to the uncanny silence of desert landscape and to the odd experience of seeing things that disappear as you approach them. Also I've discovered that what looks like a village two miles ahead is actually a village twenty miles ahead, and I've got acclimatised to fine dust permeating every crevice of self and kit. In short, I'm broken in!

There was an amusing interlude today when an American engineer going back by jeep to his work in Afghanistan pulled up to investigate me and the following conversation took place:

American: 'What the hell are you doing on this goddam road?'

Me: (having taken an instant dislike to him) 'Cycling.'

American: 'I can see that – but what the hell for?'

Me: 'For fun.'

American: 'Are you a nut-case or what? Gimme that bike and I'll stick it on behind and you get in here and we'll get out of this goddam frying-pan as fast as we can. This track isn't fit for a camel!'

Me: 'When you're on a cycle instead of in a jeep it doesn't feel like a frying-pan. Moreover, if you look around you you'll notice that the landscape compensates for the admittedly deplorable state of the road. In fact I *enjoy* cycling through this sort of country – but thank you for the kind offer. Goodbye.'

As I rode on he passed me and yelled: 'You *are* a goddam nut-case!'

I regard this sort of life, with just Roz and me and the sky and the earth, as sheer bliss. My one worry at the moment is Roz's complete disintegration. So far the rear-lamp, the rear mudguard and half the front mudguard have fallen off; the straps tying saddle-bag to saddle have both broken; the left pannier-bag holder has come apart and the right pedal has loosened. Everything is being held together by a system of rope and wire more complicated than you'd believe possible, but fortunately none of these disabilities is serious. The trouble will start when wheels or frame crack up. It's astonishing that I haven't had a puncture since leaving Teheran – a tribute to the extreme care with which I'm cycling. But obviously my claim that cycling is the best way to *see* a country just isn't valid in this region. I daren't take my eyes off the road for one second and my 'seeing' is confined to the walking intervals and to the frequent stops I make just to look around me.

This village is the most primitive place I've hit so far, with not even a gendarmerie barracks. It's a collection of the usual mud huts, very roughly constructed, and in the tea-house everything is of mud – the 'counter', the seats all around the walls and the steps leading up to an attic where men are smoking opium. I went up there to investigate sleeping accommodation and found five braves all in a trance with their pipes – that's what comes of having no gendarmerie in a place! (My right arm is so stiff tonight that I can't bend it and the pain is *intense* – but better that than frost-bite.) The three men now drinking tea here seem to be neutral towards me: they show no friendliness, but no apparent hostility either. I feel it's just as well I arrived late: the fewer people who know about my presence the better. I'll sleep on one of the long mud seats with Roz tied to me and my knapsack under my head with its straps round my neck – though it's not clear how me being strangled by my own straps will help the situation if someone tries to rob me!

BAGH-JAR, 4 APRIL

I survived last night without incident but despite tiredness slept badly as the sunburn agony woke me every time I moved. We set out at 5.30 a.m. and the whole of today's eighty-five-mile ride was through the Great Salt Desert with flat sand on either side to the horizon and only one town (Salzevar) en route. This seemed an interesting place but was full of Mullahs and turbaned youths who stoned me and cut my sunburned arm five minutes after I'd arrived, so I departed hastily before a riot started. Salzevar is in the heart of the Mullah-dominated country, where the police are afraid of the clergy and simply don't appear if there's trouble, so discretion was most emphatically the better part of valour. I'm now safe with the gendarmerie in a little village, sitting up in my bunk and feeling rotten. My right arm is half the size again of my left and tomorrow all the blisters will burst. I can't think why it's swelled so much; that didn't happen in Spain, where I also had very bad sunburn. Anyway, it's entirely my own fault.

The road was slightly improved today, except where so much sand had blown over it that one couldn't cycle without skidding. I feel quite feverish this evening; possibly it's slight heat-stroke though I didn't feel over-heated to any great degree.

NISHAPUR, 5 APRIL

I woke up feeling much better, though my arm has not burst yet. We only did fifty-five miles today as this is Omar Khayyám's town and I've stopped here to pay homage. Besides, I think I've been pushing myself too hard, so an easy day was not a bad idea.

On leaving Bagh-Jar I had a twelve-mile walk through the mountains on a ghastly road but surrounded by tremendously exciting scenery. Then we suffered more desert until reaching here.

I find the Persian fauna very un-exotic. Bird life round the villages consists of crows, magpies, willy-wagtails, swallows and sparrows. The only unfamiliar birds are little crested chaps rather like thrushes and an occasional fierce, enormous hawk; I've also heard a few nightjars. Animal life is almost nil, though today I saw four roebuck crossing the road. Insect life consists to date of houseflies (very few) and black beetles as in Ireland.

This is a very lovely town; I notice that the towns of Persia tend to be much more attractive than the cities, especially now when the gardens are so beautiful with their smooth lawns, pale green cascades of weeping willow and brilliant beds of carnations, roses, pansies and geraniums. The main streets are always wide and the sun-soaked mud walls look golden under the violet blue of the Persian sky. Almost all the traffic consists of pony-phaeton taxis and innumerable laden donkeys and bicycles. The inevitable *jube* (a channel of water flowing between footpath and road) runs everywhere but on the whole the streets are quite clean and I've come to the conclusion that Persian water is safe if you make it clear you want to *drink* it, not wash with it. Anyway I've been drinking it uninhibitedly with no ill effects.

We arrived here at 3.15 p.m. and I was immediately captured by a twenty-year-old boy who secured me as his guest for the night against terrific competition from his class-mates; the local students have to pay fifty *reals* for a thirty minutes' English lesson, so an English-speaking guest for the night is considered precious. Three days ago Khayyám's new tomb was opened to the public by the Shah (pity I missed that) and a bevy of youths, laden with dictionaries, grammars and simplified versions of *Jane Eyre*, took me there this afternoon, all bombarding me en route with their particular problems of pronunciation, sentence construction and spelling. The keenness of Persian youths to learn English is positively fanatical but their opportunities remain very limited as few competent teachers are available outside Teheran.

The new tomb represents modern architecture at its grotesque worst; I almost wept to see it over the body of such a man as Omar Khayyám. I also saw the old tomb which is very simple, dignified and appropriate. Why tens of thousands of *reals* had to be spent on this new contraption when the country is swarming with undernourished children I do not know.

The family with whom I'm staying consists of the mother (aged thirty-five), three sons aged twenty, eighteen and twelve, and four girls aged sixteen, fourteen, nine and six. The father works as a draper's assistant in Teheran and the household is obviously very poor. This being Friday (the Muslim Sunday) twelve relatives were rounded up to come and meet me at supper time, but even though the men were close relatives the mother and daughters, including the six-year-old, veiled themselves the moment the visitors appeared. Islam is so rigid around here that *no* man, except father, husband and sons, is allowed to glimpse a woman's face; no wonder the boys can't take their eyes off my poor mug – at least it's a change from mother and sisters!

I ate with the women and was relieved to get lentils instead of rice. We also had a savoury omelette and salad – which I declined, having seen it washed in the *jube* and been warned by everyone to avoid *jube*-washed salad at all costs. There were no chairs or tables or beds in the house and no cutlery – you use the flat pieces of bread to dig your share out of the communal dish. *Mast* with sugar was served as dessert and I found the whole meal very appetising.

Everyone is most concerned about my arm, which certainly looks alarming, though it feels better tonight.

After the meal grandmother and mother took turns smoking the hookah, while one girl played on a timbrel and the rest danced – the traditional Friday evening pastime. I've got to appreciate Arabic music to the point where I have my favourite tunes and I could watch Persian dancing for hours; it's marvellously graceful, particularly in the use of arms and hands. The six-year-old gave a magnificent performance and a two-year-old already had the general idea!

SANG BAST, 6 APRIL

There was quite a change in the landscape today, though none in the road surface. We covered seventy-two miles, some of them between wonderful mountains, and most through what, for this area, is fertile land – i.e. a village, surrounded by little irrigated fields, every twenty miles or so, and in between huge flocks of sheep and goats grazing on some invisible herbage. There are hundreds of tiny lambs and kids with the flocks now and they look absolutely adorable; the lambs have thick fleeces and enormous floppy ears like spaniels, and the kids are very dainty and frisky. I stopped to have lunch with a fierce-looking but actually very amiable shepherd and admired his flocks while eating: we solemnly exchanged bread and salt so are friends forever, according to local custom.

As if Persia wanted to show me what it could do in the way of fauna I saw seven more deer today and one big dog fox of a horrid yellow-grey colour. I also met a tortoise, two scorpions, a hamster and an eagle and along much of the way I was accompanied by lark-song, which made me feel quite homesick.

This village is at the junction of the Teheran–Meshed–Afghanistan road, so I'll be returning to it tomorrow evening after a detour to see the sights of Meshed and to collect my mail. The local gendarmerie are exceptionally nice and sufficiently sophisticated to diagnose my sex so a flea-bag has been put on the office floor for me.

There was a strong east wind against us today – very wearing combined with the atrocious surface. It got quite cloudy too – there might be a nice bit of rain tomorrow, but that's not likely, though last week they did have their first inch for four years in South Persia.

One of the things that most intrigues Persians about me is the fact that I have no brothers and sisters: obviously only children are quite unknown here and they have the greatest sympathy for me. They're certainly a very family-minded people: brothers and sisters show tremendous mutual affection and in times of family trouble do all they can to help each other.

This was the first evening my expired visa was spotted, as a Lieutenant is in charge here; usually there's only an NCO as illiterate as his men. But the Lieutenant is a nice young man who winked and took twenty American cigarettes and said I could be fined over £50 for having American cigarettes in Persia.

SANG BAST, 7 APRIL

We arrived outside the British Council office in Meshed at 7.50 a.m. – ten long minutes to wait for mail! It was a perfect metalled road for the twenty-five miles and I met with no hostility from the locals, who were friendlier than in many other places; but I had to avoid going to the shrine area alone, though I would have given a lot to explore it. Meshed is by far the nicest of the four Persian cities I've seen and it *did* rain this morning so all along the fine wide boulevards, which are lined with birches as big as our oaks, the new green leaves were freshly sparkling. A car was kindly laid on to take me round the city yet it was most frustrating just to glimpse the out-of-bounds beauties of the mosques and shrine and museum and library. That quarter was teeming with Mullahs; I saw three in green turbans, which means they are descended from the Prophet. An American girl who took herself off there two days ago against advice was badly hurt by stones when trying to get colour-shots of the domes and minarets.

One is told the most blood-curdling tales at each stop. Here the *pièce de résistance* is about three Americans who, when motoring from Meshed to the Afghan frontier, stopped for a picnic and were all shot dead by bandits, who then escaped into Afghanistan but were hunted, by the Afghan police, back into Persia, where they were captured by the Army and publicly hanged in the main square of Teheran. Mr Jones of the British Council said there's no question of me going to Kabul via Mazar-i-Sharif as that area has lots of Communist-inspired trouble. The Russians are really trying hard at the moment to take over the whole of Afghanistan and there's a terrific tug-of-war going on between them and the Americans.

I left the British Council at 2.45 p.m. after lunch with the Joneses. (Very nice – both lunch and Joneses – and the British Council premises, which used to be the Consulate quarters when Britain had a Consul in Meshed, are really magnificent, with gardens and grounds that seem like Paradise when one comes to them from the desert.) I had decided that Roz would have to go to hospital before tackling Afghanistan so I took her to the city's biggest cycle shop where a few jobs which should have taken half an hour took two and a half hours so that we didn't get out of Meshed till 5.30 p.m. This sounds incredible but everyone who has lived here knows it's true: Persians will *not* use a screwdriver – instead they *hammer* every screw into place, and all other repairs and readjustments are done with corresponding brutality. You can't imagine what I suffered, sitting on a stool beside the patient, chain-smoking and drinking my emergency supply of Courvoisier through sheer nerves, while they attacked that unfortunate, long-suffering cycle with hammer and chisel. Eventually we left, having abandoned the back mudguard. I am now anticipating the worst, as no machine could survive an assault like that without dire repercussions.

It was dark, though with a bright moon from 6. p.m., and I would have enjoyed the ride through the cool evening but for being badly scared by five men (plus a rifle) in a car who kept stopping and trying to persuade me to go with them to Sang Bast. Maybe they meant well but twelve miles from anywhere after dark I didn't relish their attentions and they disappeared with what looked like guilty haste when two gendarmes on horseback came patrolling up the road. I'm now safely back with my friends in the barracks here, who are all very worried about my arm (which at this stage looks a lot worse than it feels) and have just given me a soothing cream to apply – what they use for 'Marchers' Feet'. I notice it's Swiss-made.

TIEABAD, 8 APRIL

This morning my flat length of breakfast bread (called *none*) was covered with snail-tracks – much to my astonishment, as I wouldn't have thought snails to be a feature of such a dry country. This seemed slightly off-putting at first but then I reminded myself that some people are *outré* enough to *eat* snails and as there can't be much chemical difference between a snail and a snail-track I went on from there. It was rather disillusioning to discover that a gendarme – it couldn't have been anyone else – stole sixty American cigarettes out of my saddle-bag last evening, but I suppose this is not really astonishing in a country where the C-in-C of the Army is at present on trial at the Teheran High Court, for large-scale corruption. Anyway it was entirely my own fault: I know by now that American cigarettes are much coveted here (if you had smoked Persian ones you'd realise why!) and I should have kept them in my knapsack. On the whole, apart from a few incidents, I've found the gendarmerie a very decent, kind and reliable lot of boys; they are the Shah's special interest and he does all he can to keep up the standard of the corps.

We left Sang Bast at 5.15 a.m. and had covered just over forty-five miles when, at 11 a.m., the inevitable happened and the back wheel came off; fortunately we were going very slowly up an incline at the time, so I wasn't injured myself. Investigating the situation I discovered that the thread of the relevant screw had been ruined, which seemed a natural enough consequence to it having been hammered into place. At this point I was twenty-five miles from the last town and twenty miles from the next and Roz couldn't be wheeled so I ate my lunch and went to sleep till such time as something might come to rescue me. (Since leaving Ireland I've acquired the habit of sleeping whenever I want to, which is very convenient.)

Only two trucks had passed all morning, taking petrol to Herat from the oil refinery at Meshed, and it was nearly 2 p.m. before the next one woke me as it came rattling along the execrable road. The driver was a barefooted Afghan with a flowing turban and as you can't put a bicycle on top of an oil-tanker he nonchalantly roped Roz to the engine; the fact that she completely obscured his view of the road was quite irrelevant since Asian drivers never look where they're going. As I was getting into the cab he noticed my sunburn and was appalled. Before I could try to explain that if not touched it didn't hurt he had coated my arm with Premium Pure Motor Oil, applied on a filthy piece of cotton wool out of his own First Aid box. He was so gentle that the treatment didn't pain me in the least but it remains to be seen whether Premium Pure Motor Oil on raw sunburn is a cure or the beginning of a lingering, fatal illness!

The cab of this truck had no doors and no windscreen glass and no seats but an upturned box for the driver; it seemed to be entirely home-made and the petrol engine stank so strongly that, despite all the fresh air, I was feeling violently ill in less than half an hour. Only the fact that we had three breakdowns in less than a hundred miles saved me: I was able to get out then and recover. The driver told me that there was no bicycle shop before the frontier town of Tieabad so here I am a day ahead of schedule; actually the road was so bad for the last sixty miles that even if Roz hadn't succumbed I would probably have given up the unequal struggle and hitched a ride over that stretch for both our sakes: the only alternative would have been to walk every yard of the way.

The first thirty miles today was through quite prosperous country with an unusual number of cattle and many acres of wheat, well up. The people, who are supposed to be even more unreliable than those of Azerbaijan, were very nice to me at both the villages where I stopped for tea and water. A minority of them are Mongolians, which is quite thrilling – a proof I'm nearing Central Asia! One point that intrigued me was that there do not appear to be any half-breeds: one sees either pure Aryan features or pure Mongolian, so there must be no intermarrying, which seems odd, as they're all Muslims.

I had a second lunch at 2.30 with the driver at a tiny village eating-house. The mutton soup was delicious (if you like your soup twenty-five per cent grease with lumps of fat floating in it, as I do) and was followed by perfectly cooked and beautifully flavoured mutton stew with beans, bread, raw onion and Pepsi-Cola (Persia's national drink!). I find the style of building evolved to suit mud very attractive; there are no corners or angles; everything is rounded and arched and curved. I've now got used to the Eastern way of sitting silently doing nothing whatever for an indefinite period. These people don't indulge in conversation as a pastime: they have occasional fierce arguments about some particular point and the rest is silence. I found it very pleasant today, just sitting cross-legged on my carpet (a posture which is no longer agonising as my joints are in training) looking out through the arched doorway at the blue sky and the few green trees growing beside the stream and the pale gold landscape and the donkey-traffic – little boys galloping by, old men walking their steeds sedately, and young men leading donkeys which were almost hidden under enormous leather pannier-bags filled with earth for some new building. The stream (which is also the local fridge) was flowing eloquently over boxes of bottles of Pepsi and the water was bubbling companionably in the men's hookahs all around me. I couldn't help wondering what all these millions of people think about during all these countless hours spent silently sitting – they have so few mental stimulants that it's difficult to believe they think at all. My Afghan driver was much more alert than the average Persian; he's an awfully nice bloke, giving a good first impression of the 'savages' of Afghanistan.

On arriving here I took Roz to the cycle shop and after infinite trouble found a screw to fit, seized it by force from the proprietor and personally did the job with my own screwdriver. In future, if anything goes wrong I, myself, am coping – or dying in the attempt.

I seem to have lost the thread of my narrative somewhere – I was going to say that after thirty miles the rest of today's journey was through sand desert, with only a few tiny villages. This town is a pleasant little place, where I am staying at the hotel, having been through the Customs and got an exit stamp on my passport, so that I'm all set for Afghanistan first thing in the morning. Not one word was said about the expired visa, which shows what you can get away with if you try – thirty-two days on a fifteen-day visa!

I'm quite sorry to be leaving Persia. Beneath all the physical dirt and moral corruption there is an elegance and dignity about life here which you can't appreciate at first, while suffering under the impact of the more obvious and disagreeable national characteristics. The graciousness with which peasants greet each other and the effortless art with which a few beautiful rags and pieces of silver are made to furnish and decorate a whole house – in these and many other details Persia can still teach the West. I suppose it's all a question of seeing one of the oldest and richest civilisations in the world long past its zenith. But I've decided that the Persians, though it's impossible for me to *like* them as I do the Turks, are more to be pitied than censured. Hundreds of years of in-breeding and malnutrition have undermined the race and it is only when you approach them from that angle and treat them with the necessary patience that you can come to terms with them.

I've gone completely native myself and now wash face, hands, teeth and clothes in the *jube*, though I remember being shocked five weeks ago at the sight of the Persians doing just that. However, I've now realised that the dreadful colour of the water is partly due to soil erosion, one of the chief national problems; there's no such thing as a clear stream here. But I do draw the line at drinking the *jube* water!

At the moment I'm sitting in the hotel courtyard, writing by the light of a full moon, beside a nimble, sparkling fountain, with richly scented shrubs all around me and the mountains of Afghanistan jagged against a royal blue sky on the eastern horizon. The air feels like silk as a little breeze moves among the birch trees that enclose two sides of the courtyard. The town's electricity supply has broken down and the tall pillars of the verandah look very lovely by moonlight.

Actually I shouldn't be here – on arrival the proprietor told me that no women are allowed outside the Women's Quarter. I meekly went off to same but it consisted of a tiny room with six beds and just enough space to walk between them. One bed was mine; the other five were occupied by women who possessed a minimum of two infants apiece – all being fed and changed at the time of my appearance. Both window and door were tightly sealed and the stink was appalling, so I got hold of an Indian, also staying here, and used him as interpreter to tell the proprietor that (*a*) The Shah condemned the segregation of women, (*b*) The Government was trying to encourage tourism and (*c*) I was prepared to respect religious conventions within reason but was *not* prepared to lock myself up for hours in a room like that when I could be sitting in a courtyard like this. The proprietor said, 'Very well, if you don't mind being stared at', to which I irritably replied that I'd been getting stared at by every man I met for thirty-two days and that if they had nothing better to do I didn't really mind.

GHURION, AFGHANISTAN, 9 APRIL

We left Tieabad at 6 a.m. with nineteen miles to go to the Afghan Customs, though the actual frontier is only ten miles away. The road ran through more sand desert, and lots of sand had been blown over it, which was an advantage in a way on such a rough surface. We crossed the frontier at 7.45 a.m. and whoever said the weather in Afghanistan would be ideal for cycling was wrong because even at this hour it was almost too hot. Those 150 miles I came south yesterday have made an extraordinary difference to the temperature. However, last winter remains so vivid in my mind that I am still grateful for too much sun.

The only indication of the Persian-Afghan frontier is a seven-foot stone pillar, conspicuous from far across the desert, which lucidly announces 'Afghanistan'. Here I stopped to photograph Roz. Three miles further on a long branch served as Customs barrier and beside it lay a very young soldier in a very ragged uniform, sound asleep with one hand on his rifle. I quietly raised the barrier for myself and continued towards the Customs and Passport Office two hundred yards ahead.

There, no one took the slightest notice of either my kit or my passport, no uniformed officials appeared and no series of dingy, uncomfortable offices had to be visited. Instead, I was ushered into a cool, dim, carpeted room and entertained by three men who, though ignorant of any European language, made me feel welcome and at home. They all wore baggy cotton trousers and loose, cleverly embroidered shirts hanging below the knees and turbans piled high above broad, smooth brows. As we sat cross-legged, performing the ritual of tea-drinking, I felt myself being happily weaned from the twentieth century by their reposefulness.

I was two hours at the Customs and might have been sitting there yet if another petrol truck hadn't arrived en route from Meshed. The driver wanted to take me to Herat but after yesterday's experience I know that the one thing more deleterious than being fried on a cycle in a desert is being rattled through a desert by truck. However, I asked the driver to take two petrol cans of water and leave them fifteen and thirty miles away on the roadside, as I couldn't possibly carry enough water on Roz to replace the gallons of sweat lost.

The village near the Customs – Islam Qu'ala – which I had expected to look like an East Persian village, didn't look like anything but an Afghan village: every house was a miniature fortress, with special apertures for firing at your neighbour when there's a feud on. At a little distance from the houses was an encampment of black goat-hair tents similar to one I had passed on the outskirts of Meshed, with a few camels lying chewing the cud beside it; it would have been good for a photo but I decided I'd like to get the 'feel' of the country before drawing unnecessary attention to the fact that I was about to cross forty miles of uninhabited desert.

We arrived here at 6.30 p.m. after a most gruelling struggle; I thought nothing could be worse than Persian roads but of course Afghan roads are much, much worse. Poor Roz – how long will she survive?

Ghurion is off the 'main' road so I decided to spend the night in a little tea-house at the junction, which is run by a delightful old man. I'm still working on the principle that the fewer people who know I'm around the better. (Despite myself all the fuss about the dangers of Afghanistan is having its effect on my nerves: probably a few days among the Afghans will soothe me down.)

The tea here comes by the tea-pot, instead of by the glass as in Turkey and Persia. You get about a pint of it and a little china bowl half filled with sugar into which you pour the tea and by the time you've had four bowlfuls the sugar is all gone. Having seen nothing of Afghanistan but a Customs House, a desert and a tea-house, there's no more to report till I get to Herat tomorrow morning.

3

Compulsory Bus Rides

HERAT TO KABUL

HERAT, 10 APRIL

I slept very well last night in my roadside tea-house, curled up in a corner of the one-roomed building, with moonlight streaming through the doorway that had no door and the 'proprietor' curled up under his camel-hair rug in another corner, rifle and turban to hand. He was a dear old boy, who seemed quite shocked when I attempted to pay him before leaving at 5.30 a.m.

It took me four and a half hours to cover the thirty miles to Herat but I enjoyed the wide silence of the desert in the cool of the morning.

This is a city of absolute enchantment in the literal sense of the word. It loosens all the bonds binding the traveller to his own age and sets him free to live in a past that is vital and crude but never ugly. Herat is as old as history and as moving as a great epic poem – if Afghanistan had nothing else it would have been worth coming to experience this. Even the loss of my wallet containing over £12 hasn't been able to depress me today. (It was not stolen but just slipped out of my pocket somehow, as I was exploring.) Of course I'd feel worse about such a loss in Europe; the fact that every Afghan I've seen so far obviously needs £12 even more than I do is quite a consolation. During a long trek some disaster of the sort is inevitable.

The Afghans impress me as a people with very clear-cut personalities, in contrast to the rather characterless Persians. Everyone I've met so far stands out as an individual; for example, the three servants at this hotel. One is an elderly man, very slim and sad-looking and withdrawn from the world. When not working (and that means most of the time) he sits in odd corners sipping tea or stands at strategic points of the stairs and corridors looking through everyone who passes and giving the impression of being in a mystical trance. When I arrived he came to my room with the book to sign and the whole scene was like some solemn religious ritual. The door curtain was pushed aside to admit this individual, wearing a long, pale pink muslin turban and bearing the book open at the relevant page. He bowed very low and glided across the floor in bare feet, laid it on the table before me, bowed again and glided backwards towards the door where he stood erect with arms folded looking into the far distance while I filled in details. Then he glided back to collect the book, bowed, backed to the door, gave a final and most profound bow and disappeared soundlessly – the whole performance without attempting to utter a word and, despite all the bowing, there was not a trace of servility.

The waiter is equally fascinating in a different way. Aged about twenty and very handsome, with pale, clear white skin, luminous brown eyes and wonderfully clear-cut features, he has a princely bearing and paces slowly round the dining-room; he is extremely efficient, in a quiet way, and looks as though he has some special private joy which makes him supremely happy. The little 'boots' is a character too; aged about twelve, he has a round Mongolian face, a big permanent grin and a bouncing friendly manner. Watching me washing my teeth is for him an entertainment beyond compare – he positively holds his breath at the sheer excitement of the spectacle!

This is a 'Grade A' hotel: i.e. it has an Eastern lavatory but with flush attached (when I pulled the string the whole apparatus collapsed and I was drenched in rusty water – but perhaps I used immodest vigour!) and there is also a holder for lavatory paper on the wall which makes one feel that if one stayed here long enough it might have paper too some day. The establishment sports electrical fittings as well – but the supply failed an hour ago and I am now writing by oil-lamp – and my room has a door with a padlock and a window that opens, and clean though very threadbare sheets and blankets on the bed. Other amenities include a bathroom on this first-floor landing; the cold water is contained in a zinc barrel with tap attached and, as you wash, it drains away through a hole in the wall down into the yard. For all these luxuries one pays *6s. 2d.* per night.

Afghan 'fashions' for men look marvellously dignified, even when in tatters. The most common garment is one piece of cloth (usually cotton) which is worn so that it provides both a shirt and loose trousers to halfway down the calves. (Is this the 'seamless' garment of the Gospels?) Waist-length turbans, to protect the spinal cord against the sun, often have beautiful fringes and come in pastel shades of blue or pink or yellow. But there is no uniformity about dress – some wear sleeveless leather jackets inlaid with gold and silver, some fabulous brocade knee-length shirts, some heavy brocade coats, thrown over the shoulders in this weather, some brown homespun cloaks and others the flowing white robes which I have always associated with Arab countries. About fifty per cent go barefooted, even on horses and cycles – the latter being almost the only evidence of the twentieth century in Herat. The men, if Aryan, are considerably taller than Turks or Persians and are very handsome indeed. The women I simply haven't seen; very few appear on the streets and those few are completely veiled – not in the *chador* of east Turkey and Persia, which leaves eyes and nose just visible, but in the *burkah*, a garment like a tent with a piece of lace at eye-level. This lace is of such fine mesh that you have to be right beside them to distinguish it from the rest of the material and seeing the wearer standing still you don't know which is back or front: they look like people dressed up as ghosts. This afternoon I saw two women riding splendid ponies and asked their husband if I might photograph them, but he very vigorously refused permission. The only female face I've seen in the city was that of a Mongolian tribeswoman down from the mountains, bringing cloth to sell in the bazaar; she was galloping along the main street, astride and bareheaded with a baby tied to her back and its father galloping along behind on his silver-grey pony stallion.

I notice that most of the phaeton ponies are stallions who dash spiritedly around, their vehicles taking the corners on one wheel. This is all right if the mares are kept in purdah too – and evidently they are! It's a joy to see these ponies after the miserable specimens in Persian cities; they are well groomed and well fed here and their coats ripple with reflected sunlight. Oddly enough, they're the only clean looking objects, animate or inanimate, to be seen in the streets. Another point of contrast with Persia is that I haven't seen any beggars here, except for a few cripples in the immediate vicinity of the mosque.

The Afghan has not yet learned that tourists were invented to be fleeced and twice today my money was refused when I attempted to pay for tea. I am a guest of the country, so it pleases Allah when someone provides me with free refreshment . . .

During one of these pauses in a tea-house a man, whom I had never seen before and will never see again, silently approached, laid a packet of cigarettes beside me and vanished before I even had time to thank him; I couldn't help thinking then of my kind European friends who had warned me so often of the dangers of being a woman and a Christian in Muslim countries.

Strolling through the bazaar I was delightedly conscious of the fact that when Alexander's soldiers passed this way they must have witnessed scenes almost identical to those now surrounding me – bakers cooking flat bread in underground ovens, having spread the dough on leather cushions stuffed with straw and damped with filthy water; blindfolded camels walking round and round churning *mast* in stinking little dens behind their owners' stalls; butchers skinning and disembowelling a sheep and throwing scraps to the yellow, crop-eared dogs who have been waiting all morning for this happy event; tanners curing hides, weavers at their looms, potters skilfully firing pitchers of considerable beauty, cobblers making the curly-toed, exquisitely inlaid regional shoes and tailors cutting out the long, fleece-padded coats which when thrown over the shoulders of an Afghan makes him look like a fairy-story king.

On my way back to the hotel I observed hens importantly leading their excited broods to unrevealed destinations, tiny boys sitting cross-legged on the pavement meticulously cleaning oil-lamps, diminutive, anxious, furry donkey-foals who had temporarily lost their mothers, and youths squatting in doorways preparing hookahs for the men to smoke. It's unlikely that the other Afghan cities will be equally attractive; Herat is now so cut off from everywhere on every side that it's just gone jogging along happily while the rest of the country is being modernised by the US and the USSR.

The 'traffic' police here take my fancy particularly; obviously they're trained in the French system and they stand on little platforms with batons, wearing caps to prove they're police but otherwise keeping to the national costume. The joke is that you see them making a quick sweeping movement with one hand and a 'stop' movement with the other and in answer to the 'come on' signal, with its flourish of the baton that should herald the rush past of a stream of high-powered cars, twelve camels appear, heavily laden and chained together, and pace solemnly by the police-box taking about ten minutes to clear the junction. Meanwhile the 'stop' signal has briefly halted a horseman who pulls up his steed on its hind legs, looks from the camels to the policeman with a curl of the lip and then proceeds to canter round the caravan and gallop away up the main street. Occasionally a truck appears from Persia (because of the Pakistan blockade, everything now has to come from the outside world via Russia or Persia), and then there is real commotion which the police are helpless to control; donkeys, horsemen, camels, phaetons and flocks of sheep and goats all flee in the wrong direction at the wrong moment, the camels looking outraged at having to amble faster than usual.

This morning I went to the outskirts of the town just to wander among the green woods and sit on green grass beside a little stream in a beautifully kept public park. Many of the streets are lined with enormous pine trees and a glorious garden of lawns and lavishly blooming rose bushes stretches in front of the mosque. There were no restrictions about me visiting this mosque (without a camera) and it is so very beautiful that I felt it compensated for the Meshed frustration. I sat on the shady side of the enormous courtyard for almost an hour, enjoying the mosaics and the gold of the brickwork glowing against the blue sky. It was very peaceful there with no sound or movement except for a myriad twittering martins swooping in and out of the cool, dim passages between the hundreds of pillared archways. Meshed is probably as beautiful but it would be difficult to surpass this. The predominant colour here is blue of all shades, with yellow, black, pink, brown, green and orange tiles blended so skilfully that from a certain distance a façade or minaret looks as though made of some magic precious metal for the colour of which there is no name. Also, quite apart from its colouring, the proportions of the whole vast series of buildings are superb.

ROBAT, 11 APRIL

There was so much to say yesterday that I failed to mention the big route problem. My original intention was to go to Kabul via the northern road as this is by far the most beautiful and interesting, but that plan has been ruled out because of the current tricky situation with Russia. Therefore, when I reported to the police in Herat yesterday I told them I wished to go by the central route, which is the next most interesting – but the Commander said, 'No!' Apparently this road is closed to all traffic because it is too infested with bandits to be adequately policed. Even if I had wanted to have fun and games with the authorities, as in Persia, I realised that I couldn't as they're quite a different type here – clearly their 'No' means 'No'; so now I'm on the third, southern route, via Khandahar, and am lucky to have my permit to cycle confirmed by the police who took a very dim view of my ambitions and tried to get me aboard a bus. In fact I may have to give in at some stage on this road as it would be silly to risk more than fifty miles unbroken desert with Roz and there may be one eighty-mile stretch. I'll investigate the situation fully when we get to that point.

We left Herat at 4.45 a.m. because it will get hotter every day now, going due south. A glorious eight- or nine-mile oasis of green fields and woods surrounds the city and the wheat and barley are within a few weeks of harvesting. Then – about five miles out – the road became perfect! I nearly fell off with astonishment and joy and Roz really let herself go and whizzed along at an average of 15 m.p.h. Our unexpected bliss lasted all day – God bless Russia! There's an average of one truck and two buses a day on this route so the Russians certainly didn't build a flawless road here for the convenience of the Afghans; but at the moment I couldn't care less who built it or why – I only hope it lasts.

A double row of pines, alternating with a richly pink flowering shrub, lasted well beyond the green belt out into the desert. Then, just as it was getting hot enough to make me fret slightly about having no hat, the road began to climb through mountains that were great barren piles of grey, slaty rock, but, because of the good surface, we covered just over eighty miles today despite much walking. I used my chlorinated pills for the first time in some doubtful-looking water obtained during the afternoon from a nomad camp, where the people were very courteous and kind. They invited me to have a meal with them and served some sort of porridge mixed with cheese and camel's milk; I suppose I'll get used to it but at the moment I wouldn't actually say that camel's milk is my favourite beverage. Huge herds of camels were being grazed around the encampment; goats or sheep wouldn't survive this terrain. I asked if I might take photographs but though they didn't refuse they were obviously against the idea so it would have been an abuse of hospitality to insist.

We arrived here at 7.20 p.m., just after dark. This is a small town with some rather grim-looking characters around and I'm almost sorry I didn't stay for the night with my nomads, where I would have felt safer. But one can't judge yet; the Afghans seem very reserved and distant people and what I feel as 'grimness' may be merely aloofness.

From the map it looks like more lovely mountains tomorrow – if only the road keeps Russian! Early bed now.

KHANDAHAR, 12 AND 13 APRIL

For reasons that will soon become apparent I'd no opportunity to report on the day's activities last night, so I'm doing both dates now.

I was up at 4.30 a.m. yesterday morning, after a good sleep on carpets in a corner of a tea-house. I have decided that Afghans are much more 'comfortable' people to travel among than Persians, despite their unbending gravity – or perhaps because of it. A dense, curious throng surrounded us every time we stopped in Persia but though here our arrival must be equally a rarity, no one crowds us out – you'd think they were used to a continual flow of cycling women through their villages! They are very interested to know where one has come from and what route was taken to Afghanistan, but they ask no questions – just listen and look politely if you choose to explain by mime and a map. I find the contrast very intriguing; Afghanistan never attained the heights of civilisation that Persia did, nor has she ever descended to Persia's present depths. Is it that if a nation expends sufficient energy to get to a peak she hasn't enough left to maintain herself there and falls far, whereas if she remains at a certain restricted level a limited degree of national well-being can be maintained indefinitely? I suppose history proves that this is the pattern.

But to get back to 4.30 a.m., when I set off down the road and after fifty yards was held up by two police, this time wearing the jackets of their uniforms to emphasise the solemnity of the occasion. They said I'd have to go by autobus to Khandahar, and I said, 'What rot!' and showed my pass from the Commander in Herat. Then they pointed to a petrol-tanker and signed that it couldn't go on either, and to their own jeep containing two soldiers with machine-guns! (You never saw anything quite so unhappy as an Afghan soldier wearing Western uniform – the poor lads looked as though they were in a torture-chamber.) I began to wonder now whether (*a*) World War III had started or (*b*) a little local war with Russia was brewing. Anyway something was happening somewhere so I retired to the tea-house and went asleep again until 7 a.m., having been told that the bus was coming at 7.30. Eventually it came at 10 a.m. and all the passengers tumbled out for *chi* and hands and face washing in the *jube*, and lavatory work in an adjacent field; unlike Turkish and Persian tea-houses, Afghan tea-houses have no lavatories attached. Two women were travelling on the roof amidst everyone's goods and chattels – very symbolic! I simply can't imagine what torture it must have been for them. Of course they don't often travel at all and my horror was multiplied by ten when I discovered that these two were going to Kabul hospital because they were very *ill*; yet for 1,000 km they had to adhere to the top of a bouncing bus on an awful road through blazing sun and cold night air and choking dust.

The bus looked like something left on a municipal dump for a year and then retrieved during a National Emergency. It was almost entirely home-made with no cover on the engine and no doors or windows. You could read on the ceiling inside that it was constructed partly from wooden boxes in which something had been imported from the USSR. The wheels had belonged to a truck and were far too big for the body and the seats were planks across which you scrambled to get to your place as no space was wasted on an aisle down the middle. The bus had been so overcrowded on leaving Herat that my entry made no difference to the general misery (not that the Afghans seemed to regard it as misery) of being tightly wedged with nothing to lean on back or front and no chance to move an inch in any direction once you sat down. Eventually at 11 a.m. we set off and about ten miles from Robat the road petered out – not merely the good road, but any road at all. For the next two hours we bumped on over the hard rock and baked sand of the desert till the faintest trace of a track reappeared – which was worse than the desert. In the agony of the journey I'd forgotten to wonder why we were being compelled to travel in convoy but towards evening we passed a Land-Rover with its windshield shattered and its doors riddled by bullet-holes and two soldiers on guard.

I won't go into all the harrowing details, beyond saying that it took us twenty-two and a half hours to cover 420 miles. Apart from some eighty miles of sheer desert it would have been good cycling country with lots of mountains – not in the least as monotonous as I'd expected. But the road – or lack of road – would have made it very gruelling. With the seven days I estimate I've saved I'm planning to go up from Kabul to Mazar-i-Sharif via Bamian and return via Kunduz – I think it is permitted to go up from the east side.

The one compensation last night was the beauty of that wonderfully desolate landscape by moonlight, never to be forgotten. We stopped often as, apart from praying and eating sessions, the bus had two punctures and the truck three. Also the bus frequently threatened to come apart at the seams and then the driver leaped out with a mallet and went round giving it unmerciful bangs on the vital spots. Of course no one minded all these delays: people here have no concept of time as we understand it. The majority wear watches as ornaments and I was diverted to discover that they can't read the time and don't see why they should learn! Yesterday is over, today is something to be enjoyed without fuss, and tomorrow – well, it's sinful to plan anything for the future because that's Allah's department and humans have no business to meddle with it. This basic tenet of Islam is obviously one reason why Muslim countries are so materially undeveloped; after a thousand years of living by such a doctrine it is difficult to think ahead constructively.

The majority of Afghans practise their religion very seriously. Yesterday evening at about 6.30 the convoy suddenly put on terrific speed – I thought my whole unfortunate carcase would be disjointed – and after some ten miles pulled up before a tea-house beside a stream. Then the truck drivers, the soldiers and the bus passengers all rushed together to the water for ritual washing, before taking off their cloaks, which they use as prayer mats, and spreading them on the dusty ground. By sundown the whole surrounding desert was dotted with standing, bowing and kneeling men: no wonder they remain so supple in old age for this performance five times daily would keep anyone fit. They had been through it all before at 3.30 p.m. and were to repeat it at 4.10 a.m. today. Meanwhile those two unhappy women were cowering in their burkahs up on the roof among the crates and bales and Roz. They didn't even come down for meals though their husbands passed them up bread and tea occasionally.

When I first boarded the bus the men simply ignored me, but after a couple of hours they thawed out and became very pleasant companions. Of course they wouldn't allow me to pay for anything en route (it was poetic justice that I lost my £12 in this country) though they were not forthcoming with the conventions we're used to – opening doors, ladies first, and all that; in fact it was taken for granted that I should be served *last* at meals. We had a very good stew last night with mincemeat balls and deliciously prepared spinach and the ubiquitous rice. After one mouthful of the rice I admitted defeat – it tasted as though cooked in *jube*-water and most Afghan *jubes* are stagnant. So I concentrated on bread (probably mixed with *jube*-water) which is darker here than in Persia and much more palatable. Breakfast was a bowl of hot sheep's milk with bread in it and a tea-potful of very sweet cocoa made of milk and finally green tea. Having toured Khandahar today and studied the butchers and the flies and the 'sanitary' conveniences, I've reluctantly decided to avoid meat, good though it tastes, and concentrate on boiled eggs for protein – I haven't forgotten my last Spanish trip and what dysentery feels like. In Turkey and Persia it wasn't the fly season, but here everything is permanently black with the pests.

We arrived in Khandahar at 9.30 a.m. and I said goodbye to my buddies and wished them joy on the next 515 km to Kabul. The armed guard went off to get a few hours sleep before going back to Herat with another convoy made up of a bus, two trucks and two Australians motoring to England and wishing they weren't. I'm afraid I've very little patience with people who complain indignantly about places like Afghanistan being primitive. Why didn't they (*a*) find that out before coming here and then (*b*) fly from Lahore to London?

I came straight to the hotel, got my sore bones into bed and slept till 2 p.m. This hotel is a filthy building, but again my bed is clean and the only furniture in the room, apart from bed and chair, is a fine solid writing desk which compensates for a lot.

When I went off to explore at 2.30 p.m. it was overcast so not too hot. This is quite an attractive city but after Herat anything would be an anticlimax and it's disquieting to find the place teeming with Americans and their works. Obviously a terrific battle is going on to win over Afghanistan, but I hope neither side succeeds.

The Afghans smoke fewer cigarettes than the Persians. Not one passenger smoked in the bus but many chewed a green powdery stuff out of little tins kept in their pockets and the results were spat out incessantly on to the floor. No cigarettes are made here; Russian blends cost 9*d.* for twenty (pure poison) and English blends, specially ordered by the Afghan Government from England and labelled to that effect, cost 2*s.* for twenty. All the popular American blends are also 2*s.* a packet.

I've a bad sore throat this evening, which is not surprising, as last night it turned very cold from about 3 to 5 a.m., when we were crossing the mountains, and I was chilled through – I am still thinking of those two unfortunate women.

An hour ago a fierce southerly gale blew a sandstorm over the city; I felt very glad that Roz and I were not exposed to its horrors.

Undoubtedly (despite clean beds) the Afghans are, on balance, *much* dirtier in clothes, personal habits and dwellings than either the Turks or Persians. And I thought Persia bad enough when I got there! The light here goes out every ten or fifteen minutes for about five minutes, which is very right and proper; it would be too boring to travel all the way to Central Asia and then have an infallible electricity supply.

In many ways English influence is apparent here: most of the Afghans I met today spoke a little English and addressed me as 'Memsahib', which I find infuriating. Also a number of shop and public signs are in English as well as in Pushto or Pharsi; one sees some lovely spellings – 'CLOADS DRI CLEENED'! But nearly all the few Afghan-owned cars, jeeps and trucks seem to be Russian. I must write to Mr Khrushchev and tell him that a few buses would not be superfluous in the next consignment.

I hope to make Kabul in five or six days, depending on heat, roads and other contingencies such as mountain passes. Of course one never knows – we could be there under escort in forty-eight hours if the bandits move the scene of their activities.

KALAT-E-GHIZLOT, 14 APRIL

I woke this morning at 4 a.m. and leapt energetically out of bed, stark naked, to see a fine bearded warrior in each of the other two beds, which had been empty when I retired; happily they missed the fun, being sound asleep. This intrusion didn't really surprise me because I had already observed the craziness of the hotel key system. There was only *one* key to twenty rooms, and as all the rooms were occupied – which here means families of up to ten members in a room containing four single beds – with people coming and going and wanting their doors locked and unlocked and relocked, or their womenfolk incarcerated while they went out to town, the distraught lad in charge of the key had been kept in a state of perpetual motion on the previous evening.

Roz and I left Khandahar at 4.30 a.m. and the road was good for all of today's ninety miles – and will continue good for the first ten miles tomorrow. This time it's 'God bless the Americans' who within four years expect to have completed the 320 miles from Kabul to Khandahar. On the outskirts of Khandahar I passed various other evidences of American A.I.D. – little factories, a new school and an electricity power plant.

It was very hot today, with only two little villages en route. I would have been tormented by thirst but for milk obtained from various nomad camps (there were plenty of them) and now I'm quite muzzy in the head after so much sun. At 11 a.m. the heat compelled me to stop for four hours at a village; I slept for two hours and then wrote a sheaf of 'duty' letters to be posted in Kabul.

We arrived here at 7.15 p.m. This local hotel is inexplicably vast and I'm the only inhabitant; as food is not served I went to an eating-house in the village and gorged on bread and mutton-stew. (I felt too hungry to keep my good resolution about not eating meat!) The roof of the eating-house was so low that big six-footers in flowing robes had to bend their heads while walking to the carpet they had chosen to sit on. More wood than usual is in evidence in the buildings around here – though one sees few trees growing – and the ceiling and 'pillars' were of big, crudely-hewn trunks blackened by years of lamp and hookah smoke; but everything else, including the cooking stove, was of mud. I love the washing-ritual. Here, as in Persia, a special boy is employed for the purpose. Serious as an acolyte, he comes to each person with a brass or copper jug, round-bellied and long-spouted, containing very hot water, and with a basin shaped like a witch's hat turned upside-down. Having poured water over the hands into the basin he then presents a filthy towel and as cutlery is unknown here, this rite is repeated after the meal. It is fascinating to sit on the floor in a corner watching it all by the soft light of oil-lamps suspended on chains from the ceiling to about eighteen inches above floor level. This light reflects on the copper jugs, and glows in the quick dark eyes of the men, their faces strong-featured beneath high turbans. Huge shadows stir on the walls when someone arrives or departs, moving lithely in bare feet, and then the small room seems even smaller. The rapid trickling of the washing-water mingles with the meditative gurgle of the hookahs as they are passed from man to man, puffed at ceremoniously and then repacked and relit no less ceremoniously, with embers carried from the stove in lieu of matches. And always there's the other ritual of *chi*-drinking, so that when I left I had to pick my way carefully among a litter of little Japanese tea-pots and bowls. By now I'm in love with Afghanistan – with its simplicity, its courtesy and its leisureliness and with the underlying *sanity* of an area fortunate enough to have remained very backward indeed . . .

Despite the heat, today's was a glorious ride, across vast unpeopled widths of sand and barren sun-split clay. Lines of naked peaks, like broken swords, were just visible along the horizon and the only alleviation of the surrounding flatness was the deep, dead canyons which are waiting for the floods to revive them. When I came to the oasis at midday its green orchards and meadows seemed passionately fertile amidst the unproductive wastes and on entering its shade the temperature dropped by 15°. It is just as well I'm moving north because I couldn't stand much more of this – at 3.30 p.m. furnace blasts of hot air were ricocheting off the face of the desert and even my hair was soaked with sweat. I'm deadbeat now so early to bed.

MUKUR, 15 APRIL

We only covered sixty-eight miles today; the road was appalling once the American contribution to my comfort ended and we wouldn't have got even this far but for a deliciously cool northerly breeze which blew all day.

Prepare for shocks. At 10 a.m. Roz had a puncture and by 11.15 a.m. *I* had repaired it. Even more sensational – at 1.30 p.m. the chain broke and again I, myself (alone and unaided!), got out the spare links and after one and three-quarter hours of intense concentration figured how the thing operated and mended it! It is astonishing what latent talents are suddenly revealed by breakdowns in mid-desert.

The first half of today's ride was through comparatively fertile country with many streams and consequently many little villages surrounded by acres of wheat and lucerne and by groves of poplars. Then we were back to the desert and the nomad camps. One of these donated water for mending the puncture, which was jolly decent considering that they have to bring water-skins about ten miles on camels to the nearest well. At this camp I saw a pure white, new-born camel, whose mother was ill, being fed out of a leather bottle by an adorable nomad infant aged about four years. After the broken chain interlude came some dramatically beautiful gorges and extraordinary landscapes of fissured earth. Afghanistan is certainly living up to my expectations; it's a pity brainwashing tactics were used to dissuade me because I must admit that I'm now aware all the time of a slight underlying tension which mars what would otherwise be a completely enjoyable experience. I suppose *all* the people can't be wrong *all* the time and every Afghan I've met has said that he personally would *not* cycle alone through his own country.

We arrived here at 6.45 p.m. and I asked for the chief's house as there is no hotel or police barracks and I funked the tea-house after one quick look. A young man led me to the outskirts of the town and through a most beautiful orchard, where the trees were gay with bell-shaped, flame-coloured blossoms and a cool, deep carpet of lucerne lay beneath them. Then we came to an enormous mud compound, where the chief, his *five* wives, fourteen sons and uncounted daughters, thirty-eight grandchildren and sundry cousins all live in various apartments around a courtyard through which flows a swift stream with weeping willows and birches lining its banks.

Several of the chief's sons speak English and/or German, and I had a long conversation with one of them, aged nineteen, whose seventeen-year-old wife has borne him three children and who is about to acquire a second, fourteen-year-old wife. When I asked him what his wife thought about a second wife arriving on the scene, he said that Afghan women don't talk to their husbands and anyway it's none of her business *how* many wives he has! His father's fifth wife, aged eighteen, was acquired three years ago when the senior wife, now aged forty-eight, retired from stud. A total of 135 members of the family plus twenty-two servants live in the compound.

I'm writing this sitting by the stream waiting for supper (I suggested bread and boiled eggs but very much fear rice will come) and one of the servants has just glided up with a new lantern to give me more light: it's all deliciously like the Arabian Nights. Tonight I'll sleep in the maidens' (eleven- to fourteen-year-old girls) quarters and of course this has been my first chance to *see* any Afghan women. Physically they're very beautiful (the men being so tanned, one doesn't realise that Afghans are as white-skinned as we are) but the effect on their mental development of the purdah-system, as practised here, is horrifying. We should feel grateful for having been born 'free' and 'equal' – something we take completely for granted though the majority of the world's women do not yet enjoy this right.

Most Afghan village houses have no windows and the walls are lined with little alcoves which serve as cupboards. One misses the Persian carpets; coarse matting is more usual here. I can now see a servant coming with my supper on a tray; obviously I am considered not really fit company for the women of the family, so I must eat in solitude!

GHAZNI, 16 APRIL

I went to bed last night *dead drunk*. I was enjoying my 'Irish stew' of mutton, potatoes and onions when one of my host's sons arrived with a bottle and said he'd heard Christian women liked alcohol and would I have some wine? It is hardly necessary to record my reply. He then filled a tumbler ('Made in Czechoslovakia') with what looked like white wine and I, being thirsty and having eschewed the muddy water served with the meal, took a gulp of it in all innocence – and nearly collapsed! I don't pretend to know what it was, but it certainly was not wine as we know it. My gullet must be fairly leathery by now but I felt as if my mouth, throat and tummy were being cauterised. When I'd stopped choking the boy said, 'With water, yes, it is better?' and I nodded, feeling that however many lethal bacteria the water contained they would all die instantly on meeting this brew. So I finished it diluted and then, to my horror, found myself almost incapable of standing up and going to bed, and quite incapable of talking coherently. It comes to something when *one* drink can knock me out! I was in a besotted coma by 9.30 p.m. but up at 4 a.m. as usual – without a 'head', to my astonishment.

It was much cooler today and the road was slightly less agonising, so we covered the seventy miles from Mukur by 2.30 p.m. I was pushing myself to allow time to explore this city which I guessed would be congenial because of historical associations and no Americanisation; in fact it's a good second to Herat.

I tried to buy a film here, but none was available, which was very frustrating as the fine old fortifications, ruined mosques (which you may photograph), the river and camel-market make Ghazni even more photogenic than Herat. However, as things developed I was perhaps lucky to be without a film today.

Leaving Roz in the hotel, I went off to explore, still carrying my camera in hope of finding a film. For some time I strolled around the base of the old city – which looks like a more primitively constructed Avila – doing no harm to anyone and scarcely noticing the battalion of inconceivably scruffy soldiers who were marching past me, until suddenly two privates broke rank, seized my arms and hustled me about a hundred yards up the street to a military police barracks. There they asked for my passport, which I explained was in the hotel, so my camera was promptly confiscated and I was locked for fifty minutes in a cell which had been used as a lavatory by all its former occupants and never cleaned out. Then an officer appeared in a frenzied flurry of profuse apologies and said that it was all a mistake – the army was on manoeuvres in the locality and his men had been instructed to look out for 'hostile observers'. He saw by my passport that I was harmless and hoped I would forgive the incident and would now have vodka with him. I told him there was no offence taken but explained that unhappily I hadn't time for vodka as I wanted to see the old city of Ghazni and the Moghul tomb – so by way of atonement he laid on an army car to drive me there.

The tomb of Afghanistan's most famous poet, whose name no one could reasonably be expected to remember, is a very impressive marble affair in a little mosque all to itself on a hilltop outside the city. I walked up there at sunset and stood overlooking a rich spread of grain-fields, orchards dense with blossom, and groves of slim, graceful sinjit trees. The bird-song in these oases is continuous and very sweet; now, apart from swallows, the birds are all unfamiliar to me.

I've just been informed that the Americans are moving in here soon; I'm glad I saw it first. It's quite cold tonight, with snow on the hills to the east and the sky overcast – what a change!

KABUL, 17 APRIL

Today was a repeat of the Robat performance. I slept late, having had no siesta yesterday, and woke at 6.45 a.m. to find a tremendous thunderstorm in progress and *rain* (of all unlikely things!) coming down in buckets. I enjoyed a leisurely breakfast of omelette and bread as I had only intended covering forty-eight miles today (to Top, the village midway between Ghazni and Kabul) and when the rain stopped at 8 a.m. we left the hotel. But then, outside the town, came another road block, with what was by local standards a vast convoy of two buses, five trucks and a motorcyclist, all lined up outside a tea-house. I joined the queue and asked what it was this time. No one knew definitely; some said that a Danish engineer working for an American company had been shot at and wounded while others maintained that two Indians going to Europe had copped it yesterday evening twenty miles north of Ghazni. I wasn't surprised at this vagueness; the authorities here are extremely sensitive about such 'incidents' and cover them up as best they can. Anyway, whatever the cause, the effect was that Roz and I boarded one of the 'buses' at 9.30 a.m. and arrived here, having covered a distance of only ninety-three miles, at 10 p.m. A young army officer who sat beside me on the bus said that Pakistani tribesmen were behind all the trouble; he accused them of coming over the frontier and shooting up travellers (especially foreigners) to discredit Afghanistan in the eyes of the world. Maybe that's partly true, but it certainly wasn't Pakistanis who attacked the Land-Rover on the road between Robat and Farah.

I have just been told that Afghan time is one hour and ten minutes ahead of Persian time – a comical refinement in this land where ten hours or ten days more or less mean nothing whatever to the average citizen.

4

Misadventure with a Rifle-butt

KABUL TO BAMIAN

KABUL, 18 APRIL

I have just registered the fact that Easter happened four days ago – that's what comes of travelling in 'Eathen Lands! It gives me all I can do to cope with the date and I've long since given up the unequal struggle to distinguish one day of the week from another; when Friday is Sunday and Thursday is Saturday and Saturday is Monday it seems hardly worth the effort. But presumably I'll register the significance of 25 December when the time comes.

Kabul, though so much of it has been recently rebuilt, is an attractive little city. Many of the new buildings and public monuments are hideously *avant-garde* but their incongruity is so extreme in this country that the total effect is comic rather than offensive. The city streets were paved (by the Russians) only a few years ago and today I saw a traffic policeman abandoning his post to kneel on the footpath and say his prayers at the appointed hour.

This frank devotion is for me one of the most impressive features of Islamic culture. If we accept that it is more than a superstition then there is something very wonderful indeed about mixing one's daily deeds and one's daily prayers in such an unselfconscious fashion, instead of keeping each in an airtight compartment.

Kabul reminds me of Sofia in that the traffic is virtually nil by capital city standards; you can cycle happily around with only camel caravans, herds of pack-donkeys and droves of fellow-cyclists to impede the way. Among the injuries which Roz sustained in Meshed was a damaged back brake so I took her into a cycle shop today and she was efficiently cured in five minutes.

One sees a few women and quite a number of girls unveiled in the streets here and many men wear European suits, though happily these are still in the minority. I bought a first (and last) souvenir for myself this morning – one of the famous Afghan sheepskin coats. It's a second-hand (or more likely fifth-hand) model and looks and smells exactly like a dead sheep, which is logical enough, as the Afghans haven't a clue about curing skins. Anyway the main thing is that it cost only 28*s*., whereas a new one would have cost about £6. It still has years of wear in it, if the Irish public can bear the stink.

The weather here today is just like April at home – showery, warm sun, cool breeze – but with growth about two weeks ahead of us. This is the month when northern Afghanistan gets all its rainfall – heavy showers and thunderstorms nearly every day.

German seems to be more widely spoken than English among Afghans educated before the war. At that period the country was teeming with Germans – it is now beginning to teem with them again – and I am told that German is still the first foreign language of the ten per cent who go to school. Russian is widely understood too, even by the illiterate majority. In each city I noticed that the radio news from Russia was switched on regularly and listened to attentively. Russians seem to handle the propaganda tool of aid to backward countries much more intelligently than the Americans do. They achieve lots of *little* things – electricity for small towns, paving city streets, building silos and presenting superior seeds for crops – as well as launching big projects such as roads, whereas the Americans concentrate on enormous schemes – roads and dams that cost five times what the Russians spend but will take years to complete and make no impression whatever on the minds of simple people. The more I see of life in these 'undeveloped countries' and of the methods adopted to 'improve' them, the more depressed I become. It seems criminal that the backwardness of a country like Afghanistan should be used as an excuse for America and Russia to have a tug-of-war for possession. Having spoken to nine or ten young Afghans who have been exposed to Western influences, I notice an impatient feeling of contempt for their own country, an undiscriminating worship of everything American and a general restlessness, rootlessness and discontent. They repudiate their native culture yet cannot succeed in adopting an alien civilisation which they imagine is superior, though they don't understand the first thing about it. Give me the nomads' outlook every time – they haven't heard of America yet. I don't claim to know the right answer to the 'underdeveloped' problem but I feel most strongly that the Communist answer is less wrong than the Western; the Communists have much more imaginative understanding of different national temperaments, as two Russians I spoke to here today revealed very clearly. They want to impose Communism as a way of life, but with the minimum of damage to the traditional foundations of the country concerned, whereas Westerners have told me repeatedly that they want to bulldoze those foundations right away and start a nice, new, hygienic society from scratch – an ambition that seems to me almost too stupid to be true.

I have just discovered that the sale or consumption of alcohol in Afghanistan is strictly forbidden by law – a piece of information handed to me with a glass of Scotch by my hostess in the Diplomatic Enclave! Even tourists can't get permission to have it here as they can in the prohibition states of India.

My plans for the immediate future are in 'a state of chassis'; my host wants to drive me to Bamian tomorrow (a Friday, so the Embassy will be closed) and I, of course, want to cycle there and, if possible, on up to Mazar-i-Sharif. But no one seems to know whether the road beyond Bamian is free of snow or not.

I had to register with the police as a tourist this morning, which involved going to three separate offices and waiting hours in each. The head of the Tourist Department, Mr Tarzi, is a great buddy of our Mr Driscoll, this year's President of the International Tourist Board. I couldn't believe it when I met an Afghan who knew Dublin! He's an exceptionally nice man and is now trying to find out about the Mazar road before issuing me with my permits to move from Kabul. But everything is so slow here that, tomorrow being Friday, Saturday is the first day I can get my papers straightened out and make definite plans. Everyone agrees that the business of being a tourist in Kabul involves so much paperwork and waiting in offices that one has no time to see the sights. Not that there are many; apart from the magnificent museum, the city itself, with its lovely semicircle of mountains curving round it, is the chief 'sight'.

KABUL, 19 APRIL

If my arrival in Teheran was a sensation, it has been a riot here! The Tourist Office and Press photographers, complete with flashlights, were on my heels the whole day, and my 'Impressions of Afghanistan' will be in the *Kabul Times* tomorrow. 'Everyone' wants to meet me – not that I'm surprised or imagine that it's because I'm me. Kabul is wonderful from a visitor's point of view, but if one had to live here for two years, and if one were accustomed to cars (which only senior officials can have) and to TV, daily papers, mod. cons, pubs, cafés, cinemas and theatres, life without them must seem rather monotonous. This is rated a 'hardship post' by foreign services and everyone is paid a twenty-five per cent bonus to come to Kabul. It's funny to see the sedate Embassy staffs scooting round on bicycles or walking, but it does mean that for at least two years of their existence they lead healthy lives with daily exercise.

KABUL, 20 APRIL

Cheers! By signing a statement to say that I was cycling alone to Mazar entirely on my own responsibility I obtained the necessary police pass, so off we go first thing tomorrow. I spent eight and a quarter hours in four different offices getting the pass because forty-five Hajis were looking for permits to go on a pilgrimage to Mecca and I was at the end of their queue in every office.

I'm only taking the saddlebag with essential kit as there is no point in dragging my panniers and knapsack from here to Mazar and back again.

QU'LAH DOAB, 21 APRIL

I've decided that when I suspected the Afghans of a narrow hostility to emancipated women, I was being unfair. Many of them give the impression of being almost frightened by the spectacle of a lone woman roaming around their land – a phenomenon so startling to their simple minds that they are at a loss as to how they should react. Obviously this situation throws the onus on the more flexible-minded Westerner and, now that I've realised how much depends on my approach to them, relations are far easier to manage. I already love the country and the people and somehow language barriers don't matter when one feels such a degree of sympathy with a race which responds so graciously and kindly to a smile or a gesture of friendship.

We left Kabul at 7 a.m. in perfect cycling weather with a brilliant, warm sun, a cool breeze behind us and the air crisp and clear. Beyond a doubt today's run up the Ghorband valley was the most wonderful cycle-ride of my life. Surely this must have been the Garden of Eden – it's so beautiful that I was too excited to eat the lunch my hostess had packed for me and spent the day in a sort of enchanted trance. High hills look down on paddy-fields and vivid patches of young wheat and neat vineyards; on orchards of apricot, peach, almond, apple and cherry trees smothered in blossom, and on woods of willows, ash, birch and sinjit, their new leaves shivering and glistening in wind and sun. Lean, alert youths, their clothes all rags and their bearing all pride, guard herds of cattle and nervous, handsome horses and donkeys with woolly, delicately tripping foals, and fat-tailed sheep with hundreds of bounding lambs, and long-haired goats whose kids are among the most delightful of young animals. At intervals there are breaks in the walls of sheer rock on either side and then one sees the more distant peaks of the Hindu Kush rising to 18,000 feet, their snows so brilliant that they are like Light itself, miraculously solidified and immobilised. The little mud villages remain invisible until you reach them, so perfectly do they blend with their background, and the occasional huge, square, mud fortresses, straddling hilltops, recall the cruel valour of this region's past and have the same rigid, proud beauty as the men who built them. The 'road' – narrow and rough – alternately runs level with the flashing river and leaps up mountain-sides to give unimpeded views for miles and miles along the valley.

This is the part of Afghanistan I was most eager to see, but in my wildest imaginings I never thought any landscape could be so magnificent. If I *am* murdered en route it will have been well worth while! Not that I think there's much chance of that; the seventy-eight miles of my route today were patrolled by armed soldiers in pairs, apparently for my special protection as the last pair went off duty when they had led me, at dusk, to the home of the Provincial Governor in this village. I should think that if solitary travellers do get killed here it is because they've not told the police, as requested, where they are going and when. It seems to be beyond dispute that Afghanistan has slightly more than its share of bandits, yet almost everyone who travels through is favourably impressed by the treatment they receive and it's high time the silly nonsense about the extreme dangers of this land were 'exposed' as exaggeration.

The average Afghan is at once hard-working and easy-going and retains lots of things that industrial psychiatrists are now laboriously struggling to rediscover. He is good-humoured but not very talkative. He loves music and often sings quietly to himself for hours on end. He also loves bird-song and flowers, is very sensitive to natural beauty and on the whole treats animals well – not only his superb horses, but also his pack-donkeys, who are pushed in the required direction more often than beaten, his strings of cynical camels, who show few signs of returning affection, and his flocks of goats and sheep, one of whom is usually a special pet. Most of all, he loves his children, who may well number up to thirty if he can afford four wives. He is, of course, hot-tempered and uncontrollably ferocious when roused, but once a dispute is settled without loss of honour on either side he embraces his opponent and they sing a duet. (One must applaud Mohammed's common-sense in prohibiting alcohol among his followers; if they stopped at pubs as often as they do at tea-houses the populations of the Islamic countries would long since have exterminated each other.) He is indifferent to hardship, on which he has been nurtured, he endures acute pain without a moan and he is among the most fearless of soldiers. In short, he's a man after my own heart.

The latest hair-raiser I heard in Kabul concerned a four-man team of Western surveyors who were recently shot up by the tribesmen because the tribal chiefs don't want the Government to know how much land they own, since a new system of land taxes is soon to be levied. Obviously the tribesmen had been given orders not to kill, as the surveyors were only wounded, and no Afghan would miss a man-sized target. I've often seen them potting tiny birds from fantastic distances just for the hell of it, which sounds a horrid hobby but is no worse than shooting such a glorious thing as a cock-pheasant for its food value. By now I've got quite used to all the men around me carrying rifles as Irishmen carry umbrellas and I've learned to beware of falling over the stacked weapons when entering a dark, windowless tea-house from bright sunshine.

This house reveals what some might describe as the poverty of Afghanistan but what I prefer to call its simplicity, since poverty denotes a lack of necessities and simplicity a lack of needs. The Governor is the most important man in the district yet the poorest Irish peasant would have a more elaborate home, though when one examines it every essential comfort is here.

The family consists of Mohammad Musa – my thirty-one-year-old host – his elderly mother, his seventeen-year-old wife, their five-months-old first baby and four servants. They are natives of Kabul and Mohammad, who speaks fluent English, is extremely well educated. At first he was most uncomfortable about entertaining a Westerner in such a home but my very evident happiness here has reassured him. His is, of course, a 'made marriage' but it seems very successful, although the young wife, who attended a Kabul Secondary School, tends to rebel against wearing the veil and would like to meet her husband's friends – concessions which he will never allow.

Mohammad's mother is a tremendous character – one of those old people who make the young realise that old age is not something to be dreaded, when it can give such mellowness and balance and contentment to a human being. I would have readily forgiven her for being distant to someone who represented, according to her traditions, the complete negation of womanhood but, although she speaks no English, the warmth of her welcome has made me feel truly 'one of the family' this evening. Not for the first time, I am astonished and humbled by the tolerance of Muslims, who so easily accept the fact that my standards differ from theirs, yet give me no feeling of being regarded as inferior on that account. Even more remarkable, the liberty which they recognise as my inheritance does not deter them from treating me with a courtesy too rarely found in modern Europe; by this civilised fusion of our two cultures I have all the advantages and none of the disadvantages of their own womenfolk. I think it is fair to say that the modern Muslim, even if he is an uneducated peasant, shows less prejudice towards other religions than we Christians do, with our persistent tendency to brand any religion not our own as 'ignorant superstition'. This Muslim tolerance makes it all the sadder that politicians so often artificially stimulate religious differences for their own ends.

As I write, sitting in a corner on a rug on the floor, with a roll of bedding at my back and a dim oil-lamp beside me, prayer-time has come and the old lady has gone off to her room for private devotions. Mohammad is kneeling on his prayer-mat in another corner, just now touching the ground with his forehead, his wife is sitting near me, breast-feeding the baby, and a manservant is spreading a cloth on the floor in front of us for supper. When my host heard that I was coming he took one of his guns (five of them are stacked beside the door) and went out and shot a deer – the answer to unexpected guests in this region! So it's venison and rice for supper, cooked on a mud stove in the compound.

BAMIAN, 22 APRIL

Another day of incredible, unforgettable and indescribable beauty, plus our highest climb yet – 10,380 feet over the Shibar Pass; I felt like a fly going up a wall.

At breakfast this morning Mohammad tried to persuade me to go by truck as he simply didn't believe a cycle could be got over the Shibar but when I reached the foot of the pass I was very glad I hadn't agreed to his kind suggestion. At the moment there is heavy traffic on this route because Afghanistan and Pakistan are not on speaking terms and their frontier is closed, so that many of the goods which would normally be imported via Karachi and the Khyber Pass are coming from Russia via Mazar-i-Sharif. But this track was never meant to be a grand trunk road and the sight of grossly overloaded and mainly 'home-made' trucks negotiating these fantastic hairpin bends, with inches between the outer wheels and a 1,000-foot drop, made me sweat with vicarious terror – and thank God that it was only vicarious as I pushed Roz up, keeping close to the cliffside. In fact, the climb wasn't as stiff as I had anticipated, because the foot of the pass is itself about 7,000 feet above sea level; yet over the last thousand feet I did notice the effects of the altitude – shortness of breath and aching calf-muscles. But it was worth it all to rise gradually from that fertile, warm valley to the still, cold splendour of the snow-line, where the highest peaks of the Hindu Kush crowd the horizon in every direction and one begins to understand why some people believe that gods live on mountain tops.

There's an astounding change on this northern side of the range. Within a few miles the whole landscape has altered from early summer to late winter; trees are almost bare, grass and wheat are just beginning to show and the temperature is many degrees lower.

The downward gradient is much less severe and at one point the road goes through a glorious narrow gorge of red-brown cliffs; these are so close, so high and so sheer that standing between them, looking up, one has the sensation of being a midget dropped into some ruggedly built edifice with a slight crack in the roof.

It was at the end of this gorge that disaster hit Roz; she suffered two vicious rips in the back tyre and I doubt if they can be patched. The road is excruciating but personally I've got used to the feeling of being dislocated in every joint at one bump and relocated at the next. However, it's different for poor Roz and today's calamity was my fault; I let her go too fast down the pass. This was because of the back brake again giving trouble so that the alternative to cycling too fast was walking, and when you've walked up to 10,380 feet you don't feel much like walking down. At this stage it was 5.15 p.m. and we were some twenty miles from Bamian, near the junction of the Mazar–Bamian road where there is a tiny village called Bulola. I asked about a bus and one was pointed out as going to Bamian 'in a few minutes', so Roz was loaded up and I sat in. My other buses were luxurious compared with this one. The floor was covered in sheep and goat droppings and the steering-wheel was held together with sticking-plaster – a device not calculated to soothe one's nerves on a journey in this terrain. We finally set off at 6.20 p.m., by which time I was frozen stiff – it had been raining hard and there was no glass in the windows, as usual – after sitting patiently watching huge piles of hides being roped together and tied to the roof till the whole rickety contraption looked gruesomely top-heavy. And just before our departure nine men had climbed up and settled down on top of the hides, wrapping themselves in their huge rugs.

About two miles beyond Bulola the engine broke down; it was now dark and raining, and the repairs, during which the headlights were put out of order, took very nearly an hour. At 7.30 p.m. we resumed the journey up and over a 10,000-foot pass on a corkscrew 'road', barely wide enough for one vehicle, with sheer drops which I could imagine, but happily not see, as there was no light. Then quite soon there *was* light – lots of it – when the daily spring thunderstorm began. For several minutes lightning was continuous – not flashes as we know them, but glaring sheets of blue illumination, revealing gaunt peaks on one side and sickening ravines on the other; yet it was all so beautiful and awe-inspiring that one simply forgot to be afraid. The thunder reverberating in the mountains was deafening – peal after peal, the echoes of each being drowned in the crash of the next. With all this came gusts of gale-force wind carrying enormous hailstones which took the skin off my nose where they struck it as I sat next to the window-that-wasn't. There are limits even to Afghan toughness and when this demonstration started the bus stopped for the nine men on the roof to come below. As the 'inside' was already overcrowded beyond belief this meant that I had three children on my lap for the rest of the journey; I had only one two-year-old at the beginning. We waited for about fifteen minutes until the worst was over because to attempt to negotiate that winding track with the driver intermittently dazzled by lightning would have been suicidal. (To my mind the whole trip wasn't far short of suicidal anyway.) Yet what an experience to see a landscape, dramatic in itself, under such melodramatic conditions – like some inspired choreographer's setting for *Faust*.

Soon after we had restarted a melodrama of a different kind began. The system on these privately owned buses is that the owner-driver's assistant, usually an adolescent known as a *bacha*, collects the fares during the journey. The *bacha* now asked twelve *afghanis* from everyone and a number of passengers protested that ten had been agreed on before the start. Hell then broke loose and while I was bundling the children under the seat an infuriated tribesman, brandishing his rifle, climbed over me, trying to get at the driver; the *bacha* pushed him, and he fell backwards, striking me a frightful blow on the ribs with the rifle-butt. I looked round to see a terrifying forest of rifle-barrels behind me – terrifying because in a jolting bus I imagined them going off accidentally; but of course these men know exactly what they are doing with their triggers, if not with their butts, and nothing of the sort happened. The unarmed *bacha* continued his heroic defence of the driver, the bus stopped yet again, the driver got out and stood grasping *his* gun and refusing to go another yard until everyone had paid their twelve *afghanis* and I hastily produced mine, vaguely hoping to set a good example. But I was completely ignored while the verbal battle raged and everyone fingered his trigger menacingly as though it wouldn't be verbal much longer; the angry shouts of all concerned almost drowned both the thunder and the hiss of the hail slashing down. Finally one of the passengers threatened to smash the inside light with his rifle-butt. Then a compromise of eleven *afghanis* was accepted, whereupon the driver resumed his seat and off we went again. This time – rather to my astonishment – we kept on going, at some 15 m.p.h., until reaching Bamian, where Roz and I were decanted in total darkness and I was told that the hotel lay on my left. As I was switching on Roz's light a policeman appeared and almost wept with joy when he saw me – he'd been expecting me hours earlier. He had a storm-lantern and led me on a mile-long walk up a very steep hill to the hotel; we were halfway up when we encountered a car, stuck in deep, loose gravel and being pushed by two softly swearing men. Afghanistan's tourist trade is so flourishing that after a few weeks in the country most tourists are on christian name terms with each other, so I yelled 'Hi, what's wrong?' having recognised three very nice Indians I'd met in Kabul. They said that after the 140 miles from Kabul everything that could go wrong with a car was wrong and now they just wanted to get her as far as the hotel, to avoid leaving her unguarded all night. So Roz was dropped by the wayside and the policeman and I added our pushes, during which operation I began to suspect that my lowest right rib has been fractured by the rifle butt. When we eventually got the unfortunate machine over the crest of the hill the policeman said that he'd go back to the village as I had found friends and then, having retrieved Roz, I walked on with two of the Indians, who had stayed out of the car to save it extra weight. We were trotting along, numb with cold and exchanging our harrowing experiences of the road, when a blood-curdling yell halted us and we found ourselves looking down the barrel of a rifle held by a very young soldier. We gave a chorus of little yelps of terror and said 'Hotel! Hotel! Tourist's Hotel!' But the sentry wasn't at all sure that three strangers – one with a bicycle and two without luggage – coming suddenly out of the black, cold night, could be genuine tourists, so he kept us covered until another soldier had examined our passports. This second lad then led us to the hotel, some 200 yards away from what is apparently a military barracks.

It was depressing, if not altogether surprising, to discover that here there was (*a*) no food or drink of any description, (*b*) no light, (*c*) no water, (*d*) no heating and (*e*) only one thin blanket on each bed. As we were now 8,550 feet above sea level (*e*) was not funny. I had coffee and sugar and bread with me and the boys had some tinned sausages and pineapples so we scraped together a meal of sorts by the light of oil-lamps borrowed from the military, making coffee with the boys' emergency water supply. (The side-splitting part of this story is that Bamian Hotel is listed as Luxury, Grade A!) Then we raided a vast number of empty bedrooms and accumulated six blankets each; I am now sitting up in bed swathed in my six, with numb hands and feet and a howling gale blowing through the loose window-frame. But I suppose I should be grateful for glass in the windows . . .

BAMIAN, 23 APRIL

I woke this morning, looked through my window and almost fell out of bed with excitement. This hotel is built on a 1,000-foot cliff rising sheer from the valley floor and across the valley, distinct in the brilliant, early sunshine, I saw a 120-foot-high statue of the Lord Buddha standing, as it has stood for over 2,000 years, in a gigantic alcove in the golden sandstone mountain – both alcove and statue having been carved with extraordinary skill out of the rock. The whole face of this mountain is pitted with the caves of Buddhist monks and another, eighty-foot, statue stands about a quarter of a mile east of the giant one. Quite apart from this unique spectacle the valley itself is superbly beautiful; a depression in the centre of the mountains, fertile and neatly tilled, dotted with tiny villages and criss-crossed with lines of silver-barked sinjit trees, whose diminutive rosy buds were glowing softly in the early light. Even though I was mentally prepared for those Buddhas the impact was tremendous when I actually saw them presiding impassively over the valley.

After breakfast of two boiled eggs, dry bread and tea, I investigated Roz fully; there are five severe cuts in the back tyre and eleven punctures in that tube and three in the front tube. Definitely this is where I gracefully accept defeat, admit that Afghanistan is not a suitable country for cycle-touring and get on the next bus for Mazar. No one knows when another bus will come to Bamian but that aspect doesn't worry me – I could happily spend a month here. The spare tyre is in Kabul, yet even if it were here I'd hesitate to put it on as it would probably be in shreds before we got back to Kabul and the next spare is with the British High Commission in Peshawar. So a bus to Mazar and back is the obvious though acutely disappointing solution. From Kabul, where I'll put the new tyre on, much of the road to Peshawar via the Khyber Pass is metalled.

My experience to date of Afghan buses leads me to expect that the trip to Mazar will be (*a*) infinitely more dangerous than by cycle, (*b*) a thousand times more wearying and uncomfortable and (*c*) at least as long in travelling hours. It will also be fraught with frustration – so many places where I'll want to stop and be alone – but better to go by bus than not at all.

Having discovered the worst about Roz I went with the Indians to see the Buddhas and caves. This is one of Afghanistan's main tourist attractions (hence a 'luxury' hotel), but what a contrast to our idea of a tourist centre! Apart from the hotel the whole valley is completely unspoiled; nothing comes between the ancient past and the moment when you walk beneath the shadow of those immense monuments of an era when Bamian was the centre of the Buddhist religion. The statues, however, look far less impressive close-to than from the other side, or centre, of the valley. There the effect of so many centuries of weathering is not apparent, although, considering their great antiquity, the damage is very slight and much skilful restoring has recently been done; even the paintings executed on the arches of the alcoves and in the caves are still traceable. The monastery of caves is fabulous; one could spend days wandering (chiefly on one's tummy) through the maze of connecting passages between one cell and another. Similar caves, all blackened with the smoke of fires that burned so long ago, are located in other mountains around the valley and I hope to explore these tomorrow on my own; delightful as the Indians are, I prefer being alone in places like this.

After a lunch of tea and dry bread and two boiled eggs (the variety of the menu here is *fascinating*) I wandered off to a little village at the foot of the massive, snowy mountains that overhang this valley to the south. The fields were being ploughed by the most primitive methods, which involve tremendously hard work on the part of the men as well as the yokes of bullocks, and irrigation channels were rippling smoothly along between the cultivated patches. In the village, of well-fortified houses, the little children were so terrified at the sight of me that they fled like chickens before a fox. Yet to my extreme astonishment when a group of ten- to fourteen-year-olds gathered to investigate me and asked where I came from and when I replied 'Ireland' they immediately said 'Dublin!' in unison. They were dressed in the usual filthy rags, but instead of begging from the tourist they offered me revolting fly-blown sweets, nuts and raisins out of the (probably lousy) recesses of their garments. I didn't like refusing but one has to draw the line somewhere. They also organised a bird-fight for my entertainment; this is one of the most popular sports among the villagers. Two birds, about the size of hen-pheasants, but in build and plumage like doves, are released from their cages on the ground and go for each other; the fight lasts until one bird has the other pinned to the ground so that it can't get up. There's no bloodshed and no killing, only plenty of feathers flying, and since the tactics are quite beautiful to watch it was a lot more enjoyable than I had expected. Of course my last film had been used on the Buddhas; I've discovered that one of the chief griefs of a photographer's life is that the last film has always been used immediately before a 'special' picture presents itself.

After this I went off to explore the ruins of 'The City of Sighs', where the King of Bamian was successfully besieged by Genghis Khan in 1222. It stands on a hill isolated in the centre of the valley and the climb is so sheer that I was completely breathless by the time I got to the top, with its remains of two watch towers. The view of the valley would be well worth climbing Everest to see; I had deliberately chosen this time, to watch the sunset from here. Bamian valley runs from east to west and the hilltop is 900 feet above the valley floor. Looking down I could see right into the compounds of all those inscrutable blank-walled villages and watch tiny figures of unveiled, red-trousered women scuttling around at their household jobs. Across the fields men were moving home with their pairs of oxen and down from the hillsides came little shepherd boys driving their flocks of sheep and goats and frisking lambs and kids. I must digress here to expatiate on the loveableness of Afghan kids, so nimble and playful and alert of expression and beautiful to look at, with their short, glossy coats and upturned tails and almost snub-nosed faces and delicate bones. They come in jet-black, nigger-brown and an extraordinarily lovely shade of blue-grey. Their elders look very dignified before shearing, with coats sweeping the ground and horns curving handsomely back – quite a contrast to the comical fat-tailed sheep with that vast bundle (weighing from 100 to 140 pounds) swaying along behind them. Arab sheep are also fairly common, bred exclusively for their skins as the wool is of little value; these sheep are very lightly built and can be confused with short-haired goats at a distance. I haven't yet seen any of the breed from which comes genuine Persian Lamb – most unjustly misnamed. The cattle here are small and dainty; some remind me of Kerries but they're mostly like Jerseys.

North of this valley are the sandstone mountains of the statues and caves and to the east lie low hills like vast mounds of velvet dropped from the sky and delicately shaded in violet, brown, pink and beige. (Such formations are very common in Persia, too, where the colouring is usually brown or grey.) To the south, in complete contrast to these soft contours and tints, rears a craggy range of 14–18,000-foot peaks, covered in fiercely white snow which turned to radiant gold a few moments before the sun dropped behind the lower, bluish-tinged peaks at the far western end of the valley, leaving one splendid billowy cloud of bronze behind it.

The ruins among which I stood were equally moving in their way. Archaeologists reckon that 'The City of Sighs' must have had between seven and eight thousand inhabitants and as I climbed the silent laneways between those houses – some still in an excellent state of preservation, with many traces of paintings on the walls – a curious feeling of melancholy crept over me. Local techniques of building seem to have remained unchanged over all those centuries; the Afghans one sees building new houses today construct them in exactly the same manner with identical materials.

Climbing down in the rapidly fading light was almost eerie; the locals, who firmly believe in an endless variety of ghosts and spirits, wouldn't come near the place day or night. On reaching level ground I found two soldiers, complete with the usual armoury of revolver, rifle and sword, posted one on either side of the hill, and when they had escorted me back to the hotel the manager explained that some years ago a German boy was murdered among those ruins, so now tourists are always supervised there. Then I had supper of dry bread and two boiled eggs and tea (sorry for the monotony!) followed by a most interesting discussion with one of the Indian boys on Hinduism and Christianity.

BAMIAN, 24 APRIL

How stupid can one be? I woke this morning to find my rib markedly worse; then, as I was having breakfast (bet you can't guess the menu!) the Police Commander called and said that since there was no sign of a bus going from Bamian in the foreseeable future perhaps I'd like to spend the day riding up the valley? Commonsense prompted me to say, 'No, thanks; it's very kind of you but not with a cracked rib.' However, the temptation was too strong – a day on horseback in the Hindu Kush is the nearest thing I can think of to Heaven. But half an hour later, looking out of the window, my heart sank at the sight of a gleaming, rearing chestnut stallion on the gravel. I then proceeded to disprove the theory that if you go up in a plane – or whatever – immediately after an accident you won't lose your nerve. Last October I remounted an Aran Island demon of a mare three times after being thrown, yet the moment my steed appeared this morning I began to positively tremble with terror. But I needn't have worried; he was a darling and seemed to understand the situation perfectly as soon as he felt me shivering fearfully on his back. The Afghan saddle further demoralised me – no fancy leather, but solid wood and make the best of it. I did register a protest about the girth being too loose and the stirrups too long and had both adjusted; the Persians ride very short stirrups but the Afghans in this region go to the other extreme. After about twenty minutes I regained my nerve and from then on enjoyed myself thoroughly – *what* a day! I had my usual two guards who combined business with pleasure by shooting three deer and two foxes between them. It was tremendously exciting to sit watching them galloping along mountainsides in pursuit of deer and bringing them down with magnificent shots fired while going at full speed. (Not that I really approve of shooting deer, but one has to admire the skill and it *does* mean venison instead of boiled eggs for supper!) We went deep into that magnificent range of snowy peaks, through lush green ravines and across streams and up hillsides and through woods. Quite apart from my normal inability to convey the beauty of it all, I'm too exhausted tonight even to try. After nine and a half hours in the saddle I'd have been a stiff mass of agony tomorrow, however fit at the start, but with that rib it was just idiotic to ride. The day's beauty so excited me that I didn't heed the pain increasing every hour; time will tell what damage has been done.

5

The Oddities of Afghan Trucks

BAMIAN TO PUL-I-KHUMRI

DOAB, 25 APRIL

My body was suffering such universal torture when I dragged it out of bed this morning that I can't yet determine the precise extent of damage to my rib. At 7 a.m. the Police Commissioner appeared again to say that a bus was leaving for Bolola at 8 a.m., but I've been long enough in Afghanistan now to know what that means, so I crawled down to the village at 9.30 and sat in the sun, drinking tea and watching the Bazaar Day crowd, till the bus was ready to go at 12.15 p.m. In these parts no bus will start until double the number of passengers that it was designed to hold have been crammed into and on to it. If there's room for just *one* more, it'll wait hours for that one to turn up, with the *bacha* standing out in the middle of the road hoarsely yelling the bus's destination to attract the necessary extra passenger. As Afghans are so indifferent to time (the vast majority have no idea how old they are) it follows that every passenger comes when it suits him so that it can take up to six hours to fill a bus. Afghans are equally vague about distance: a truck-driver who goes from Kabul to Mazar once a week won't have the remotest idea how far it is; he just knows that if he keeps driving long enough, and if Allah is willing, he'll get there some day. Personally I find all this most endearing after a lifetime of being tyrannised by the clock.

Next to food, fuel is the scarcest thing in this region at this season and on Thursdays dozens of donkeys come in from the surrounding few hamlets laden with bushes of some herb which smells like incense and weighs so light that one donkey can carry a load twice the size of itself. Everyone lines up to bid for these loads and the owners of tea-houses, who need it most and can bid highest, go off with the bulk of what's available.

The winter is so cold round here that no potatoes or other vegetables will grow and the pasturage is so poor now that neither cows', sheep's nor goats' milk will make butter or cheese. Within a few weeks all that will be changed; even during the days I've been here the trees have turned from bareness to greenness and the grass and wheat have come up well. Meanwhile, the people live on tea and dry bread and eggs.

I got a very pleasant surprise when the bus stopped to take us on, having loaded up elsewhere; it was the bus which had brought us here and the driver promptly handed me the two water-bottles and the plastic mug I thought I'd lost for ever. Not bad in an alleged 'nation of robbers' – it hadn't even occurred to me to enquire about them.

One significant thing I notice in Afghanistan is that many men with severe physical disabilities are seen doing the same jobs (although more slowly and perhaps less efficiently) as their healthy brothers. In Persia, these men would be lying on the sidewalks begging.

Officially Mongolians are supposed to form less than fifteen per cent of the Afghan population, but anyone can see that this is nonsense – forty per cent would be more like it, and around this region sixty to seventy per cent. In the centuries following Ghenghis Khan's invasion the Mongolians were important and prosperous citizens; now they are all in the poorer class.

The first twenty miles today was back along the stretch we came over by the light of heaven the other night and seeing the road by the light of day I realised that our survival was a miracle. This road is marked third-class on maps and when one remembers that a first-class Afghan road would be marked as a track on any European map – well, you see what I mean! (A recent United Nations survey declared Afghan roads to be the worst in the whole wide world – a description which I now have no difficulty in accepting.) This goat-track crawls around mountains, overhanging a river the whole way, and in these twenty miles I saw the remains of two recently crashed buses: mercifully the lightning didn't reveal them the other night. In several places the river has eaten away so much of the track that one can only drive at

5 m.p.h. with inches to spare and it took us one and three-quarters hours to cover those twenty miles. Actually I was very glad, for this stretch is just about the most beautiful part of the Hindu Kush I have seen. The glory of those mountains makes one feel that it must all be a dream. Every peak and slope and outcrop is different in shape, texture and colour, the rock and shale and clay shaded purple, rose, green, ochre, black, pale grey, dark grey, brown, navy and off-white. Then, below those arid, soaring cliffs – so vertical that not even an Afghan goat attempts them – is this narrow vale of Bamian, all graceful with willows and poplars, and soft with new grass and filled with bird-song and the rush of the river. Towards the end of the vale, the mountains closed in ahead and we entered a permanently shadowed gorge no more than fifty feet wide, where the river was forced into a deep channel, half-filled with gigantic boulders through which it roared and foamed in a series of waterfalls. When the gorge ended we crossed a bridge built entirely of wood and mud.

A few miles further on, at the junction village, I transferred to a truck going to Mazar; this must be one of the easiest routes in the world for hitch-hiking because so many empty trucks go to Russia from Kabul to import essential supplies. Afghanistan's closing of her border with Pakistan was a classical example of biting off one's nose, etc.; the gesture hurt no one but Afghanistan and benefited no one but Russia, who now has almost a monopoly of trade with Afghanistan. (What makes me so sick in Afghan vehicles is the nauseating reek of Russian petrol, which is very inferior stuff; I'm told it ruins cars.) A lot of people thought that when the old pro-Russian Prime Minister 'resigned' (i.e. was dismissed by the Emir) the border would re-open, and perhaps it will soon. Its closure means that the prices of all imported goods in Kabul are almost as high as in Teheran.

Afghan trucks are unique. To make up for the absence of windows, wipers, mirrors, handbrakes and all the other refinements we take for granted, their exteriors are so brilliantly painted with a series of elaborate pictures that they look like circus caravans; also they have a railed-in compartment built on top of the cab which can carry extra goods or four humans – or both. I chose to ride up there, (*a*) so that I wouldn't miss anything of the scenery and (*b*) so that I wouldn't get sick. Of course it all depends upon what makes you sick – if you'd a bad head for heights those fantastic valleys and gullies and ravines and gorges, seen from the top of a truck crawling along with no margin of error, might make you feel sicker than any Russian petrol fumes could. The situation on this route is one that could only occur in a deliciously crazy land; during the two years since the border closed eighty per cent of Afghanistan's traffic has travelled on it, yet it's the country's worst road.

The *bacha* acts as rear-mirror, horn-blower (the horns are fabulous things like trumpets, eighteen inches long and audible miles away) and windscreen wiper if the truck is posh enough to have a windscreen. He also leaps down whenever the truck stops and inserts a huge wooden block to act as a brake beneath a back wheel. Every mile or so the road widens enough to let two trucks pass if one remains stationary and you can imagine the chaos involved. The really exciting part of the performance comes when you have to *back* down this track, overhanging a gorge for about a quarter of a mile, because your truck is the one nearest the passing point; that's when it's wiser to look up rather than down. For this manoeuvre the *bacha* is of course out on the road, walking backwards shouting instructions to the driver.

The average speed of forward progression is 15 m.p.h. and allowing for frequent reversings, and for one puncture or other breakdown every two hours, it takes four hours to cover forty miles – at this rate I'll be in Mazar for Christmas! But these Afghan drivers are really magnificent – good-humoured about their hardships, brilliantly resourceful when mechanical improvisations are required, and very sensible and cautious. The only thing that terrifies me is the appalling state of repair of the trucks; if a brake went or the steering column broke on this road the best drivers in the world couldn't avoid disaster. Fortunately, the beauty of the landscape leaves little time for these morbid broodings.

For about the first twenty of this afternoon's forty miles we were going through a narrow gorge overhung by mountains eroded to many grotesquely beautiful shapes – some were like the ruins of colossal

Gothic cathedrals, others had crags worn by wind and water into parodies of sculptured human faces and always there was that incredible display of colours. Then the valley widened slightly and we came to a region of devastation, a shattered wilderness where giant rocks, the size of cottages, lay strewn everywhere, and wide fissures in the mountains warned that at the next earth tremor – and they are frequent here – the whole appearance of the area would change. Before the border trouble this track was often blocked by rock-falls; now the Russians have teams of men camped at intervals to clear away the débris as soon as it crashes down.

I reckon that today's forty miles were only about ten miles as the crow flies, so tortuously did the road and river wind back and forth through the mountains. After such a jolting on top of the truck, added to yesterday's gallivanting, the rib is neat hell tonight and the rest of my ill-treated carcase feels not much better. 'Bed' in a tea-shop corner now.

DOSHI, 26 APRIL

It took us eleven hours to cover ninety miles today; we were afflicted by two punctures and three engine breakdowns. This obviously suited my purpose as, while the repairs were being done, I could wander off and absorb the beauty of a landscape no less spectacular than yesterday's. But I couldn't wander far or do anything energetic – merely climbing into the truck this morning was agony. Definitely I'm in for real trouble with this rib and I must take it to a Russian doctor in Mazar, if we ever get as far.

The valley was wider and more fertile and more populous today. Women in this region lead a very active life and lovely splashes of crimson against grey rocks or green pastures indicate that a shepherdess is on duty. Almost all the villagers here seem to be Mongolians, who are much less conservative than the Aryan Muslims. The women have elaborate patterns tattooed on their foreheads and chins, and girl-babies wear silver ornaments permanently embedded in their noses. Both men and women use massive silver bangles and ear-rings and their curly-toed shoes are inlaid with silver and gold. They all look sturdy, rosy-cheeked and healthy beneath the dirt of bodies that certainly do not know what water feels like.

This is the centre of the Afghan horse-breeding area, where herds of magnificent animals graze beneath the mountains on velvet pastures, with scores of frolicking foals, and to see them galloping away from the sound of the truck is a heart-stopping sight. Here too the famous sport of Buzkashi is most popular. This involves two teams, of up to a hundred horsemen each, who try to drop a sheep's carcase in a hole in the centre of a mile-long pitch; I hope to see it before leaving the region. This explains the wooden 'handle' on my saddle the other day – riders hang on to it with one hand while they bend down to spear a sheep off the ground with the other.

Tonight I'm again staying with a Provincial Governor, one who spent seven years in an American university and speaks perfect English. His house is so primitive that his wife prefers to remain in Kabul with their children; only one room is fit to sleep in and despite his foreign education he takes it for granted that I won't mind sharing it with him. As it happens he's quite right in this case, since by now I equate 'Afghan' with 'gentleman'. He's a very nice fellow who paid me one of the most valued compliments I've ever received when he said that he had never before met a foreigner who had become so completely adjusted to Afghan life in so brief a time. I replied that it isn't difficult to get adjusted when you love a country as much as I love this one. He had been warned by the other Governor to expect me, so there was quite a banquet for supper – fried chicken, spinach beautifully prepared, hard-boiled eggs, the usual flat wholemeal bread, sheep's butter, goat's and sheep's cheese and masses of sultanas; sultanas eaten with unsalted goat's cheese are quite a gastronomic experience and on that course I made a pig of myself. Then we had hot cow's milk with lots of sugar in it and finally green tea, and the more I filled my tummy the sorer my rib got – from expansion!

PUL-I-KHUMRI, 27 APRIL

I slept very little last night and couldn't stand up without help this morning; I was in too much pain to eat an elaborate breakfast. While drinking my tea I coughed involuntarily and at once fainted clean away because of the agony. When I had come to, my host and I held an emergency conference and he advised me to go to the German-built hospital in this town, fifty-five miles from Doshi. I'll skip details of the journey – I did *not* observe the landscape and fainted twice more: I'm getting quite expert at it. A young Afghan doctor said that three ribs are broken; he plastered them and ordered me to bed and banned cycling for a month.

This hospital is exactly what you would expect an Afghan hospital to be – even one built by Germans. A male nurse undressed me and two police officers and three other officials stood by as interested spectators while I stood naked from the waist up being plastered. There are a few women nurses here – elderly widows without sons or husbands or fathers to restrain them from leading such immoral lives! A bathroom-cum-lavatory leads off my room but the water supply has been broken down since the Germans left in 1945. However, this doesn't deter everyone from using the lavatory: it would be so much healthier to have an Eastern one outside instead of a Western one, minus water, inside. I can't see myself escaping from this dive without dysentery – the room is *dense* with flies. Fortunately it opens on to a verandah and the bed is beside a big window with a wide view of the heavenly garden which is like a miniature forest, full of chestnuts heavy with blossom and Scotch firs and many other big trees, unfamiliar to me, in early summer foliage. There are also blazing flower-beds, smooth lawns and a little bubbling stream. Possibly I'll survive; a Czech doctor is going to re-examine me tomorrow.

PUL-I-KHUMRI, 28 APRIL

A grim night, and now I know what it feels like to be a guinea-pig. The Czech doctor arrived at 7.30 a.m. (an odd chap, who has been here sixteen years; he might be a Graham Greene character), and having taken one look at my ribs he sent for the Afghan doctor. I was made to stand in the centre of the floor and told to turn round slowly while the Czech demonstrated that this was how *not* to strap broken ribs. Then the plaster was removed and the Czech doctor put on a new lot whilst the Afghan watched respectfully; my ribs feel much better now. The Czech said that I could probably cycle in about two weeks, as all the breaks seemed to be clean. I asked why they were so painful, as I always thought broken bones not such agony, but he said broken *ribs* are, because of nerves that run from the spine between them. He told me that I could return to Kabul by the next jeep going there, but not by truck as it would be too jolting. Mazar-i-Sharif has to be abandoned as it would involve another 300 miles on these roads, which might be unwise. It would be all right if I could fly there and back but the Mazar airport has been swept away by spring floods and won't reopen for three or four weeks. (It's swept away every spring with monotonous regularity.) When I get to Kabul I'm to rest until my two weeks are up, and longer if still painful, but my injuries always heal very quickly so I should be in working order by 12 May or so. I feel that Fate has dealt very kindly with me: if I had had to choose a country in which to be delayed I would certainly have chosen Afghanistan. I'm considering returning home this way to see the bits I've had to miss.

Not a dull moment today. By 10 a.m. my room was overflowing with roses, polyanthuses and geraniums, and a myriad visitors were in attendance.

This is one of Afghanistan's very few industrial centres – it has cement, sugar and textile factories, run by Russians and Czechs – so I don't feel too frustrated at not being able to explore the town. There is a big secondary school (co-educational) and the girls come streaming in after classes to look at me and beam. They go unveiled and are extraordinarily beautiful; unlike the Turkish and Persian girls, who rarely have any colour in their cheeks, these youngsters are all roses and cream, with glossy, wavy waist-length hair. When you see how good-looking they are it makes the veil seem either more iniquitous or more prudent. Undoubtedly the Afghans must be, by our standards, the best-looking people in the world. They have everything; height, proportions, carriage, features and complexion.

The food is atrocious here and even dirtier than usual, or perhaps it's just that there's more light to examine it by.

6

A Medical Break

PUL-I-KHUMRI TO JALALABAD

PUL-I-KHUMRI, 29 APRIL

Here in Afghanistan, the majority are Sunni Muslims, with a minority of Shias in certain areas and, as usual, no love is lost between the two sects. Sunnis consider Shias a pack of unwholesome fanatics and Shias consider Sunnis a gang of lukewarm no-goods – there's nothing like religion for spreading brotherly love!

I have at last, after ceaseless querying, got a definition of Afghanistan's government; it's a Theocracy, all laws being based on Islamic Law (Sunni interpretation) and the Emir's first duty is to defend Islam. For this reason I think it unlikely that Afghanistan will ever, in the foreseeable future, turn Communist, however many Russian helpers and however much Russian money she accepts.

One aspect of the Divorce Laws seems very odd: a husband has to return to his wife's family all the dowry cash, but he automatically retains custody of the children. However, if he can't return the cash, having spent it, he gives *half* the children instead (it's not clear what happens if there are nine or eleven children – another case for Solomon!). The manager of Bamian Hotel told me all this. He was married at eighteen to a fourteen-year-old wife and they have six children. Now he has just divorced her to marry the twenty-two-year-old daughter of an American posted to Afghanistan. The girl must be badly bitten if she's willing to take on six Afghan infants as well as an Afghan husband, who rather peevishly pointed out to me that he's losing a lot of money because of the tiresome American habit of having only one wife at a time. Normally he wouldn't dream of divorcing and forfeiting all that cash.

I had such a bad night and the pain was so grim this morning that the doctor said travelling today was out, though the police had a Russian jeep going to Kabul all lined up to take me. I feel better this evening so may get going the day after tomorrow in a Swede-driven UN jeep. Meanwhile I'm quite happy here.

PUL-I-KHUMRI, 30 APRIL

The ribs are much better today, *Deo gratias*, and the doctor said that I could go tomorrow if a jeep is available and if I sit in front. However, after today's developments I'm not all that keen on going tomorrow. The centre of life in this town is a textile company founded by Germans in the late 1930s and now run by Afghans. It owns the hospital and also the local hotel, built by the Germans as a club for themselves when they settled here. At 10 a.m. today the manager of the hotel arrived and invited me to stay there as a guest of the textile company till I could find transport to Kabul, so off I went with him in his jeep to this palatial outfit, built in a semicircle around a garden that is quite breath-taking, with a superb view of mountains in the near distance. I was shown over the whole building and in one of the vast lounges the manager said casually, 'That's a radiogram and there are some records in the cabinet.' I made a dive for the cabinet and the first thing I picked up was Schubert's Trout Quintet. Further investigation revealed four Beethoven symphonies, Mozart's Jupiter Symphony, Brahms' Violin and 2nd Piano Concertos, and a selection of opera – what *bliss*! They were, of course, the old 78s, but so are all my own at home. I had the Fifth on before 12 o'clock lunch and was edging back towards the relevant lounge when the factory manager collared me to come and tour the works. I could hardly refuse and found it quite interesting watching the whole process, from raw cotton leaving the growers' sacks to the finished product – some quite lovely fabrics – emerging at the other end. Two thousand are employed, including four hundred boys and girls in the ten to fourteen age group; for certain jobs their small fingers are best: pretty grim. As a result of the industrialisation of Pul-i-Khumri one sees more unveiled women here than in Kabul, and there are hundreds of neat little houses built by the Germans for their workers. The two electricity plants were also built by them and this is the only place in Afghanistan where you can depend on the electricity supply.

PUL-I-KHUMRI, 1 MAY

The ribs are very much better today but my big toe got bitten by a scorpion this morning, so I'm having serum treatment. It was a very traditional scorpion, lurking in my boot, and I've never seen anything quite so horrifying; the sooner the better I wake up to the fact that I'm now in Asia and act accordingly. I'd no idea the creatures were so enormous; my picture was of something about the size of a black beetle but this brute was as big as an adult mouse. I've decided that even the fattest and hairiest spider would be companionable in comparison. The morning was spent nursing my foot with Brahms to soothe the nerves.

DOAB, 2 MAY

Life is becoming dangerous! I was hardly out of bed this morning when a hornet stung me on the neck, but evidently the scorpion serum is still operating as there were no ill effects, apart from the immediate pain.

All the jeeps that might possibly have been going to Kabul today (two in number) were not going after all, so I was entrusted to a svelte Russian oil-tanker instead. With my infallible instinct for being in every country at the time of the national annual Big Feast (end of Ramadan in Turkey, Now Ruz in Persia) I find myself stranded this evening in central Afghanistan on the eve of their five-day Id holiday, when no trucks will be travelling. As other traffic is almost non-existent it's anybody's guess when I'll get to Kabul. The idea today was that I'd go all the way with the Russian tanker, but (*a*) I didn't want to travel in darkness through this lovely region and (*b*) the ribs, which seemed almost cured when I was sitting in Pul-i-Khumri, became acutely painful again on the road.

Today's journey taught me that despite the tribulations incidental to travelling by Afghan buses and trucks, they are in fact the vehicles best adapted to Afghan roads. On being helped into the Russian tanker this morning I felt as disconcerted as though I'd been transferred without warning from a local eating-house to Dublin's Shelbourne Hotel. Sinking back in the well-upholstered seat (with arm-rest) I stretched out my legs and put down the window (with glass) and watched the clean-shaven driver in his neat Western clothes hanging my wind-cheater from a hook. Definitely, I thought, this is the next best thing to the comfort of an ambulance. Then as soon as we started I realised that Comrade Ivan, lacking that native Afghan philosophy which alone makes such journeys tolerable, was in a *hurry*, which jarred me in every direction; mentally it was incongruous and physically it was hell. Holding my semi-knit ribs together with one hand and hanging on to the door with the other, I found myself being bounced off that excessively well-sprung seat every five minutes; I longed then for a vehicle with no springs and six passengers in a space meant for three, each keeping the other firmly wedged. We passed a total of eight happily broken-down Afghan trucks surrounded by little groups of ragged, barefooted, undismayed men; looking enviously at them I pondered the symbolism of luxury trucks being so uncomfortable on Afghan roads. Our smug engine had no breakdown though we did suffer four punctures, which even the best bred tanker could not avoid on such a surface, but each time the wheels were changed with disgusting speed, giving me no opportunity to see what lay beyond the nearest hill. Russians use a newfangled thing called a 'jack'; Afghans, on the other hand, dig a hole in the road beneath the relevant wheel . . .

Many changes have been taking place since I first travelled this way a week ago. Melting snow on the high peaks has transformed what were mere streams into wide, frenzied rivers, the colour of café-au-lait, which forcefully sweep giant boulders along their course. Several new rock-falls are keeping the Russians busy, the wheat is almost turning colour, blue and orange migrant birds flash splendidly across the sky and shrubs that were just coming into leaf are now feathery masses of pale green, like enormous ferns, showing a profusion of tiny, mauve blooms. Right over the tops of the rounded, earthy mountains (2,000 feet above the valley floor and over 10,000 feet above sea level) patches of cultivated land are visible in neat squares of green or brown. (Who's going to get up there with a tractor?) The few flat expanses where the valleys widen are covered by a thick, smooth carpet of dark golden moss. The tender rice shoots have sprung up, the blossoms have fallen from the fruit trees and, now that the lambs and kids are of grazing age, sheep and goats have bound udders to save milk for butter and cheese.

I saw an unusual sight in the middle of the road today – an eagle killing a snake about two and a half feet long. We stopped and watched him start to eat it, then, when the engine revved, he picked it up and swept off to the mountains to lunch in peace.

Tonight I've rejoined Roz at the home of my good friend the Provincial Governor, who has been cherishing her since I went to hospital. A few moments ago he announced that he himself is going to Kabul tomorrow, to be with the family for Id, but his jeep is so decrepit that he regretfully advised me against accompanying him; he thinks an ordinary truck, if such were available, would be better for the ribs. He has promised to bring Roz with him in the jeep – so now I have only myself to worry about.

. . . 3 MAY

I can't give an address, for God alone knows where we are; an hour ago we found ourselves stranded in the mountains miles from the nearest tea-shop, not to say village. This Afghan truck rolled up to Doab at 8 a.m., on a day when none was expected, because it had had nine engine breakdowns and four punctures en route from Russia yesterday. But now it's the road which has broken down – a rock-fall, estimated by the Russians who are blasting it away at 500 tons. There is no hope of the job being done before morning so we will sleep on the tyres that are our load: they should be comfortable enough. I'm writing this by the light of Roz's lamp, sitting on a rock by a crashing torrent under a sheer precipice in magically bright moonlight. I notice that the authorities seem to have given up trying to cope with the situation and have left me to my own devices. In the circumstances it's just as well I'm over my initial nervousness of Afghanistan. This is the only country I was ever in where not one single man of any type has made the slightest attempt to 'get off' with me, so I feel no qualms about a night at the mercy of my five companions. They all look as though murder was their favourite hobby (and maybe it is – among themselves) yet they're as gentle as lambs with me. The Russians wanted me to spend the night on a camp-bed in their tent but as all except the foreman are convicts I prefer to stick to my Noble Savages. We're all desperately hungry but there's nothing to be done about it; the Russians have so little food and are so isolated that we couldn't accept any from them.

KABUL, 4 AND 5 MAY

It cost me 7*s.* to post the last instalment of the diary on my arrival here at 4 p.m. yesterday and this was such a shock to the system that I couldn't bring myself to start writing it again last night.

I'm feeling rather miserable today, having left the Hindu Kush behind, yet the past weeks have given me something that I know will prove permanent. It may sound ridiculous, but I feel I've been privileged to see Man at this best – still in possession of the sort of liberty and dignity that we have exchanged for what it pleases us to call 'progress'. Even a brief glimpse of what we were is valuable to help to understand what we are. Living in the West, it's now impossible for most of us to envisage our own past by a mere exercise of the imagination, so we're rather like adults who have forgotten the childhood that shaped them. And that increases the unnaturalness of our lives. So to realise this past through contact with a people like the Afghans should help us to cope better with our present – though it also brings the sadness of knowing what we're missing. At times during these past weeks I felt so *whole* and so at peace that I was tempted seriously to consider settling in the Hindu Kush. Nothing is false there, for humans and animals and earth, intimately interdependent, partake together in the rhythmic cycle of nature. To lose one's petty, sophisticated complexities in that world would be heaven – but impossible, because of the fundamental falsity involved in attempting to abandon our own unhappy heritage. Yet the awareness that one cannot go back is a bitter pill to swallow.

KABUL, 6 MAY

Today I met a twenty-five-year-old American boy in the Museum who was typical of a certain category of youngster – European, Commonwealth and American – I've met all along the route. To them, travel is more a *going away from* rather than a *going towards*, and they seem empty and unhappy and bewildered and pathetically anxious for companionship, yet are afraid to commit themselves to any ideal or cause or other individual. I find something both terrifying and touching in young people without an aim, however foolish or even wrong it may be. This young man was pleasant and intelligent but wasting himself and resentfully conscious of the fact. He doesn't want to return home in the foreseeable future, yet, after two years of it, is weary of travelling, probably because he always holds himself aloof from the people he travels among – not through hostility or superiority but through a strange unconsciousness of the unity of mankind. Is this something else our age does – on the one hand make communication easier than ever before, while on the other hand widening the gulf between those who are 'developed' and those who are not?

KABUL, 7 MAY

Continuing the 'gulf' theme – what an artificial life is led by the foreign colonies in these Asian cities! The sense of their isolation from the world around them is quite stifling. At a dinner party tonight I met a European couple who have been in Kabul for eighteen months without once entering the home of an ordinary Afghan – and they are not exceptions. The attitude is that the 'natives' are people to be observed from a discreet distance and photographed as often as possible, but not lived among. The result is boredom and an obsessional longing for home leave. The collecting of souvenirs seems to be a substitute for the cheaper and richer experience of being temporarily integrated in the life of the country. Apparently if you can bring home to Malvern or Minneapolis or Munich a sufficiently overwhelming bulk of 'typical native products' this concrete evidence of your travels is enough.

This evening I also met a young Dutch couple who arrived in Kabul a fortnight ago, on their first assignment abroad, and who are still wondering what hit them. I must admit that I do see their point and am duly grateful that I approached Afghanistan gradually. Had I flown direct from Dublin and landed in Kabul as a wide-eyed, sensitive-nostrilled newcomer to the East, I too might well have been unable to appreciate the finer points of Afghan life and culture. As it is, during my two months' travelling from Istanbul to Meshed, the roads became daily less road-like, the mountains higher, the atmosphere rarer, the clothes stranger, the chairs scarcer, the Moslems more Islamic, the sanitary arrangements more alarming, the weather hotter, the stenches stronger, and the food dirtier. By the time I arrived at the Afghan frontier it seemed quite natural, before a meal, to scrape the dried mud off the bread, pick the hairs out of the cheese and remove the bugs from the sugar. I had also stopped registering the presence of fleas, the absence of cutlery, and the fact that I hadn't taken off my clothes or slept in a bed for ten days.

KABUL, 8 MAY

I had dinner this evening at the home of the Provincial Governor with whom I had stayed in Doab. His young nineteen-year-old brother came on a cycle to guide me to the house and I tried out my ribs by going the two or three miles on Roz – an experiment of which the ribs did *not* approve.

The party was by way of being an Id family reunion. However, since the ramifications of even the average Afghan family overtax my brain I didn't so much as attempt to grasp who was related to whom, or how, in this re-united family; but they were all equally hospitable and gracious and sincerely welcoming.

The large two-storey house was built – of mud, as usual – round three sides of a courtyard whose fourth side, facing the road, was a high secretive wall behind which the women could move about the garden unveiled. One small ground-floor room had been furnished in Western style and when I arrived everyone was dressed in Western clothes and sitting Western-fashion on the chairs, half of them with bouncing, gurgling, cherubic offspring on their knees (Afghans make very doting Daddies). They all spoke English or German with varying degrees of fluency – including the Governor's wife, who is a university graduate in economics – and conversation flowed easily. After about half an hour, by which time we had become the best of friends, first one and then another rose and disappeared for a few minutes, to return in Afghan dress and resettle themselves, comfortably cross-legged, on their chairs. They could have made no more eloquent gesture of acceptance than this tacit admission that it was unnecessary to impress me by affecting Western ways.

While the younger women were helping the servants to prepare dinner their elders and I sat listening to the family orchestra playing the sort of traditional music that gets into your blood. I loved every minute of it and one of the young men was a quite exceptionally talented musician who afterwards played several solos on an eight-stringed instrument.

Dinner was served at 9 p.m., the dishes being laid on an enormous cloth spread on the floor of a room completely bare of furniture. It was a banquet such as I have not had since leaving Turkey and I feel now that I won't need to eat again in the foreseeable future.

During the meal we discussed the 'progress' now being made by Afghanistan. The Government has recently produced a very fine book called *Afghanistan: Ancient Land with Modern Ways*, which, as the title implies, gives a rosy picture of the present situation – but that is understandable. What alarms me is that the general tone of the book reveals the Afghan Government's unquestioning acceptance of progress along Western lines as being something entirely good and desirable. This educated Afghan family held the same tragic belief in the superiority of our ways over their ways. It is frightening to belong to, and be in a fractional way responsible for, a civilisation that has such a hypnotic fascination for simple people everywhere – people whose very simplicity leaves them totally at our mercy. And so far we have shown little mercy, if that means anything more than the distribution of vaccines and the building of roads. With our mad lust for Uniformity and a Higher Standard of Living and Expanding Markets, we go to a country like Afghanistan and cruelly try to jerk her forward two thousand years in two decades, giving no thought to the profound shock this must be to her national psychology. The present state of our own national psychologies is a good enough advertisement for the need of a far more gradual change. I tried to point out to my friends that once they have created this terrible idol of the Modern State it will enslave them for ever and then it will be too late for them to see that 'the good old days' were best; they will be forced to continue worshipping their idol whatever the cost to their humanity. However, they thought I was mad to find more happiness and peace in an Afghan village than in a European industrial city.

One of my most pleasant memories of Kabul will be the walk home after dinner tonight, with the moon spilling silver over the mountains into the streets and the perfume of the acacia, in full bloom now, rich on the damp air, and not a mouse stirring from one side of the city to the other. I wonder is there any other capital city which one could cross at 10.30 p.m. without seeing a solitary person or a car or any sign of life.

KABUL, 9 MAY

This afternoon I changed £30-worth of travellers' cheques in the bazaar and got Rs 20 for each £1, which is one-third more than the official Bank Rate. Of course the whole thing is madly illegal and I'll have to smuggle the currency into both Pakistan and India, but it does mean only spending 1*s.* instead of 1*s.* 6*d.* every time I part with a rupee. In Teheran the money-changers work openly but here it's all frightfully hush-hush and melodramatic. You go down into a maze of smelly little alleys and walk along with your hands held in a certain position, indicating that you've been initiated by someone the changer already trusts. Then a little boy of about seven or eight appears, wearing an appropriately significant expression, and he looks at you and you look at him, after which he saunters casually off and you follow and enter a bakery and go behind the scenes where you sit sipping tea and haggling in a leisurely way about the rate of exchange; it's all wonderfully unlike the respectability of changing a cheque in the West.

When I set off for Jalalabad in the morning I'm leaving behind the two pannier-bags and knapsack and all kit that would be superfluous during the next few months; I'll collect it on the return journey. My friends here are paralysed with horror at the thought of anyone going on a five-month trip with only a saddlebag of luggage, but the fact is that the further you travel the less you find you need and I see no sense in frolicking around the Himalayas with a load of inessentials. So I'm down to two pens, writing-paper, Blake's poems, map, passport, camera, comb, toothbrush, one spare pair of nylon pants and nylon shirt – and there's plenty of room left over for food as required from day to day. It's a good life that teaches you how little you need to be healthy and happy, if not particularly clean!

JALALABAD, 10 MAY

I left Kabul at 6.30 a.m. and covered 115 miles today. The ribs are still uncomfortable but not actually painful and a strong east wind tempered the fierce sun while Roz and I were moving. The road was atrocious for forty miles, though excellent for the rest, and it was an odd sensation to be going gradually but steadily *down* over most of the way, just pedalling automatically – but think of the return journey! Kabul is at 7,000 feet and, though I don't know what the altitude here is, the air feels positively thick with oxygen after so long on the heights. Roz got one puncture in her new tyre this afternoon and a truck-driver stopped when he saw me struggling with it and did the job in less than ten minutes. Of course he would *not* accept the gift of a packet of American cigarettes.

We passed through some tremendous scenery and saw a most awe-inspiring engineering feat – the road through the Tangi Sharo Gorge. Here the mountains are almost sheer walls of solid grey rock and the road pirouettes its way down thousands of feet to river level. The surface has not been metalled yet so I walked, which was safer anyway with no back brake. From the top the Kabul river looks a mere thread of water, though in fact it's a torrent in a mad, foaming rush to join the Indus.

During the afternoon I had a most exciting bathe (not swim) in the Kabul. I picked a spot where the current would wash me up about a quarter of a mile downstream on a bank of gravel, and just went with it, enjoying the thrilling sensation of being swept along at such speed by the flood; I went down four times and watching Pathans obviously thought me too mad to be quite true! That was near here, where harvesting is in full swing, wheat being cut by hand with the most primitive sickles and carried home on men's backs. It is very lovely to see rows of trees in early dense fresh greenery standing amidst fields of pure gold corn, with low blue mountains behind and beyond them again the massive ranges of the southern Hindu Kush burning against the sky like a white fire. Orchards of (I think) pomegranate trees sometimes line the road and look like a new sort of Christmas tree with their profusion of scarlet, bell-shaped blossom. I can't attempt to describe the various exotic shrubs of the region; they line the streets of this city and their scent defeats even the stagnant *jubes* – which are equally remarkable in their own way.

I have left a dozen broken hearts behind me in Kabul, which is not as romantic as it sounds, since they are all in the Tourist Bureau! Obviously, *qua* tourist, I'm the answer to an Afghan's prayer – they admitted I was one of the few to enter their offices without a list of complaints from here to Eternity. Anyway I implored them, almost with tears in my eyes, not to pander to outsiders and defile Afghanistan with cafés on every mountain pass and juke-boxes in hotels and souvenir shops in Bamian. Tourists who want these extras can get them in practically every accessible country of the world.

The poor chaps at the Tourist Bureau were in misery about my accident on the bus, yet, as I pointed out, it could as easily have happened in Ireland, only there it wouldn't be a fight about fares but a drunken brawl going home from a hurling match and a hurley instead of a rifle-butt!

At midday I went asleep for about half an hour on a mountainside, having been up since 5.30 a.m., and woke to find myself in a *tent*. I had decided that I was still asleep and dreaming when a filthy old man of the Kochi (nomad) tribes appeared and explained by signs that they'd noticed me going to sleep with no shade, which they thought very bad, so he erected one of their goat-hair tents over me – without loosening a pebble, they move so very stealthily. The moral here is that the basis of a successful psychological approach to Afghans is *not* to be afraid of them. Yet it's literally true that the same old man would think nothing of murdering his own daughter if she ran away and married into an enemy tribe. It does take a while to sort out the fact that such people don't want to murder *you*!

This city is full of Sikhs, who are undoubtedly the most forthcoming people on my route since Bulgaria. They told me that I could stay as long as I like in their Golden Temple at Amritsar, where a bed and three meals a day are given free to all travellers of every colour, class and creed – one of these religious 'things'. The complexity of Eastern religions is quite beyond me – when you think of how Sikhs and Muslims massacred each other in 1947–48! Yet it's absolutely true that once you leave Europe you could, if you were stingy enough, live entirely free on the generosity of people with about a twentieth of the average European income. The other day in a tea-house I made a casual remark to a total stranger about the postal rates here and he immediately offered to pay all my stamp bills – a man with no shoes to his feet! This is typical. Again, on my return from Pul-i-Khumri I found an envelope with 500 *afghanis* (£3 10*s*.) in my writing case, and no one could have put it there but the Afghan doctor. This anonymity is characteristic; they don't want to impress with their wealth or kindness, they just want to please Allah and obey Mohammed by 'helping strangers in the land'. I realised that this gift was made to me under false pretences as my destitution, judging by outward appearances, is now beyond all, with trousers, shirt and shoes in small shreds, just hanging together – I hope – till I get to Peshawar. (This is why I didn't give the ribs more time to recover; they could have been a good excuse to stay longer in Afghanistan.) I sent the money, equally anonymously, to the TB Centre, which is desperately short of funds.

One of the current scandals of the world – I've been hearing about it from the Americans and British ever since I got to Asia – is the number of so-called Christians who take advantage of this Muslim doctrine to 'borrow' from the locals in these countries. The classic case concerns an Englishman and his wife driving home from Australia. They stayed with a doctor who befriended them in Tabriz, went to town on Persian rugs, 'borrowed' all the poor man's savings (over £300) to pay for their souvenirs – and that was that. Of course this sponging is usually on a smaller scale and is chiefly done by hitch-hikers. Personally, I haven't the slightest objection to accepting hospitality from *Westerners* – they can usually well afford it and their religion doesn't forbid them to accept farewell gifts – but it enrages me to think of 'our side' being let down by such scroungers.

7

Anticlimax

JALALABAD TO PESHAWAR

LANDI KOTAL, PAKISTAN, 11 MAY

As far as I'm concerned the Khyber Pass hasn't had a chance so far. It's quite beautiful, though not comparable to the Shibar Pass, but I simply wasn't in the mood to give it credit since for me it's the route out of my beloved Afghanistan. From the top you can see Kabul, 156 miles away, with all the intervening mountains in a wild jumble of peaks below you. Then you say goodbye to Afghanistan – a sad moment – and turn a corner round the mountainside and it's all Pakistan ahead, beautiful and friendly and primitive enough to satisfy anyone not newly parted from Afghanistan!

Now I'd better begin at the beginning. We left Jalalabad at 5.45 a.m. with fifty-six miles to go on a perfect road to reach the frontier. At first the level plain was wide and cultivated to the foot of distant, snow-crested mountains; then we came to rough brown hills overlooking the road and dotted with fortresses, in case we might forget that this is territory where trigger-happy tribesmen have been busy for centuries. By this stage, at about 10 a.m., the heat was so intense that I had to pack it up and retire to a nearby nomad camp where I slept till noon. I woke to find the sky full of lovely rain-clouds and Kochis grilling lamb for my lunch – a very classy menu in this camp. It was almost as though they knew how I felt about leaving their country, they were so kind to me.

There is little traffic on this road, because of the frontier being closed. I arrived at the Afghan Customs at 3 p.m. and at once I could feel the twentieth century ready to pounce on me. The Customs building here is positively contemporary compared with the one at the Persian frontier and the officers wear European clothes, speak a little English and smoke cigarettes . . . They said they hoped I had enjoyed my stay in Afghanistan and didn't I think Sarobi hydroelectric plant (which I passed yesterday and tried not to notice) was wonderful? I said I'd enjoyed myself more in Afghanistan than in any other country of the world but that the cycle run from Kabul to the frontier was the least enjoyable part, because here 'progress' is fastest. They stared at me as though I were a lunatic and then we parted.

On crossing the bridge which marks the Durand Line, the first thing I saw was a Pakistani bus, all spick and span and not in the least likely to break down or do anything unexpected within the next five years. Then there were *signposts* – a phenomenon unknown in Afghanistan – which gave distances in miles, and a 'Drive on the Left' sign, and a detachment of the Khyber Rifles, who looked quite the smartest soldiers I've ever seen anywhere; their uniform is distinctive and gay, and apparently newly issued from the Army stores every morning! Their drill is of course equally impeccable – shades of Sandhurst! Unmistakably I have entered a Commonwealth country. (Afghan privates literally have their behinds showing through their ragged pants – just like me now – and are paid 3*s.* 2*d.* per *month.*)

A great fuss was made of me in the Pakistani Customs' Rest House (complete with bathroom, armchairs and electric fans) but though I appreciated being given such a welcome and having a pot of tea served as at home – for the first time since leaving England – I couldn't adjust happily to the change, and haven't yet. The five-mile walk up took me one and a half hours and I didn't arrive till 5.30 p.m., an hour after curfew, but no one fussed. I saw my first railway since leaving Meshed (Afghanistan and Tibet are the only countries in the world without railways) and while going through the bazaar here met my first beggars since Persia and heard the old baksheesh whine. Landi Kotal's is a notorious bazaar where you can buy almost anything from any country in the world, presumably all smuggled, and it's rather startling to come on this exotic sort of supermarket in the middle of nowhere. By now it's to some extent a tourist attraction, yet I bought a very nice new watch-strap for 2*s.* which would probably have cost 5*s.* at home.

But then it's fairly obvious from my present attire that I'm not a tourist within the meaning of the act. I left my cigarette holder by mistake on the counter of the watch-stall and five minutes later a boy came rushing through the alleyway shouting for the Memsahib from Ireland and brandishing the holder; this makes one wonder if Landi Kotal's nickname, 'The Town of Ten Thousand Thieves', is quite fair.

Muslim hospitality is continuing unabated here and I have just had an excellently cooked, though simple, dinner in the home of a local official, where I'm invited to stay the night. It certainly makes travelling more interesting when one can converse freely with the average citizens of a country, but it also makes for embarrassments, as at dinner this evening when the conversation was all political – on the Kashmir and Pakhtoonistan problems. The former was easy for me as I'm with the Pakistanis on Kashmir, simply because I like things carried to logical conclusions, and if India had to be partitioned and the basis of partition was religious then Kashmir should be part of Pakistan. On the other issue, however, I was torn between loyalty to Afghanistan and politeness to my hosts, so I made a big effort and remained silent. Granted that the advisability of giving independence to Pakhtoonistan is debatable, in a world of tedious amalgamations I can't help favouring the idea. Here again, as at every frontier I've crossed, I notice that enmity between neighbouring nations which is one of the most depressing features of travel. Even the closest racial and religious ties don't tone it down – in fact they seem to heighten it in the present case. But I always blame the politicians for this. The man-in-the-bazaar is easily led and the virulent propaganda that emanates from all the National Radio Stations in this part of the world is proof of how grossly his leaders abuse their authority. To me this type of propaganda is so blatant as to appear childish but in an Asian context it's criminally clever.

Landi Kotal, being at the top of the pass, is deliciously cool and this evening it's raining steadily; my room is filled with the scent of huge mulberry trees on the lawn outside. Peshawar is thirty miles down the pass – I hope it's fine by morning. I'm now covered in funny things acquired in the nomad tent today; they look exactly like lice but hop like fleas when you try to catch them.

PESHAWAR, 12 MAY

I was awakened at 1 a.m. by thunder and was kept awake for two hours by its continuous crashing and by torrents of rain on the tin roof. It was still raining in an Irish sort of downpour when I rose at 6.30, and my host said that this would go on all day. Therefore (since sitting on top of the Khyber Pass unable to see your hand in front of your face is not my idea of fun) I decided temporarily to abandon Roz, come down here by bus for my mail to cheer myself up and return to collect Roz when the rain stops. Judging by the way the road drops to the Plain of Peshawar in a sort of convulsion of twists around mountains it must be a thrilling run, but I didn't *see* anything except what looked like mist imported from Connemara. It's still pouring here, which means there's no great heat yet, and it's just like a July day in Ireland. Everyone says it's fantastic weather; normally they have no rain in May and the present torrent has nothing to do with the monsoon due next month.

Peshawar is like an English city with a few water-buffaloes and vultures and lizards thrown in. I'm installed in a dak bungalow, which is the cheapest accommodation for tourists in Pakistan and India. These bungalows were originally built by the British for the comfort of their officials on tour and I'm told one finds them in even the remotests spots. My bearer here supports nine children on £2 10s. a month. His two-year-old son has seven fingers on one hand and he's so proud of this that he's bringing the infant for me to admire tomorrow.

PESHAWAR, 13 MAY

I'm getting over my mourning for Afghanistan today and settling down to make the best of this country. To be objective about the Indian subcontinent – discarding my inherited anti-colonialism, and a temperamental bias towards mediaeval Afghanistan – even two days in this one city make nonsense of the argument that Britain exploited the country without compensation. Of course she exploited her, but in what city between Constantinople and

Peshawar do you see good and plentiful schools, hospitals, homes for the blind, orphanages, clinics and Christian churches that are allowed to function? And where in the Middle East do you find efficient transport services, reliable communications, an army that *looks* like an army, well-trained civil servants, electricity plants that actually produce electricity and roads that *are* roads? Britain grew fat on Indian wealth, but enough was ploughed back to make the familiar picture of her as a heartless bandit look just plain silly.

Of course the social atmosphere of Afghanistan is much more congenial. There the poorest peasant looks you in the eyes, instead of cringing because you're a white memsahib, as the Punjabis here do. (My bearer is different; he's a Pathan and it wasn't hard to train him to sit down and talk sociably instead of squatting eternally outside the door ready to dart in and turn on the fan if I tried to do it myself.) Yet you can't blame the British for this servility either: if the Indians had had as much guts as the Afghans they'd never have been conquered – Afghanistan wasn't!

Yesterday was Sunday, which *is* Sunday here – very confusing after ten weeks of Friday being Sunday. I set off after lunch to buy something to cover my nakedness but the bazaar was shut, so I went on to see the Irish priests, with hordes of children running after me pointing to the unsewable split in the back of my slacks and enjoying the fun like mad. The good priests, dressed in unclerical garb, were themselves almost as decrepit. Going on to the Peshawar Club I found that Mr Beck from the British Embassy in Kabul had come down for a few days and he took me to dinner with Indian friends of his, which was very enjoyable. Afterwards we saw the sixteen city gates being shut for the night to keep the tribesmen out – and it's quite a ceremony.

Today is, if possible, even wetter than yesterday. I went off first thing to the bazaar and got a second-hand pair of men's trousers for 7*s.*, plus my old ones in exchange. They're a bit long in the leg but I'm not planning to feature in any fashion show in the immediate future, so why worry! (I've had the most adorable lizard on my wall all day – he makes a very companionable sound as he scampers up and down industriously catching flies – so hygienic of him!) I was given tea and Marie biscuits – made in Karachi – by the second-hand clothes merchant, while he sent his peon off with my boots to be resoled. Thick new soles cost only 2*s.* and I got a second-hand khaki shirt for 3*s.* On arriving back here I was absolutely soaked; the rain has been coming down persistently all day.

Before returning to Landi Kotal for Roz I must get a permit to re-enter the Khyber area so I'll go round to the office now and be ready to leave early in the morning if it's fine. This Khyber set-up is a curious one; the region is politically in Pakistan but is legally independent and the road through is not *owned* by Pakistan but is leased from the tribes and maintained by Pakistan for the convenience of people going and coming via the pass. That's why the area is rated as dangerous: Tribal Laws only are in force.

Today I heard the sad story of two motoring tourists who were driving to Quetta when, east of Khandahar, a Kochi child ran in front of their car and was killed. They naturally, although in those special circumstances unwisely, stopped and the men of the tribe attacked the husband and knifed him in the lungs – he's now in Quetta hospital seriously ill and would have been killed if a bus-load of Afghans hadn't intervened; two men on the bus were injured during the fight.

Later. This really is a very pleasant city, with trees and flowering shrubs lining every street in the Cantonment area and acres of lush grass stretching in all directions. There was no trouble about getting my pass so I'm all set for the morning. One sees the funniest little taxis here – called rickshaws – with three tiny wheels and plastic awnings and motorbike handlebars and engines. These take three passengers and cost 6*d.* per mile. There's very little traffic in Peshawar and the standard of driving is quite good.

PESHAWAR, 14 MAY

At 6.30 a.m. it was not actually raining and looked as though the skies might clear, so I went to catch the 7.30 bus back to Landi Kotal, reaching the terminus at 7.28. The bus started at 7.29, which shook me badly; I'm not yet sufficiently reconditioned to be able to take this sort of thing in my stride!

The Khyber Pass is very fine, but, after the Hindu Kush, something of an anticlimax. Its fame is based on history rather than on scenery, and one has both in Afghanistan, though British travellers find the Khyber uniquely significant, with all its sad little graveyards on the mountainsides and the regimental plaques on the cliff-faces. I spoke to several Pathans who said that the British were the soldiers most worth a Pathan's ammunition!

I thought rifles common in Afghanistan but around the Khyber Pass every male over twelve years old carries one, and often a revolver as well, with as much ammunition slung across his chest as one human body can accommodate. Family blood feuds are still carried on, though not quite with the old fervour, and among the Afridis and Shinwalis wives are expected to be able to take over the defence of a compound in emergencies. I stopped at four villages on the way down and was told in three of them that I looked like a Pathan woman; this, naturally, is the highest compliment a Pathan man can think of! Today every one of these hardy warriors was solemnly holding an umbrella over his head – probably to keep his ammunition dry, for instead of improving, the day got damper hourly.

There are two roads through Khyber. The old one, which has been in use for the past 3,500 years, follows the river most of the way at the foot of the mountains, but the new one, built around the side of the mountains by the British, is considerably shorter. However, as it avoids the tribal villages the old one seemed more attractive so, having collected Roz, I followed it for much of the descent, enjoying many lengthy stops in teahouses, talking to the tribesmen, some of whom speak a little English. I'm invited to spend 'as long as I like' in one Afridi village on my way back in November – a date I hope to keep. One of the most impressive things about the pass is the railway – a stupendous piece of engineering which thrilled even me. I was lucky enough to see one of the very rare trains go up, with an engine in front pulling and another behind pushing, as the gradient is so steep. On almost every hilltop (and there are a good many hilltops) stands a fort, commanding the stretch of road to the next bend. These are not now manned but of course the big HQ fort of the Khyber Rifles – Jamrud – is still very much in use.

PESHAWAR, 15 MAY

Today the local British Council opened an exhibition of books on Afghanistan, so I spent most of the day browsing amongst these; they were very interesting though of course they didn't form as rare a collection as that in the British Embassy library in Kabul. At midday I stopped browsing for long enough to lunch with the family of a Pakistani Army colonel. They were delightful people, who of course all spoke flawless English, though my hostess and her eighteen-year-old daughter both observe purdah. The daughter was educated by Irish nuns at Murree (Pakistan's hill-station) and is anxious to study medicine but her father wishes her to marry now and be a good, traditional wife to the man of his choice. Her mother, who is only thirty-five, told me when we were alone before lunch that she fully supports her daughter's bid for liberty. I hardly knew what to say; obviously she expected me to agree with her completely, but I'm not yet long enough in this environment to have evolved definite personal opinions on the subject. At first glance this is, by our standards, a monstrous situation. Yet the colonel, far from being an unreasonable tyrant, is a most kindly and humorous man, truly cultured, tolerant without being indecisive and, I feel, *wise*. So what's the answer? Perhaps the mistake is to give daughters a glimpse of Western freedom by educating them at European-run schools, and then to expect them to revert unprotestingly to their own traditions. Of course one condemns without reservations that perversion of the Koran which leads to the subjection in which the majority of Afghan women are kept. But in this milieu things are very different, the women being treated with affection and respect and, on the deepest level, as equals, even though the father is so decidedly the ruler of the family when it comes to practical matters. Today I felt sympathy both towards the daughter who had acquired a taste for what we consider basic human rights, and towards the father who knows the value of Islamic traditions and the danger of exchanging them for ours.

After lunch a friend of my host called and the women of the family retired to purdah quarters before the visitor was shown into the sitting-room. During the conversation that followed it became very clear that the Colonel's apparently irrational conservatism was based on a sincere desire to protect his daughter from what he considered the worst evils of Western society – materialism, sexual promiscuity and general godlessness. I put the point that in our view youngsters have to be turned loose to take their chance in these matters and he quickly challenged me to deny that the results of such liberalism had proved disastrous, both for individual youngsters and for society as a whole. To this I could only reply that it's entirely a matter of one's inherited way of thinking. Clearly this stratum of Pakistani society is now the scene of a rather pathetic struggle to achieve an honourable compromise between old and new, and one hopes that the Muslims can preserve the most valuable elements in their traditions despite mounting pressure from the West. The Colonel argued that the worship of God and keeping the women by the hearth form a better basis for human happiness and stability than the worship of mammon and women in the professions. At this point I was tempted to ask how and where one drew the dividing line between God and mammon when human nature has a foot in both camps and our reactions in either direction can be so variously interpreted; but feeling that the Colonel might not relish this question I restrained myself. Perhaps it's because I am so conscious personally of the results of godlessness that I failed to follow my first instinct and argue wholeheartedly for his daughter's freedom.

PESHAWAR, 16 MAY

Today I called again on the Irish priests and on the convent of Irish Presentation nuns. The Catholics run two schools here, one a very expensive college for the sons of rich Muslims and the other a free primary school for poor Christians. I'm intrigued by the subtlety of making Muslims pay for Christians to be educated! The teaching of Christian doctrine is, of course, absolutely taboo at the Muslim college, which is packed to overflowing with all the local (and other) Big Men's sons avid for good teaching. Seemingly the standard of teaching at Pakistani-run schools, where the staffs are incredibly underpaid, is appalling.

I can't even begin to imagine what it must feel like to be a Christian missionary in a Muslim country where one daren't ever attempt to convert anybody, except by the vague method of 'example'. But then to me Christian missionaries in Muslim countries, however genuine their fervour, are at best unattractive manifestations of self-righteousness and at worst an impertinence. Yet that attitude is narrow too in its own way. If you are convinced of your duty to spread the gospel there is obviously a certain nobility in settling in a place like Peshawar, without hope of any material gain whatsoever, and in patiently leading a Christian life for the purpose of influencing those around you.

This evening I went to dine at the home of Mr Mohammad Ali, the Vice-Chancellor of Peshawar University, to whom I had an introduction. The new university is four miles outside the city, beautifully situated in the centre of a semicircle of mountains, with the snowy Central Asian range to the far north. A big, purring, chauffeur-driven Mercedes came to fetch me but the Vice-Chancellor's family is unassuming and homely and Mr Ali himself kindly took me around all the new buildings – the majority are very handsome indeed – in which he takes a fatherly pride. Like most men of outstanding intellectual abilities he is simple and easy to get on with and I felt very much at home in this family. They have invited me to stop with them on my return journey and if possible to come for their second son's wedding festivities in October. This son, who is a senior lecturer in English (BA Cantab.) at the university, earns £20 a month, and other salaries are in proportion, although prices of commodities here are *not* correspondingly low, as one would expect.

8

Welcome at the Waliahad

PESHAWAR TO SAIDU SHARIFF

BAGDADA, 17 MAY

This sounds as though I've somehow got to Iraq overnight and forgotten my spelling en route, but in fact it's a delightful frontier village forty-five miles north of Peshawar where I'm staying with the chief in a vast but primitive house. My spirits are completely restored now that I've escaped from Peshawar and its European luxuries. Suinabhayat Khan, my host, is a brother of Colonel Zeb, whom I met in Teheran, and is a son of the official who helped rescue Miss Molly Ellis from the Afridis. As I can still remember the day some twenty years ago, when I first read an account of this adventure, you can imagine the thrill I got out of being shown the handwritten report submitted by my hero on his return.

I've had a most enjoyable evening – back to eating with fingers off plates on the floor, surrounded by Pathans. My Colonel host from Peshawar also came up, by car, today, and looks much more handsome in his Pathan garb than in a European suit. (He is another brother: why they all have different surnames is one of the local mysteries I haven't got around to solving yet.) In the middle of supper we heard gunfire from the direction of the bazaar and the chief dashed off to investigate. He came back in fifteen minutes and reported that a policeman had been shot dead, while sitting in a tea-house, by a tribesman whom the police couldn't capture as the crowd were 'with him'. I'm sure you'll agree that though regrettable, this is the sort of thing that *should* happen during supper in the NWFP (North West Frontier Province), as everyone here still insists on calling the region.

A few days ago at a nearby court the magistrate awarded a case to A against B. B promptly stood up and shot A dead in front of the magistrate, who equally promptly and very wisely dived under a table. Perhaps, after all, Pakistan is not *quite* the same as England.

I learned a lot this evening about the habits of Pathans. These sons of Moghul Baz Khan don't wear guns when motoring with their wives and children because if they did so and were held up – as is quite likely around here – they would have no alternative, according to the code, but to shoot at the bandits, who would then shoot back, possibly injuring the wives and children. And however long any of these men may have been in English schools or universities or military colleges they still adhere most rigidly to the Pathan code. The inheritance laws are the same here as in Afghanistan – Islamic. When a man dies, his wife or wives get one-eighth of his property and sons get a portion each of the rest and daughters a half of what the sons get: Muslims disapprove violently of primogeniture. But as they often produce ten to twenty sons apiece this doesn't seem to make much sense. More than one wife is now illegal here, but I doubt if that will make any impression on anyone in the immediate future. My host told me that his twelve-year-old daughter, now at the Murree convent school, has insisted on putting herself into purdah although he has assured her that she needn't if she preferred to go unveiled. He also told me that when he took his wife to Europe last year he could not persuade her to take off her *burkah* in Paris, London or anywhere else. This contrast in the attitude of two brothers reveals the extent to which Islamic traditions are currently in the melting pot.

I left Peshawar at 7.30 a.m. today and the traffic on this road was the heaviest I've met since Italy. It's grim to see so many buffaloes and horses and dogs half-starved. The people en route were very friendly and I was frequently pursued by loud cheers. After the desolation of Afghanistan the density of population seems extraordinary. I cycled twenty-two miles looking for a 'quiet corner' and finally was driven to emulating the natives and not bothering about spectators – one gets adjusted, I suppose! The stinks are even worse than Afghanistan – obviously, since so many more are contributing to them per square mile. At one tea-house the stench was so overpowering that I simply couldn't sit there and drink tea; no wonder there's so much typhoid in the area. I collected more mail from Nowshera and here I must pause to record for posterity a word that definitely deserves its place in the *OED*. It is the property of one of my correspondents who in his last letter begged me not to become too 'Afghanatical'. The fact that I had become rabidly and irreparably 'Afghanatical' before the plea arrived is irrelevant.

The whole of today's cycling was over level, rather dull countryside that looked heavily wooded in comparison with Afghanistan. The road seemed very good to me although the locals complain bitterly about it. I whizzed along happily at 16 m.p.h. and was just congratulating myself on the perfection of the weather for cycling when a blue Morris Minor overtook me, slowed up and drove ahead for a few minutes, then stopped and decanted a worried-looking European woman who held me up and began a lecture on heat stroke being the consequence of anyone cycling at that speed in that heat. While moving I'd felt perfectly comfortable but the instant I stopped the sweat began to run off me as I stood in the sun. I said meekly that I hadn't felt hot and she said that that had nothing to do with it. Apparently heat stroke is a cumulative thing and you don't notice it happening till you drop like a stone. Then she noticed the sweat that was streaming down my face and neck and arms, non-stop, and said, 'Oh well, if you sweat like that I think you're safe enough and probably that's why you don't feel it so much.' Before proceeding on her way she kindly invited me to lunch at Mardan, and when I arrived there I found that she was the wife of the Danish Lutheran Bishop of NWFP. They are a very charming couple who have been forty years in this area and speak Pushto like Pathans. I was told this evening about their son's murder thirty-five years ago. Their Pathan gardener wanted to have their Christian Indian ayah as his second wife but the Bishop vetoed the marriage, so in revenge the Pathan shot the ayah and their seven-year-old son and then fled back to his Shinwali tribe and was never heard of again. The Bishop's wife very understandably wanted to go back to Denmark after that and leave the Pathans to stew in their own heretical juice, but the

Bishop said, 'No, let's turn the other cheek', and they've been turning it ever since.

I went round the local cane-sugar factory – the biggest in Asia – after my siesta. The men are paid £5 per month for an eight-hour six-day week. It's a very interesting process but would put you off sugar for life.

TAKHT-I-BAI, 18 MAY

Last night, in honour of some village wedding, a band played throbbingly outside my window until 2 a.m.: the wild, martial airs were not sleep-inducing but I was happy to lie on my charpoy enjoying the concert. I was wakened again at 5.45 a.m. by quite different sounds – fierce arguing in the courtyard. Looking out I saw my host sitting in the shade of an awning of rushes surrounded by villagers, two of whom were arguing like demons – and an angry Pathan-Afghan has to be seen to be believed, as I know to my cost. Later Sai Rab told me that this is a daily routine; from 5.30 to 8.30 a.m. people come with disputes for him to settle and he has such a tremendous personality and such authority over the local branch of the Afridis that they usually accept his decisions, which are based on Tribal Laws. This is all part of President Ayub's effort to re-introduce what is known here as 'Basic Democracy' and is in fact a reversion to things as they were before the British came. It works smoothly when men like Sai Rab Khan are available to take over; but men of his type are, unfortunately, rare in any country.

We only covered eight miles today because of three detours involving over twenty miles of walking and the climbing of three mountains to inspect some fascinating Buddhist ruins. It was a most enjoyable day although from 5 p.m. I was being saturated by another downpour of rain. An introduction to a Scots engineer at a sugar factory here led to my being invited to his home, where we've just been listening to a Communist broadcast in English accusing America of nuclear tests above the atmosphere which have completely upset the world's weather.

SAIDU SHARIFF, 19 MAY

What a deluge! I left Takht-i-Bai at 8 a.m. and it poured non-stop till I arrived here at 4 p.m. However, it's good training for India, where I'll have to endure something similar every day during the monsoon. I found the Malakand Pass baby-food after my efforts in the Hindu Kush: it wasn't necessary to dismount once although we climbed 5,000 feet in seven miles – but of course the road is beautifully surfaced and well graded. Unfortunately, I missed all the views because of mist and saw only enough of the renowned valley of Swat to make me recognise it as the nearest thing to Irish scenery met with since leaving home.

My arrival here was one of the classic episodes of the expedition. On the outskirts of Saidu I asked for Aurang Zeb's house [sic] and was directed to one end of the town. I went there and asked again. A policeman pointed down the street and I pedalled off in the indicated direction, noting en route a palatial-looking building complete with sentry-boxes. Not seeing any house that looked a 'likely' I returned to the crossroads and repeated my query. The policeman pointed again, rather impatiently, and I shook my head and repeated 'Aurang Zeb's house.' The policeman nodded and said, '*That's* his house.' I said, 'That's not a house – it's a ruddy great palace!' The policeman nodded yet again and said, 'Yes, Wali of Swat's Palace.' 'Blast it, I don't *want* Wali of Swat's palace – I want Aurang Zeb's house.' The policeman continued nodding and said 'Aurang Zeb is Wali's prince and lives in father's palace.' I said nothing for a moment after that, then murmured 'Thank you,' rather faintly, and wrung some water out of my hair in a vague way, to make myself look slightly more respectable before approaching one of the two sentry-boxes. The sentries immediately came to attention and another soldier appeared from within the gates and said, 'Are you the lady with the bicycle?' I replied, 'I'm afraid so,' apologetically, as he obviously only credited the bicycle clause, and he continued in an 'outraged Jeeves' voice, 'You are to be brought directly in.' A few moments later I was sitting on the verandah, where a very self-possessed peke promptly took over my lap, while the servant to whom I'd been delivered by the soldier went to announce my arrival. It seemed to me as I waited that Colonel Zeb, on giving me this introduction in Teheran, should have warned me that it involved walis, princes, palaces and sentries – all contingencies which I felt singularly ill-equipped to meet. But then Begum Naseem Aurang Zeb came walking down the verandah and I realised at a glance that the complications of the situation were more apparent than real. Naseem, President Ayub's eldest daughter, is Prince Aurang Zeb's wife and her physical beauty (striking even by Pathan standards) is equalled by true gentleness of nature, sincerity and simplicity of manner and warmth of heart. She told me not to stand up because of the peke and sat down and talked to me as though we were continuing an interrupted conversation rather than getting acquainted. Naseem accompanies her father on his State Visits abroad and Pakistan is fortunate indeed to have such a remarkable young woman to represent her in other countries. Characteristically, she told me first about her three oldest children's mumps and her fear that the six-weeks-old baby might get them. As a twenty-four-year-old girl whose eldest daughter is aged seven many of her Western contemporaries might pity her, but when you have been conditioned to regard the rôle of wife and mother as the most honourable one there is for a woman, the – to us slightly premature – responsibility of a growing family at twenty-four is a source of deep satisfaction. I couldn't help contrasting the basic contentment so evident in Naseem, and in most of the young Pakistani women I've met to date, with the uncertainty as to what *is* fulfilment shown by the young of the West. Yet these Pakistani girls, unlike the simple peasants of Afghanistan, live in luxurious Western-style homes, have been educated in Irish-run schools, speak English as fluently as Pushto and are in close cultural contact with the West. It will be interesting, and probably saddening, to observe the changes within the next quarter-century; it seems too much to hope that the present delicate balance between East and West – using the best of both worlds – can be maintained by future generations.

Naseem and I had been talking only a few minutes when Prince

Aurang Zeb and his younger brother arrived to welcome me. I don't quite know what it is about the Pathans (perhaps some profound racial affinity with the Irish) but I find them extraordinarily easy to get on with; ever since meeting those three officers in Teheran every contact with this race has been an unqualified success. I'm not exactly uncritical of my fellow-beings, but I haven't yet met one unlikable Pathan. Of course their educational ties with Ireland and consequent knowledge of my own little country – which most people have never heard of – undoubtedly has something to do with this, although there's obviously a lot more to it. Anyway, whatever the cause, I become assimilated into Pathan families with delightful ease and am now as happy in my present surroundings of unparalleled splendour as though I were in a nomad camp, which just shows that it's *people* who count and that the human qualities I found to admire in Afghanistan are still present here, despite the very different material environment.

SAIDU SHARIFF, 20 MAY

The happy-go-lucky informality of this establishment effectively counteracts the outward glory and the awe-inspiring fact that all sorts of VIPs, including Mr Khrushchev and Queen Elizabeth II, have occupied one's rooms in the past. Yesterday afternoon, when it became obvious that something must be done about clothing me while my shirt and pants dried, Aurang Zeb sent for a measuring tape and personally confirmed that his trousers would fit me, to the great amusement of the family, my fellow-guests and a semicircle of delightedly grinning servants, who have assuredly never before witnessed the arrival at the Waliahad of such an unlikely looking guest.

Incidentally, I notice that in Pakistan – and I believe it's the same in India – women never wear Western dress, though in Persia and Afghanistan the majority of middle- and upper-class women wear the latest European fashions under their *chadors* and *burkahs*.

I find it very interesting that Muslim families can carry suddenly acquired wealth and power so much more graciously than their European counterparts usually do. Aurang Zeb's grandfather was an illiterate tribal leader who by a combination of intelligence, ruthlessness and sheer personality secured control of Swat State in 1917 and Aurang Zeb himself hints with a chuckle that the ethics of the take-over left a lot to be desired. Yet in this case the end appears to have justified the means, as the little mountain state (area 4,000 sq. miles, population 600,000 in 1961) is now the most prosperous region of Pakistan, with the best roads – as I noticed yesterday on reaching the state boundary – and with a higher percentage of rural hospitals and primary schools than I've seen anywhere else in Asia. There is obviously a moral here to be pointed by someone better qualified than I am in such matters.

Again, Naseem's paternal grandfather was a peasant-boy recruited to the old Indian Army from his village near Abbottabad, but in his distinguished descendants there is neither any self-conscious defensive bragging about this background nor any wish to forget it. In fact, President Ayub's strongest psychological card in the political game is probably his genuinely felt link with the ordinary village people, and his understanding of them is no doubt one of the reasons why he doesn't repeat the fatally unrealistic mistake of trying to run Pakistan as thought it were a Western democracy. Islamic countries have their own traditional type of democracy which, as I mentioned a few days ago, President Ayub is now attempting to revive in Pakistan. Whether the flair for accepting a drastic change of status with such natural dignity is due to the democratic aspects of Muslim philosophy or to the sense and sensibility of the individuals concerned it is difficult to know, but this characteristic certainly makes for a very pleasant social atmosphere.

I woke to a cloudless sky this morning and from my verandah the view of the long, broad valley of Swat was very lovely indeed. Blue mountains enclose wide sweeps of pastoral land, the cornfields shining gold between clumps of trees, now heavily green, and the river swirling brilliantly through the valley centre. The little 'capital' town of Saidu Shariff (altitude 3,150 feet), with the Waliahad on a slight rise above it, looks north towards the snow peaks and gives me the same feeling of carefree isolation as Andorra out of the tourist season. It's a comparatively clean and very gay town where the people are all spontaneous friendliness and uninhibited, but not embarrassing, curiosity. Roz has been minutely examined more times today than at any previous stop. She also had her back brake mended again (free, of course) and while the operation was being performed I was invited to have tea with a young doctor from Lahore who has recently taken up practice here. His living conditions were on a par with those of an Irish farm-labourer, but that didn't worry him. His only complaint was of the lack of cultured people with whom to talk, and his motive for moving from Lahore was that his widowed mother wanted him to marry a girl of whom, for some undisclosed reason, he didn't approve. In this he was a rare exception as the majority of young Muslims are very content with their parent's choice. I suspect him of being one of those who lose more than they gain by a university education on the Western pattern.

Unfortunately, the most interesting corners of Swat are still snow-bound and won't be accessible for at least another month so I explored the nearby excavations of Buddhist remains at Butkara and Udezhan. The latter town, captured by Alexander and known to the Greeks as Ora, was interesting enough to make up for anything. This valley, once the centre of a very advanced Buddhist civilisation, is an archaeological treasure-trove; wherever you dig something exciting comes up. The arrangement is that the Rome Academy finances Professor Tucci's expeditions and in return gets half the movable finds, Swat retaining the other half. Some of the Gandhara bas-reliefs I saw today decorating the outside walls of stupas were exquisitely beautiful and made me very conscious of the relative youth of our civilisation – which seems to be about to die in early middle-age!

SAIDU SHARIFF, 21 MAY

Being entertained by oriental potentates is fine – among other luxuries I have a complete set of Beethoven Symphonies at my disposal, presented to President Ayub by Dr Adenauer! But the position also has snags, one of them being that it's considered very bad form for a house-guest of the ruler of a state to transport herself around the said state on a lowly cycle, as I did yesterday. So today I was gently but firmly organised and driven up the length of the valley by Hassan, Aurang Zeb's younger brother. We went much too fast for my liking, but it was worth it to get to Bahrain where the Swat River, coming from its source in the surrounding 20,000-foot mountains, leaps triumphantly over cliffs on its way down to the valley floor. We drove along a rough track up the narrowing valley, and then got out and climbed mountains through cool forests of pine and walnut and larch. It had been a hot, cloudless day when we left Saidu but here the air was invigoratingly fresh. At about 4 p.m. dark clouds began to gather around the peaks and within half an hour torrential rain had reduced visibility to a few yards, but by then we were back in the little village where we had left the car and where we ate a huge tea of *paratas* and roast chicken and syrupy pastries.

Almost the best part of every day here is the interval before 9 p.m. dinner when Naseem and Aurang Zeb and I sit talking for a few hours, sometimes joined by Hassan or by Aurang Zeb's youngest uncle, the Wali's 'kid brother', who is the same age (thirty-five) as Aurang Zeb. If any visitor calls, Naseem has to retire to the women's quarters because while in Swat she must keep strict purdah, her father-in-law being the religious as well as the civil Head of State. I feel that this is very hard on someone who is accustomed to complete freedom in Pindi and who has no other educated woman in the household with whom to converse. However, the main thing is that she and Aurang Zeb are very happy together, which makes all the restrictions of life in Saidu relatively unimportant to her.

SAIDU SHARIFF, 22 MAY

Professor Tucci's excavations have made Swat very conscious of its past as a centre of Buddhist civilisation, but the proud emphasis on an era that ended *c.* AD 800 seems faintly *non-sequitur* in view of the fact that the present population is descended from the Yusafzai tribe of Afghanistan who migrated *c.* AD 1500 and chased the then inhabitants across the Indus before settling down to enjoy the comparative ease of life in a fertile valley.

This evening Aurang Zeb told me that the first Wali's grandfather (the Akhund of Swat) was a warrior saint who led the Yusafzai tribe at the battle of Ambella in 1862 when the British forces were commanded by Neville Chamberlain's grandfather.

It was after the Akhund's death in 1877 that Swat became involved in a forty-year crisis of constant tribal warfare – mainly because the Akhund's two sons had predeceased him and there was no acceptable leader. Then, in 1917, Badshah Sahib got a grip on the situation and since then Swat has never looked back. In 1949, after thirty-two years of vigorous work for his people, Badshah Sahib abdicated in favour of his son and has since spent his time leading the life of an ascetic.

Swat's legal status is that of a princely state within Pakistan – it was the first state to accede to Pakistan after independence. The Wali runs all internal affairs and only on foreign policy does the Central Government intervene; justice is imparted according to custom and Islamic law and under the Wali's orders. An army of 8,000 men and a police force of 2,000 are maintained by the state, whose annual revenue is approximately three-quarters of a million pounds sterling. There is no income-tax but the emerald mines near here annually provide one million rupees.

Today we visited a leper colony in a valley hidden away in the depths of the Bruner Range. A special mosque has been built there for the lepers, who spend most of their time praying – not to be cured themselves, but that nobody else may ever get the disease. There were appalling sights as we walked around, some too gruesome for description, but the lepers were pathetically pleased to see their Wali's son and he was very kind and gentle with them, shaking hands without batting an eyelid even when there was hardly any hand left.

9

Sweating out of Swat

SAIDU SHARIFF TO RAWALPINDI

RUSTAM, 23 MAY

This was definitely my most enjoyable day's cycling since leaving Afghanistan. We covered seventy-eight miles, crossing three mountain passes – all babies of between 6 and 7,000 feet, but so steep that they involved walking a total of over fourteen miles which is not particularly relaxing when the temperature is 102° F in the shade and you have *no* shade. I passed only two vehicles and no town, had three swims in a deep river, ate nothing but four teaspoons of salt, drank twenty-four pints of water and must have lost about forty-eight pints of sweat. (Aurang Zeb had presented me with his old army water-bottle, which holds six pints, and I had no trouble refilling it en route from the river.)

Between the infrequent villages peasants were busily harvesting barley and a little wheat, which is mostly blackened by the unusual rains. Their threshing is completely biblical – throwing the grain up in the air for the breeze to blow away the chaff. The landscape, as throughout Swat, was very green and we passed through many pine woods where the aroma of resin mingled in the hot air with the scents of a multitude of flowering wild shrubs and herbs. Weeping willows lined some stretches of the road, granting a brief escape from the sun, 'Irish' bramble hedges and ditches induced homesickness, and on the slopes of the grey, round-topped mountains little green bushes like juniper grew thickly. Crossing the last pass before coming down again to the Plain of Peshawar I saw enormous slabs of grey rock that reminded me very much of Inishmaan although they weren't quite as big as those on the island. I also saw five of the lizards for which this locality is famous; when resting under a tree I noticed the first one and for a brief, crazy moment imagined it to be a baby dragon. They're between three and four feet long and are very fat and much respected by the locals who believe that they kill snakes, which seems to me a doubtful occupation for a lizard.

I passed hundreds of nomads today, trudging along beneath that brutal sun carrying all their possessions. Obviously they're much poorer than the Afghan nomads, most of whom own huge herds of camels, goats and sheep; these people just have a few donkeys and goats and no tents. The women carry huge wicker baskets on their heads containing kettles, tin mugs, frying-pans, a hen or two and a few clothes. The men carry the babies tied to their backs and the toddlers sit on their shoulders; sick goats and lame kids travel in their arms. At this season they come up from the plains to the mountains where they live mostly on wild fruit and nuts. They're not nearly as friendly as their Afghan cousins though the peasant people of these valleys are very kind and were really distressed at the sight of me pedalling along leaving a trail of sweat behind me in the dust. On two of the passes shepherd boys came leaping down from halfway up the mountainside to take over the job of pushing Roz to the top. And they weren't looking for baksheesh – just being 'Pathanical'!

The road we followed today is classified as a track but is fifty times better than Afghan main roads, though the last twelve miles (all downhill), after I'd passed the Swat frontier post, were very tricky; the Pakistan Government has covered the surface with about five inches of fine sand for the convenience of the camels and Roz did *not* like this. After she'd skidded twice near the edge of precipices I got off and walked. These mountains are north-east of the Plain of Peshawar and the descent reminded me of going down the Khyber Pass, though it is much more desolate and beautiful here. It's extraordinary how the mountains rise absolutely sheer from this plain, with no intervening foothills – the effect is quite wonderful.

RAWALPINDI, 24 MAY

It got dark last night before I could finish with a description of my bed in Rustam – a tiny village miles from everywhere. I arrived there at 7 p.m. and after a supper of fried eggs and dry bread (shades of Bamian!) I was given a charpoy outside a tea-house under an awning of cane-leaves and wrote till it got dark at 8 p.m., when I went to sleep with the entire male population of Rustam standing around in an awestruck circle. I woke at 4.30 a.m., as it was just beginning to get light, and we started out at 5 a.m.

We covered 118 miles today over a level metalled road, through pleasant but not exciting scenery. There was heavy traffic for the last sixty-six miles, once we joined the grand trunk road, where water-buffalo carts make cycling conditions almost as unpleasantly dangerous as in Teheran.

I've evolved a new technique of cycling in this sort of weather. Instead of taking a three-hour midday break I experimented yesterday and today with quarter-hour rests every twelve or fifteen miles and found this much more satisfactory. By 7.30 a.m. today it was uncomfortably hot and I find that fifteen miles is the limit at a stretch without a feeling of exhaustion setting in. Then just ten or fifteen minutes out of the sun, with hot, *very* sweet tea, restores one for the next lap. Perhaps this technique is quite wrong medically; I'm just going on instinct as to what best suits my physique. At 2 p.m. today an American AID man in a jeep pulled up to tell me that the temperature was 102° in the shade and that I was *mad*. I thanked him and explained my technique, but just standing still under that sun for a few minutes while talking to him made me feel quite dizzy. Roz will have to get rubber grips for her brakes as I burnt three fingers today on the over-heated metal. What's really worrying me is the effect this heat must be having on her tyres.

I am staying here with a Pakistani General's family. The General himself is in London now but his wife and elder daughter gave me a very warm welcome; their house resembles a military museum as the General collects ancient weapons and armour. My room is his library, which gives me a nice homey feeling – it's a long time since I slept in a book-lined room. This is the first completely Westernised Pakistani home I've been in and a very faint but always perceptible 'pseudoness' pervades the atmosphere, which is much more formal than in Saidu. But I don't mean to sound ungrateful; everyone here is very kind and sincerely hospitable and can't do enough for me so it's just a question of *my* limitations.

Last night I was bitten all over by mosquitoes while asleep on my charpoy and I'm tormented with itch this evening. Between that and the jackals who are howling like damned souls beyond the garden wall I see no prospect of sleep tonight: unfortunately all the drinking is done before dinner here, so that by bedtime one has sobered up.

I stopped six times for tea today and at none of these little tea-houses would they accept money from me; they usually pressed me to have a meal also, which I had to refuse, as the mere thought of food in that heat made my tummy turn over – though I realise it can't be good to cycle such distances without eating.

At dinner this evening while discussing my journey to Gilgit it was casually mentioned that all pilots on the Pindi–Gilgit air-route get a fifty per cent danger bonus because flying through the Himalayas is so dicey. Then and there I almost abandoned my ambition to see Gilgit, but as usual my Scots blood won the argument and I decided that since I'm going as Aurang Zeb's guest, I'd risk it. However, not being very brave about flying, even under the best conditions, I won't be sorry when we've landed safely. Of course Roz is coming too and by mid-June (with luck) the Babusar Pass will be open again and we'll come back at our leisure.

RAWALPINDI, 25 MAY

I spent much of today rapidly sorting out Pindi Society. The 'Smart Set' suffers in general from too much money and the depressing sort of snobbery that sometimes accompanies this affliction. The Orthodox Set, though no less exalted in military rank and social standing, is very much nicer. I called on a brother and sister of Colonel Zeb and found both homes very congenial. Begum Ghawas invited me to stop with them on my return from Gilgit, an invitation which I accepted with pleasure.

The basis of wealth in Pakistan now is either inherited money or profits from one of the new industries – not, as formerly, officers' pay, which has been drastically cut. The two households which I visited today (of a Brigadier and a Major-General) were quite dilapidated and barely 'keeping up appearances': but there was such a pleasantly genuine feeling that the 'no drinking or smoking' and 'women in purdah' rules were more than compensated for by the sense that one was being treated as a *person* rather than as a circus-act, which is the feeling some of the 'Smart Set' give me.

Today the National Assembly opened a new session and Aurang Zeb came down to represent Swat. He called for me at 9 a.m. and swept me off to the Distinguished (!) Visitors' Gallery, where I met myriads of genuine Big Shots, who obviously thought someone had made a hideous mistake by admitting such a battered-looking object to their corner of the House.

The intricacies of the political system here are slightly beyond me. President Ayub appoints ministers who are not members of the Assembly, but who appear before the House to answer criticisms and defend themselves. There is complete freedom of speech within the House; members can, and do, stand up and denounce everyone from the President down, and on the whole this régime is probably the best for Pakistan at the moment even if some rich citizens dislike it. Certainly it is *not* a totalitarian régime, as Pakistan's enemies would have us believe.

All the proceedings of the Assembly are in English, which is the only practical national language when the two wings of Pakistan speak so many different tongues. One motion concerned the movement for a separate nation which is now starting up in East Pakistan; apparently the feeling among many there is – 'We've got rid of the British, now let's get rid of the West Pakistanis.'

Ethnically of course the vast majority of East Pakistanis are Bengalis and the only tie between East and West Pakistan is religious. Also the poverty in the Eastern wing is much greater than in the Western, with 950 people to the square mile as against 150 here. In 1960 a census of agriculture was taken, and the report on East Pakistan has just come out. I give a few details below.

Average Farm 3·5 acres of which 3·1 acres are cultivated.
The main crop is rice of different kinds

Owner Farms	61%
Owner-cum-Tenant	37%
Tenant Farms	2%
Fragmented Farms	90%
Manured Farms	45%
Farms with no work animals	35%
Milch Farms	38%
Farmers in debt	48%
Official loans	10%
Private loans	90%
Average Farm Family	6 people

The experiment of transplanting families from East to West Pakistan is being tried but naturally is not being very successful; you might as well expect Italians to be happy if semi-forcibly settled in Lapland. Bengali farmers just don't know *what* to make of the land around Karachi. Today there were heated arguments in the Assembly about this and when talking to a few experienced politicians I got the impression that it is possible to make a nation out of a country of which the two parts are separated without even overland communications.

RAWALPINDI, 26 MAY

This afternoon I went to visit the Presentation nuns here; there are thirty of them, all Irish. The Rev. Mother, who has been fifty years in India, had lots of interesting observations to make. She said that since Partition the only safe person in power from their Christian viewpoint was President Ayub, who is very liberal-minded. Of course all his daughters were at this school, and he knows where Pakistan would be without the Christian educationalists; also the best hospital in Pakistan is run by French nuns.

The temperature yesterday and today has remained around 110° and the strong breeze feels like a blast from the ovens of hell, even during the night.

Yesterday evening, while having dinner in the garden, we saw (at 8.40) the latest Russian satellite travelling at tremendous speed across the sky, looking just like a moving star.

I have decided that my old theory about extreme cold being better for cycling than extreme heat is now kiboshed. After all, minus 25° positively *stops* cycling whereas one can struggle on through 112° and live to tell the tale. But, In'she Allah, by this time tomorrow I'll be cooling off in Gilgit or lying in small pieces on a Himalayan peak and either alternative seems preferable to sitting in Pindi at this temperature. There was a frantic flap today about whether I could cycle back from Gilgit or not: no one knows the exact state of the pass because now all supplies and personnel go by air, but general opinion was that it wouldn't be open this year till mid-July, because of late snow.

The Muslims have a saying that 'a man's name is the sweetest sound in the language', and as a result they consider it good manners to use your name every time they speak to you – which is disastrous for me as I find their names so difficult to remember. Of course they find Dervla equally impossible, so all the way through since Turkey I've been known as D. Except in the most Westernised circles they don't use surnames – which explains why brothers have different names. What really intrigues me is the mixture of Urdu, English and Pushto spoken by all these Western-educated people; they habitually use the three languages, often in the same sentence, while speaking among themselves. A very curious phenomenon!

RAWALPINDI, 27 MAY

More chaos this morning. First my plane couldn't go as the cloud was too dense in the Himalayas; some of the peaks en route are 20–26,000 feet high, and as Dakotas can't fly *over* these they only take off when visibility is perfect for flying *between* them. Then my hostess, who really is being endlessly kind and helpful, started an elaborate series of phone calls in sixteen different directions and finally announced that the majority opinion of experts was that I *could* cycle back by the end of June. So the latest plan is that I fly up on 2 June and meanwhile go to Murree and what is known as 'Free Kashmir', starting tomorrow.

I went this morning for the inevitable interview with Radio Pakistan. It was very frustrating as I couldn't say I loved Afghanistan, took a very dim view of Persia, approved of Bulgaria and etc. Having to be non-committal irritates me more than anything else in the world.

It's quite cool today – only 96° in the shade. I've been told that my biggest risk cycling in this weather is pneumonia – of all unlikely things; but it's good to be warned.

MURREE, 28 MAY

Last night soon after I went out to dinner one of the dust storms, for which Pindi is famous, blew up so that within five minutes everything and everyone in the room was coated in dust; you could see it on the food and feel it in your mouth and smell it horribly. Then all the lights went out and, what was far more disastrous, the fans stopped and we all sat in lamplight, streaming sweat and grinding dust with our pilau.

You'd think that the people here would take this heat in their stride but the papers go to town on it with banner headlines – 'Eighty per cent of Lahore's cab-horses fainted . . . ', 'Pindi streets deserted as all flee from sun . . . ' and so on. Evidently being born to it doesn't make people immune. In summer factory-production goes down and the general efficiency level drops in the Civil Service, business, etc. Coming from sun-starved Ireland it takes time to adjust to the custom of avoiding the sun: it seems so *odd* to sit at lunch with curtains drawn and lights on.

We left Pindi at 7.30 a.m. today after what is here a 'late night' (bed at 11.15 p.m.) and covered forty-four miles, the last sixteen of which had to be walked as the road rose from 1,300 to 7,040 feet and the average gradient was one in fourteen. It fascinated me to watch the plain falling farther and farther away as we ascended and to notice the flora becoming more and more familiar until we were surrounded by daisies, dandelions, heavy blossomed chestnuts, stately pines, lavishly flowering white and pink dog-roses and many very lovely shrubs, my favourite being one with dark green leaves and flame-coloured flowers. Despite going up and up the heat remained intense. So, at 1 p.m., I abandoned

Roz in a tea-shop and retired to the depths of a silent pine wood where I slept for an hour before exploring the cool dimness of the forest. (Murree is Pakistan's only hill-station and the road was pretty busy all day as rich families in sleek cars sped up from the plains to their mountain residences. During summer the population of Murree rises from 15,000 to 50,000 so it's not exactly my sort of place . . .) At 5 p.m. I continued the sweaty crawl upwards, stopping at every tea-house to absorb sugar and salt and mango-juice, this being reputedly the best remedy of all for heat-exhaustion, from which I suspect I'm now permanently suffering; but the mangos must be *un*ripe and baked and the juice then squeezed out, so I carried a supply from Pindi.

The hour from 6.30 to 7.30 p.m. was unforgettable, with sunset colours tinting the snowy ridges of the Himalayan foothills, and long shadows stretching across the valley's steep slopes, which were terraced and irrigated in orderly patterns and dotted by tiny mud houses. Then the cool radiance of moonlight succeeded the brief dusk as I dragged myself up the last and steepest two miles to the PWD rest-house where I'm now half asleep as I write. There's a small snake in the corner of this room but he also seems to be half asleep and, as I'm too exhausted to face the fuss and flap-doodle if I report his presence to the authorities, I'll chance his company for the night: probably he's harmless anyway.

MUZAFFARABAD, 29 MAY

Now that I've forgiven Pakistan for not being Afghanistan I'm enjoying it like mad and have had a most blissful day today. I left Murree at 7.30, having called on the Irish Presentation nuns at the somewhat startling hour of 6.45 a.m. and got a terrific reception. They're always so pathetically pleased to see someone fresh from Ireland that it's worth the effort of answering all the usual questions for the umpteenth time. On the way out of Murree a carload of tourists stopped to ask was I the Irish woman? When I said 'yes' they asked if I was going to Madras, and I said 'perhaps', whereupon they gave me their address and told me I must stop with them. Then they drove on – just like that! I should be used to it by now, but I'm being repeatedly touched and astonished by the hospitality and kindness of *everyone* in this part of the world.

The first thirty miles today were all one continual sweep downhill – even finer scenery than yesterday and no traffic as this is the Prohibited Zone of Azad Kashmir. I saw my first monkeys and spent one and three-quarter hours stalking them through a dense forest with my camera – which is funny when you come to think of it. One wonders how I expected to photograph two monkeys, considering that I can't even get a moderately good picture of a mountain that stands still and waits to be photographed. Needless to say they effortlessly eluded me, but only when they had with deliberate malice led me almost to the top of a mountain so steep that I was terrified to look down and realised that I had to go back. For minutes I stayed hanging on to a shrub, gazing miserably down seeking inspiration as to how best to begin the descent, while those two sat hugging themselves with joy and positively giggling at my predicament. Then I suddenly remembered that Roz had been left unguarded by the roadside and this gave me such a fright that I just let go of the shrub and began the descent by falling six feet into a bramble bush – which doubtless rounded off the monkeys' joy – acquiring innumerable horrid scratches in the process. After that I carried the camera in my mouth and went down like a monkey myself, swinging from branch to branch of the pines and big shrubs.

I can't understand the birds here; they sing – very melodiously too – right through the midday heat, a thing no well brought up Irish bird would ever dream of doing. And such glorious colours. Some are only the size of our butterflies, and some of the equally beautiful butterflies are the size of our robins. There's masses of lovely heather too – white and an extraordinary red-gold colour, but no purple.

After thirty miles we were down to 2,000 feet and level with the river, now flooded by melting snows and tearing furiously along between high mountains. For the next thirty-five miles this road, more or less level, followed the river: a memorable cycle-ride though it was so hot that I could only cover about eight m.p.h. with countless stops to sit nude under waterfalls. I saw lots of logs going down from high up-river, being swept along at tremendous speed. There were no bridges after the one I crossed at the foot of the mountains; the locals use pulley ropes, suspended above the foaming, forty-foot deep, fifty-yard wide waters which they cross as nonchalantly as circus artistes, using only their hands. I notice the people in this region build their cottages of stones, just like the Aran Islanders, and roof them with a flat thatch of straw covered over by mud.

Here I'm still being entertained by the Army in a wonderfully primitive camp by the river-bank. This is being written sitting on a charpoy overlooking the noisy rush of water, glinting in the moonlight. Yet it's too hot even now because this is a narrow valley enclosed by rock mountains which retain and throw back the day's heat during the night and though there's a strong breeze it's hot too.

I stopped in the little town of Muzaffarabad for half an hour and talked to the locals about the Kashmir problem. On my Bartholomew's map this region is in India, but they tell me here it's in Pakistan – I give it up! Anyway, they've their own separate 'Government of Azad (Free) Kashmir' which is financed by the Pakistan Government. The people are in general the most moronic I've met since Persia, but they're friendly once over the initial shock of witnessing such an unusual arrival. I met two government officials and a local 'doctor' (who is not qualified but has a second-hand stethoscope and can give injections – so people think he's wonderful) and they all said that the only way to get Kashmir is to fight for it, an opinion shared by most Pakistanis of all types.

From the town to this camp is a two-mile walk on a dirt-track by the river, past one of Akbar's colossal forts – a splendid sight in the moonlight, overlooking a wide curve of the river and overlooked in turn by jagged mountains. It's very peaceful here with a little village near by where peasants are still sifting the grain by moonlight on their beaten mud threshing-floor. I'm going to sleep now under the stars.

ABBOTTABAD, 30 MAY

Another wonderful day. I slept from 9.30 p.m. to 4.30 and was wakened by pale light spreading over the mountains and slowly filling the valley. We were on the road by 5.15 a.m. and at the top of a tremendous pass, after a six-mile walk up, by 7 a.m. As usual, no film was left for the glorious sight of a river forming a semicircle round the base of a granite mountain thousands of feet directly below me. The mountain we were on was so sheer that I was able to drop a big stone into the water from that distance. Then came a ten-mile free-wheel down, overlooking another very different but equally lovely river valley. Next followed a very steep eight-mile climb through hushed, ancient pine woods, where massive Himalayan peaks, sharp and snow-covered, could be seen in the distance between the giant trees. After that we again free-wheeled down for five miles and the final twenty-five miles were through undulating country, with lots of trees and golden cornfields and reddish cliffs of clay and tiny mud villages. The heat is now extreme and is making me unusually irritable; if people are stupid on the road and nearly get knocked down by Roz I lose my temper and swear like a trooper at them – poor devils, it's probably just the heat softening their brains too!

Since leaving Swat I've seen very few cows, goats or sheep; it's mostly grain farming around here. One of the most appalling local sights is a cow in calf; they're so underfed that you can see plainly the whole shape of the calf in the womb. Only the poorest people use cows' milk; most prefer buffaloes' because buffaloes are immune to TB, whereas the cows are reeking with it, as are many of the human population. Buffalo milk is delicious – pure white and much richer than cows'.

The family with whom I'm staying tonight are delightful people. One daughter is a doctor now working in Lahore who previously ran the hospital here for two years single-handed, performing an average of twenty Caesarean operations per week without a single nurse or anaesthetist to help her. One of the results of malnutrition is that the mother's pelvic (and other) bones disintegrate during pregnancy, when the system's calcium is going to form the baby's bones, and as a result they can't give birth normally. Some time ago, having tried to push birth-control and failed, the Government in despair put a tax on every new-born baby, but that didn't work either and has now been dropped.

Yet eighty per cent of the girls still marry as soon as they reach puberty and produce ten or fifteen children, seventy per cent of whom are born diseased and, because epidemics are coming under control, the majority of these babies are fated to live on as semi-invalids.

WAH, 31 MAY

The temperature on the plains shot up to 112° today and your correspondent began to think that Yugoslavia in February '63 wasn't such a bad place after all! Pindi was my original destination for this evening, but I couldn't cover more than fifty-seven miles and even that felt like fifty-six too many. There can be no report on today's scenery because I was past observing it as I slogged along with my very lungs being blistered by the hot air. I only know that there were few trees and little greenery, a lack which always accentuates the heat. On every side stretched bare stubble fields and arid wastes of rock and stony soil – if you never hear from me again you'll know that I was thinking of you all as I lay expiring by the wayside! The very pleasant family I'm with tonight are friends of my Abbottabad host, as were the people I stopped with for the afternoon from 1 to 5.30. I reached here at 7.30 this evening in a state of collapse.

PINDI, 1 JUNE

When Roz and I left Wah at 8.30 a.m. there was such a strong headwind that we could only crawl at 5 m.p.h. despite the level road. The gale felt absolutely scorching, as if coming from an open furnace, and after about three hours I was suddenly overcome by headache, nausea and severe cramps in the leg muscles – the latter I believe due to salt deficiency, although I've eaten over three-quarters of a pound of solid salt in the last few days. Fortunately we were on the main Peshawar–Pindi road, where buses pass frequently, so I stopped one and was pulled on to it by a twinkling-eyed passenger who asked whether I was a mad dog or an Englishman? This immediately made me feel better, and I replied 'neither – an Irishwoman', and he said that that was obviously much the same thing. It was only five miles back to Pindi and after lying down in my air-conditioned room at the General's house, and absorbing eight pints of mango-juice and sour milk heavily salted, I had recovered by 2 p.m. – as much as anyone could recover in this infernal region.

This afternoon I had a date with one Father O'Leary at the Mission Hospital eight miles away. At 3 p.m. I put my head outside the door, felt as though my face was being burnt, retreated rapidly, rang the bell and ordered the air-conditioned Jaguar in a lordly way – poor Roz must have felt jilted!

I prefer to try to forget the sights I saw in hospital, particularly in the children's wards. Infants a month old weighing only a pound and a half, fitting on to the palm of my hand – *not* premature – and that was the least of it . . .

Father O'Leary told me that this is one of the few dioceses where Roman Catholics can get dispensations from the Bishop to marry Muslims. From the Islamic angle, if a Muslim girl marries a Christian *he* must become Muslim, but if a Muslim man marries a Christian girl, she can keep her own faith. (Christians and Jews are the only non-Muslims the sons of the Prophet may marry.)

Another fabulous dust-storm is performing now and all electricity has gone off again, so I'm writing by oil-lamp in a bath of sweat.

PINDI, 2 JUNE

I was up at 5.30 a.m. to see the sky overcast and feel the temperature down to a cool, delicious 85°. I then rang the airport to ask about flights to Gilgit but the weather is so cloudy in the Himalayas that none is going till Tuesday afternoon at the earliest: a disappointing development, yet in the relief of today's coolness nothing else seems to matter very much. Now it's 1 p.m. and the temperature is only 89° – I'm still dripping sweat but without that awful feeling of complete physical and mental exhaustion.

At breakfast we had an interesting discussion on the various Christian workers in Pakistan. I was understandably gratified to notice that everyone to whom I have spoken is very appreciative of the fact that no attempt at conversion is ever made by the Catholic teachers or medical workers. In the past thirty-five years, during which they have educated thousands of Muslim girls, the Presentation nuns haven't had *one* convert; I've spoken by now to over twenty of their past pupils and the nuns are universally loved and admired. On the other hand, all the Protestant Missions (educational and medical) stink in Muslim nostrils because their teaching and medical treatment is always accompanied by what the Muslims call 'insulting propaganda'. In their schools the children have to study the Bible and Christian doctrine and with their medicines they also dispense leaflets and pamphlets on the 'Good Path to God'. I know that this is true because I visited a Protestant Mission Hospital the other day and the matron showed me the 'literature' they distribute – awful sickly stuff that would put a Pope off Christianity for life. My host summed it up pretty well this morning when he said, 'The Protestants seem to come here because they hate Islam and the Catholics because they love God.' No doubt it's a matter of opinion which attitude is correct, but personally I'm entirely with the Catholics who have the good sense and good manners to admit in practice, if not in theory, that Islam is a different, but not necessarily inferior or wrong 'Path to God'. And, of course, the result is that in Pakistan a genuine good feeling exists between educated Muslims and Catholics, though here, as elsewhere, the semi-illiterate Mullahs hate any form of Christianity.

I suppose you've been reading and hearing about the cyclone disaster in East Pakistan. Many people I've met take the attitude that it's Allah's way of cutting down the population and there's no sense of a 'National Calamity' in the air, though the President has declared it to be such. What happens in East Pakistan is no more or less important to the average West Pakistani than what happens in Madras or Hyderabad. By now I've met very many Pakistanis who regard India as their home and who complain of not being able to go back to see their relatives there or of not being accepted by the *real* natives of this area, or of having lost all their property at the time of Partition, as well as most of their friends, who were either Hindu or Sikh. I asked several such people why they chose Pakistan when India is so much nearer and dearer to them and they said, 'for the sake of the children'. Apparently, although in ordinary Indian social life the various religions (at least among the cultured classes) meet and mingle without bigotry, *officially* the Muslim youth in the new India are discriminated against – or so they say here. I'll investigate that situation as best as I can when I get to India. What a tragic muddle it all is.

I spent the afternoon taking advantage of the coolness and the consequent return of my brain to (what I consider) normal to work on an article and after dinner went out to observe the scene in the streets. This is the end of the Shia's Muharram period, when they mourn the murder of one of the Prophet's followers by another and do penance most masochistically by lashing themselves with whips and sometimes cutting their own bodies with knives. It's supposed to be a dangerous time for women to go unprotected through the country, as the end-result of the penance is often an uncontrollable sexual frenzy, but of course there's no danger in a well-policed and (over-) civilised city like Pindi. I saw many coming from mosques carrying their whips and two men with blood actually seeping through their shirts. There are not many Shiahs in Pakistan and most of these are around Gilgit, where there's also one area populated by the Ismailis (followers of the Aga Khan). Tomorrow is a holiday in the Muslim world – their religious holidays are legion – and I've discovered that's why there's no flight to Gilgit. Anyway, the Himalayan forecast is bad; also the local forecast for tomorrow is bad – a rise in temperature! The weather here in summer is regarded as a National Emergency, with two-hourly broadcasts to tell the populace what the temperature is so that they can act accordingly and not die of heat-stroke. As far as discomfort goes there's very little difference between 100° and 110°, but from a health point of view 110° is lethal and one daren't take risks under such a sun; hence the broadcast warnings that now is the time to go in and stay in. Naturally enough, nothing much gets done at this season. There are five servants here but apart from providing meals they lie asleep on the marble floors all day and no one has the heart to point out that the whole house is coated with dust. I'm very impressed by the way Pakistani family servants are treated. In every household where I've stayed the relations between family and staff are a credit to all concerned. There's no insurance stamp nonsense and no need for it, because when a servant falls ill the family pays all expenses and some member visits them daily in hospital. When they are old and retired, and their places filled by their children and grandchildren, the servants continue to live in the household till they die and the younger members of the family love and respect them as though they were elderly relatives, and go to them with their various problems for advice and consolation. The average wage is £2 per month but they are clothed free and get the same food as the family. At first I found it very difficult to adjust myself to the business of ringing a bell when I wanted a drink or had forgotten to bring my cigarettes from another room, but now that I've got the feel of the set-up I don't mind. It outrages the staff's sense of propriety if Memsahib goes to fetch her own cigarettes, and I must admit that in this sort of weather Memsahib is damn glad to have someone else fetch them. (I've become addicted to chewing betel-nut and my teeth are being ruined – must really abandon the habit.)

One of the unsettling things about local customs is that servants never knock before entering a room. As I'm prone to nudity this weather, in what I regard as the privacy of my boudoir, the result is that all concerned are unnerved – me grabbing a bath towel at the sound of any footsteps and the bearers leaving my tea-tray outside the door in terror of what they might behold if they entered.

10

Scraping through the Himalayas

RAWALPINDI TO GULAPUR

GILGIT, 4 JUNE

Never, *never* again will I allow myself to be persuaded to leave Mother Earth, and bounce in a nightmarish way through the Himalayas. If I have to stay here in Gilgit until August, waiting for the pass to open, I am *not* going back in that unspeakable little plane over that monstrous route to Pindi. I had expected the flight to be fairly blood-curdling but it was beyond my worst imaginings.

I got to the airport at 1.30 p.m. and after the six-mile cycle run out from the city I needed to drink every drop in my six-pint water-bottle. Today was the hottest yet, with the sky an ugly colourless arc and the sun fiendishly scourging the city and its surrounding dust-suffocated plain.

There were only two other passengers waiting on the verandah – a couple of young men from Karachi named Mukhtar and Rifat, who thought the combination of a woman and a bicycle flying to Gilgit was the weirdest thing that had ever happened.

'But *why* are you going?' asked Mukhtar.

'To get away from all this,' I replied, watching the sweat trickle briskly down my arms and cascading off at the elbows on to my already saturated shorts.

They both considered this reply very witty indeed and chuckled with delight. Mukhtar said provokingly, 'You don't like our weather?'

I diverted a torrent of sweat from my eyes and answered savagely, 'I *hate* your weather,' adding, 'but it's the only thing in Pakistan I don't like, and no country can be perfect.'

Rifat then ordered a round of Coca-Colas and remarked, in a

friendly, reproving voice, 'You must know that Gilgit is a very interesting and historical place – it should be taken seriously.'

'Yes,' I agreed wearily, 'once upon a time I had lots of positively erudite reasons for wanting to visit Gilgit, but now I can only think of one moronic reason.'

Rifat sighed, 'I'm afraid you'll be disappointed,' he said, 'because Gilgit itself is quite hot.' (He was right, as I now know.)

At 2 p.m. a few figures moved lethargically across the tarmac, towards our plane, pushing a hand-cart loaded with supplies for Gilgit – plus Roz. By 2.20 p.m. I was inside the little Dakota which had been standing exposed to the sun for hours, and was so hot inside that I would have fainted if I hadn't been too afraid. Somehow it seemed even more likely that I'd be killed if I was not fully conscious when hurtling through the Himalayas in a contraption like this. As I tied my safety belt, one of the crew handed me a newspaper to distract me from my worries. On the front page I read 'Twenty-three killed in Indian Himalayan Air-crash'.

We took off punctually at 2.30 p.m., when the heat was rising up so frenziedly from the plain that we fell, rather than bumped, in and out of air-pockets, until I didn't know whether my tummy was in my head or my head in my tummy – but I thought I knew that the next time we fell, we'd fall all the way. Yet at that point I almost longed for the crash; at least my tummy would then remain *in situ*, or, if it didn't, the matter would be of no importance to me.

Soon the plain was left behind and we passed over the terrain I had cycled through on the Azad Kashmir detour. Then this region of brown, rounded foothills and deep green valleys was replaced by a landscape of naked rock peaks, giant glaciers and vast sweeps of loose shale. We were flying so low that it was, in a sense, the next best thing to trekking through this area, which even the hardiest tribes have never attempted to inhabit and which has been trodden by no more than a few of the bravest traders and mountaineers. Yet only in one sense was it the next best thing; when we passed the 26,000-foot Nanga Parbat, whose triple peak dominated the thousands of snow mountains which stretched to the horizon in every direction, I suddenly became acutely aware that this was the wrong approach to a noble range. One should *win* the privilege of looking down on such a scene, and because I had done nothing to earn a glimpse of these remote beauties I felt that I was cheating and that this nasty, noisy little impertinence, mechanically transporting me, was an insult to the mountains. You will probably accuse me of a tiresome outburst of romanticism – but I'm not sure you'll be right. The more I see of unmechanised places and people the more convinced I become that machines have done incalculable damage by unbalancing the relationship between Man and Nature. The mere fact that we think and talk as we do about Nature is symptomatic. For us to refer to Nature as a separate entity – something we admire or avoid or study or paint – shows how far we've removed ourselves from it. Marco Polo saw it as the background to human adventures and endeavours – a healthy reaction possible only when our lives are basically in harmony with it. (Granted that Roz is a machine and that to be logical I should have walked or ridden from Ireland, but at least one exerts oneself cycling and the speed is not too outrageous and one is constantly exposed to the elements.) I suppose all our scientific advances are a wonderful boost for the superior intellect of the human race but what those advances are doing to us seems to me quite literally tragic. After all, only a handful of people are concerned in the excitement and stimulation of discovering and developing, while millions lead feebler and more synthetic lives because of the achievements of that handful. When Sterne toured France and Italy he needed more guts and initiative than the contemporary traveller needs to tour the five continents; people now use less than half their potential forces because 'Progress' has deprived them of the incentive to live fully. All this has been brought to the surface of my mind by the general attitude to my conception of travelling, which I once took for granted as normal behaviour but which strikes most people as wild eccentricity, merely because it involves a certain amount of what is now regarded as hardship but was to all our ancestors a feature of everyday life – using physical energy to get from point A to point B. I don't know what the end result of all this 'progress' will be – something pretty dire, I should think. We remain *part of Nature*, however startling our scientific advances, and the more successfully we forget or ignore this fact, the less we can be proud of being men.

During the last fifteen minutes of the flight, however, I had no time for such quasi-philosophical speculations, for by then we had left behind the prosaic world of passenger transport and had entered the sphere of aerial acrobatics. Here the mountains are far too high for a Dakota to fly over them, so we were confined to a rock-strewn gorge which in my opinion is far too narrow for a Dakota to fly *through*. It is said that at this point even hardened air-travellers begin to think of alternative routes back to Pindi. The sensation of looking out to see rough rock-walls apparently within one and a quarter inches of the wing-tips is not a pleasant one. I am assured that there are twenty yards to spare on either side, but I stick to it that from the passenger's point of view this is, morally speaking, one and a quarter inches! When we came out over the valley we descended so abruptly that I got an excruciating pain in my right ear – it was so severe that I could think of nothing else and forgot to be afraid of the landing, which usually reduces me to a bundle of craven terror. Before I'd even registered the touchdown, Roz and I were being hurled out with the rest of the cargo and I found myself in the charge of a young lieutenant of the Gilgit Scouts who had been sent with a jeep to meet me. Ten minutes later I was being welcomed to the headquarters of the Scouts by Colonel Shah, who obviously thought he had a lunatic on his hands and immediately began to dissuade me from attempting to cross the Babusar Pass with Roz. But fortunately he is a perceptive man and he soon realised that every time he uttered 'impossible' my perverse determination hardened. So we changed the subject and discussed the Gilgit Agency from more impersonal angles.

My host told me that the first jeepable track from the Kagan Valley to Chilas was constructed about four years ago and is now frequently used during those three summer months when the Babusar Pass remains open. The arrival of the first jeep in Chilas was an historic occasion. Everyone turned out to see it and with characteristic thoughtfulness the peasants provided a large meal of freshly-cut grass for this strange new animal. They were then quite convinced that a jeep is the offspring of two of those curious creatures so often seen in the sky over the valleys and they assumed that it would be able to fly when mature. This, of course, is not an original story – all over the world primitive peoples react thus on first meeting machines. Nor, to my mind, is it a funny story, though it is so often told as a joke at the expense of 'ignorant peasants'.

Colonel Shah went on to inform me proudly that work is now in progress on an all-weather jeep road, which, within a few years, will greatly improve communications with the rest of Pakistan – always referred to as 'down-country' by the English-speaking residents of Gilgit. You can imagine how unenthusiastically I received this information. Granted something must be done to improve this area's economy – after even a few hours here I can see that for myself – but as usual I fear that the disimprovements will outweigh the improvements when the Twentieth Century comes bustling along the New Road. If only someone could think of a way to utilise Gilgit's natural resources – chiefly a superabundance of fruit – without destroying her individuality! After all, this region has only recently become impoverished and forgotten. Before international tensions made their terrible impact on the ordinary man's life Gilgit Town was an important trade centre on the Sinkiang–India route and was a thriving market for the sale and exchange of Central Asian, Chinese and Indian wares – a sad contrast to its present importance as a Military Centre.

It was very pleasant sitting on the smooth lawn of the officers' mess beneath plane trees so tall and graceful that it was impossible to associate them with their sooty London cousins. An orderly served us with frequent orange drinks to which everyone automatically added quantities of salt, because it *is* hot here, with an average June temperature of 94° in the shade – which I'd consider hellish if I hadn't come direct from Pindi. Behind us, almost overhanging the mess buildings, rose a 9,000-foot mountain wall of stark, grey rock which was repeated on the other side of the narrow valley; it's this confinement which keeps the temperature so high despite an altitude of nearly 5,000 feet. Down the valley snow-capped peaks of over 20,000 feet were sharply beautiful against the gentle evening sky and as the setting sun caught the valley walls they changed colour so that their pink and violet glow seemed to illuminate the whole scene.

While we were having dinner on the verandah a full moon rose and by the time the meal was over the valley looked so very lovely that I took myself off for a walk – to the unspoken disapproval of all those present! Having descended steeply for about half a mile my path turned west along the valley floor, leaving the shuttered stalls of the bazaar behind. Tall mulberry and apricot trees laid intricate shadows on the sandy path and the silence was broken only by the snow-enraged Gilgit River. The sky was a strange royal-blue with all but the brightest stars quenched, while on either side the mountains were transformed into silver barricades, as their quartz surfaces reflected the moonlight. I walked for over an hour and that walk alone made the horrors of the flight here seem well worth while.

My bed for tonight is a charpoy under a plane tree and I've written this by moonlight-cum-cycle-lamplight. Yesterday, as you may have noticed, there was no entry. I should have gone out to watch the Muharram procession at 10 a.m. but I simply hadn't the guts to leave my air-conditioned room – even within it I hadn't the energy to put pen to paper. However, atonement has now been made at the expense of my eyesight.

GILGIT, 5 JUNE

I set out at 6 a.m. to climb the mountain directly overlooking Gilgit Town from the south. The path went through a tiny farming hamlet which, if Gilgit were a city, might be described as its suburb, and filthy pot-bellied children collected in groups to stare at me. The Gilgitis are white-skinned (or would be if they washed themselves) though they are of different origins, none of which has been definitely established. Probably some have Pathan ancestors, as Afghan raiders periodically crossed the border in the past, and Afghan traders still bring their camel-caravans over the Babusar Pass during the summer months. A tradition which, as far as I am aware, has no supporting evidence, claims that the valleys were first populated by a detachment of Alexander's army which went astray in the course of his Indian campaign. Despite the lack of evidence there is, of course, nothing inherently ridiculous about this legend, and it is pleasingly romantic. Another theory refers to Arab ancestry – doubtless a lost detachment of the Arab army which invaded Afghanistan in the 9th century – but this theory is supported only by the fact that the Gilgitis carry all loads on their backs, not on their heads as in the neighbouring countries, and such tenuous support invites disagreement more than does the lack of any support for the Alexandrian theory.

I was told yesterday evening that many mutually incomprehensible languages are spoken throughout the Gilgit Agency, and most of them are unwritten. The majority of the people understand neither Pushto nor Urdu, and are of course illiterate, though every village of any size now has its school. However, throughout rural Pakistan the standard of intelligence of the average village schoolteacher is incredibly low and the children's help is needed by their farming parents – a combination of circumstances which makes it extremely difficult to cope with rural illiteracy. Many Western observers find this quite shocking, yet I must admit that it leaves me undisturbed; we have yet to prove that universal literacy as we know it advances the mass of the people in any worthwhile direction.

Walking slowly upwards through the hamlet and across the fertile strip of land at the base of the mountain I was again reminded of the Aran Islands. Here too the fields are 'made' and enclosed within high stone walls, grassy lane-ways run between the walls, little donkeys carry big loads, the sense of remoteness is strong and the tiny cottages are built of stone – though instead of thatch they have flat stone and mud roofs, laid on wooden beams. At one stage the similarity was so great that if I lowered my eyes from the mountains I could almost hear the music of the Atlantic on the shores of Inishere.

Less than two miles from Gilgit the cultivated land ends abruptly and the steepening slope is covered with large loose stones. Now all around me were jagged brown-grey rocks, and stretches of barren scree, and devastated dry water courses, revealing the savage velocity of melted snows. The only vegetation was a splendid shrub, about five feet high, which at intervals flared up spectacularly in the midst of a wide desolation of grey stones and was so laden with deep pink flowers that from a distance it looked like some mysterious bonfire burning untended.

It was quite a stiff climb to the top and at times I had to go very cautiously indeed. Once I was so 'trapped' that the only way up was through a waterfall, where the secure stones offered safer hand- and foot-holds than the loose scree on either side. It was a 'thin' waterfall, yet the power of even that comparatively low volume of water astonished me. (By this time the sun was so hot that my clothes were dry in half an hour.)

Just before this I found the corpse of a young man – dead eight or ten days I should think. His skull had been bashed in so I've officially 'forgotten' the discovery as I wish to remain on good terms with *all* the local factions while trekking here. My nose led me to the poor devil, who was pushed into a crevice between two big boulders. I notice that rifles are not carried in this part of the Agency but they evidently manage to liquidate each other without them. After investigating I was quite glad to immerse myself in the waterfall!

From the summit I had a magnificent view of a tumult of rough white peaks in every direction – including Nanga Parbat again, triumphantly conspicuous above the rest. On the way down I saw a couple of caveman types, with long, tangled hair and beards, carrying ice from the glaciers to Gilgit Town. By following them my return route was shorter – but much more hair-raising – and I got back at 5.20 p.m. utterly exhausted and ravenously hungry.

After a nameless but very satisfying meal I went for a stroll around the town. In some stalls of the bazaar goods from down-country – films, biscuits, toothpaste and the like – are on sale, but they all look excessively fly-blown and cost the earth because of air-freight charges. The townspeople strike me as a surly lot – not impolite or in any way unpleasant, but lacking the frank friendliness which so impressed me in Afghanistan and Pakistan proper. In fact, from the human society point of view it's rather like being back in Persia, except that these people are more uncouth than the Persians – and by uncouth I don't mean spitting on the street or squatting in public, but something deeper inside that governs a man's attitude to others. The actual town has nothing to distinguish it and but for its surroundings would be slightly depressing. Now (10 p.m.) I'm going to bed early in preparation for tomorrow's trek up the valley.

GULAPUR, 6 JUNE

My 'military advisers' had laughed at the idea of anyone cycling up the valley, but I couldn't bear the thought of abandoning Roz now so we left Gilgit at 4.45 a.m., soon after sunrise, to attempt the first stage of the trek together, and for a few miles it was possible to cycle – though at little more than walking pace, over a track covered with several inches of sand.

Already, taking advantage of the morning coolness, peasants were harvesting barley, reaping and binding by hand with leisurely movements. The women wear gay, ankle-length petticoats of imported cotton, but the men have homespun trousers and jackets, again recalling the Aran Islands. Gilgit's entire population is Muslim – different sects predominating in different regions – but the turban is here replaced by a soft cloth cap, turned up around the edges, which gives the men an oddly European appearance.

Today's landscape was a series of dramatic contrasts. The valley floor around Gilgit Town showed the fragrant abundance of early summer – fields of trembling, silver-green wheat and richly golden barley, bushes of unfamiliar, lovely blossoms and, most beautiful of all, a rock-plant with tiny, golden-pink flowers, growing so lavishly in the crevices of the walls that it was like a sunset cloud draped over the grey stones. Then the valley narrowed to exclude the early sun until there was room only for the river between the opposing precipices and we were alone in a barren, rough, shadowy world, where nothing moved but the brown flood-waters.

Next the track soared upwards, overhanging the river-bed, and it became so rocky underfoot that I was often carrying, rather than pushing, Roz. At one stage I couldn't get her up an impossibly steep gradient with kit 'on board', so I unloaded, carried Roz up, slithered down to retrieve the kit and, as I dragged myself up for the second time, admitted defeat. By now Roz has gallantly carried me through quite a variety of improbable terrains, but clearly she can *not* carry me through the Karakoram Mountains – nor can I carry her through them . . .

After some miles of this daredevil upward spiralling the track wriggled around a jutting thousand-foot cliff and I saw, far below, on the other side of the river, a fertile semicircle of land, hidden and tranquil at the base of a snow-capped mountain. A few of the hamlet's farmhouses were visible between willow, plane, sinjit and mulberry trees, growing tall and strong among neat little patches of corn and shimmering young meadows. Sunlight was brilliant on the dark green waters and white foam of a nullah leaping down the mountainside to join the mud-stained river, and through the still, clear air I could hear the faint shouts of men directing the donkeys which were walking round and round on mud threshing-floors.

After this the track descended to river level, before again climbing steeply, and it was almost as difficult to manoeuvre Roz down such a gradient as it had been to haul her up. My wrists ached from the strain of holding the brakes while I stumbled against rocks and slipped on the deep sand: I wished then that I'd had the good sense to heed my 'military advisers'.

Beyond the next pass the mountains receded slightly on our left and for a few miles I was able to cycle across the boulder-strewn moor, though a surface littered with sharp flints kept my speed down. Then, at 10 a.m., trees ahead showed that we were approaching the first hamlet on this side of the river, where the reaction to my appearance was rather disconcerting. Only a few old people and children were about, and the children, after one horrified look, either screamed loudly and buried their faces in their elders' laps, or bounded over the low walls and vanished. The adults, though more restrained, looked no less alarmed, and obviously didn't wish to improve the acquaintance, so I realised that apart from the physical difficulties of cycling here an approach on wheels is psychologically unsound.

Soon after midday I met the problem of finding shade – something uncommonly scarce at noon on a bare mountainside. It wouldn't have been too difficult to find a patch for myself but here again poor Roz complicated things as it was unthinkable that she should be left exposed to such a ferocious sun. So for her sake I had to walk further than was prudent, until an overhanging rock offered protection to us both.

Having slept soundly for two hours I woke to find it even hotter than before, though fortunately the track was now partly in shadow. Today's highest pass lay immediately ahead and to prepare for it I had a swim – one of the coldest of my life – at a spot where high, projecting rocks gave protection from the current and where there was a nice little 'strand' of soft silver sand between the water and the track.

From the top of this pass I could see the orchards and fields of another village about eight miles up the valley. The descent here was more gradual than most and we free-wheeled slowly down – if 'free-wheeled' is the *mot juste* for zig-zagging between boulders! Then, when the track ran level with the river, there was no space left for zig-zagging so Roz and I again exchanged rôles. Near the village a man came riding towards us – the first person we'd met since leaving Gilgit.

Colonel Shah had given me a map which shows that this village is twenty-one miles from Gilgit Town and as I reckon that I cycled no more than one third of the way it's obvious that the time has come to be disloyal to Roz and temporarily acquire a more adaptable mount.

The food situation here is very grim – an acute scarcity of flour and no tea, sugar or salt left after the winter. Most people are living on goats' milk, eggs and mulberries – not my favourite diet when served simultaneously but this evening I was too starved to fuss. I wolfed five eggs and about two pounds of white mulberries – but stuck at the milk. This is odd as I've so often taken it in my stride before: yet I suppose five eggs do make an insecure foundation for goats' milk, which so undeniably tastes exactly as a billy-goat smells! Of course, in a few weeks' time, when the maize harvest has been saved and ground, there will be no shortage of flour and by then too the camel-caravans will have crossed the Babusar Pass with this year's supply of tea, sugar, salt and cotton.

I find that the people here are much easier to get on with than the folk of Gilgit Town – who make me wonder if they have not already lost something through their comparatively close contacts with down-country. This village has one tiny shop, in which a tubercular-looking young man sits on the floor chatting with a few friends and surrounded by almost empty shelves: after eight long months of commercial isolation only a half-bale of cotton and a few boot-laces and pocket-combs remain of the winter's stock. Yet to my surprise cigarettes are available, at *6d.* for twenty, and I'm told that these are flown up regularly, though few other goods are imported by plane – air-freight charges would put them beyond the reach of most Gilgitis. But again I'm experiencing the dignified generosity of the very poor: when I produced money for forty cigarettes the young man looked quite hurt and firmly refused to accept it.

My arrival here caused no less of a sensation than in that other hamlet down the valley. However, this community is better prepared to meet an invasion by bicycle, as some of the older men have served in the Indian Army under the British and two have even been to Italy, so the peculiarities of European women are vaguely comprehended.

The village has a school as well as a shop and within minutes of my arrival the young teacher came hurrying to the rescue. He speaks Urdu, which is of no assistance whatever, and a very few words of English, which is of the greatest assistance. Supplementing these few words with scores of complicated signs, I explained my position and was assured that a suitable horse will be awaiting me at dawn tomorrow and that Roz will be respectfully cherished until I rejoin her.

I'm often astounded by the complicated explanations, discussions and arrangements which can be conducted through signs, even without a single mutually comprehensible word. Admittedly the usefulness of signs varies according to the intelligence of the local population; I found the superbly quick-witted Afghans the easiest of all in this respect. A language barrier does inevitably impede the collection of concrete information and the exchange of ideas, but it really is surprisingly flimsy when one wishes to arrange practical details and in unsophisticated societies it ceases to count where personal relationships are concerned. What can be an embarrassment when visiting Europeans, to whom elaborate signs may seem undignified, actually helps to overcome shyness and awe in primitive homes. When you ask for fried eggs by making noises like a hen after laying, followed by noises like something sizzling in fat, the whole household is convulsed with laughter and not only are fried eggs served, but you are unanimously elected as one of the family.

A local detail which absolutely astounds me is that the women knit heavy unbleached woollen sweaters for their menfolk *on an Aran pattern.* It's unmistakable – and they certainly didn't get it from women's magazines!

During the summer, in river-level villages, everyone here sleeps out of doors – either on the flat roofs of their little houses, or in their compounds, if they have them, or simply in village streets or in orchards; my bed for tonight is a charpoy under an apricot tree in the teacher's compound.

11

From One Saddle to Another

GULAPUR TO SHER QUILA RAKAPOSHI

GAKUCH, 7 JUNE

When we started our trek today at 5.30 a.m. the sun was up, but not yet over the mountains, and the valley looked very beautiful in the cool light, with the air soft and fresh, like spring grass. I was so happy that I burst into what it pleases me to call 'song', but the result obviously unnerved my mount and I had to desist abruptly. Apart from this lack of appreciation, she's a splendid pony – a sturdy, agile eight-year-old of about fourteen hands, with a curious pale golden coat, not uncommon in this region. I've rechristened her 'Rob' for the duration of our trek because her real name is so tongue-eluding, not to say unspellable. At first I found her nonchalant treatment of precipices quite terrifying; then I realised that if she avoided the edge of today's track she'd very successfully concuss me against overhanging chunks of cliff and by midday I'd become quite reconciled to the way she tripped along the very verge of the track, frequently dislodging stones which took a long, long time to reach the river. And by evening I'd become so trustful that I positively enjoyed looking down to see nothing whatever between me and the torrent, 1,500 feet below. Following the example of local horsemen I walked up the steepest gradients and rode down, so I'd the worst of both worlds, since it's far more tiring to ride down than up such sharp inclines. On some of the level stretches I had to dismount again, where the track was too narrow to take a rider, or was strewn with massive boulders which it seemed wisest for us to negotiate separately.

Over the first two or three miles beyond Gakuch the valley floor was very fertile. Then the track began to go up and up, winding round and round mountain after mountain, and the many other fertile patches which appeared below were all on the opposite side of the river. I often stopped to look down on those little hamlets – one could never tire of their beauty. In this part of the valley the river seethes along, a mass of white foam, with thin waterfalls from glaciers twinkling down cliffs to meet it, and today fields of unripe barley and wheat were being played on by a strong west wind until they too looked like rivers flowing east. A lovely shrub, with feathery, pale green branches which shade off to pink about twelve inches from the end, grows abundantly amidst the stones and sand by the riverside; usually it's a few feet high but some of the bushes were almost trees.

We met one other traveller today – a frail and half-starved-looking young man who was carrying a colossal wooden crate on his back and could barely stagger along the rough track under its weight. I gave him my lunch of four hard-boiled eggs and he ate them so fast I was quite alarmed, fearing he'd die of indigestion and that I'd have done more harm than good. Now I basely and bitterly regret my generosity, as I myself am almost dying of starvation and this village can't even produce an egg. At the moment I'm waiting while clover is being cut in a nearby field to be stewed for my supper. It's the very same as clover at home and I suppose (and hope) it's nourishing; they eat it often in Afghanistan, too, and when it was served there with grilled mutton I mistook it for spinach. I'll know now what to do next summer with the clover on my lawn!

We covered thirty-four miles today, arriving here at 6.45 p.m., and I had one delicious swim where the track dived right down to river level. Watering Rob is the big problem (I carry fodder for her behind the saddle) but we were lucky enough today with springs en route.

The filth in these villages is beyond all, the poverty is the most extreme, I've met since leaving home and the skin-diseases are too dreadful to be described. Everyone stinks to high heaven – even in the open air it's overpowering and inside the little stone huts it's almost lethal. Now two grinning boys of about twelve have just appeared beside me, carrying a hideous-looking cloth full of mulberries. The method is to lay a cloth under a tree, climb into the lower branches and shake the fruit down. I'm too hungry to resist their juicy sweetness so, in spite of the cloth, will devour them. They are, of course, the chief source of sugar for the Gilgitis – and I badly need sugar this evening after those thirty-four miles.

NAME OF VILLAGE UNKNOWN, 8 JUNE

We arrived here at 7.45 p.m. – half an hour ago – and so far there's no sign of any food appearing. I've had nothing to eat since a tiny bowl of stewed clover at 5.30 a.m.; this would be passable with salt, but without it it merely tastes like a slimy mess and anyway is *not* sustaining. Rob did much better than I today – we came to several grassy patches where she grazed contentedly while I wished that I was a horse too! The situation is maddening because in Pindi I asked those who are supposed to be authorities on this area if I should bring stores and they said that if I was prepared to eat local foods this would not be necessary: which just shows how little central authorities know about outlying areas. Though I must admit that this village is *very* outlying – if the path and my permit hadn't petered out here we'd soon be in China!

I was also told that there are no snakes in Gilgit and consequently I have been happily sleeping on the ground all over the place – yet this afternoon I met two thin, black-and-yellow eighteen inchers within an hour; they hissed at us from beside the track and Rob got very jittery. I killed them both with heavy stones, having a vague feeling that it's one's duty as a citizen to do so; then afterwards I got scruples about taking life without provocation and regretted my savagery. But now the scribe of this village, who most improbably speaks English (As She Should Not Be Spoken), has soothed my conscience by telling me that these snakes are a menace to the kids grazing on the mountainsides. He added that the adult goats never get bitten, which seems unlikely – if goats had a built-in anti-snake device it would surely operate as efficiently for kids as for adults. Possibly the answer is that this poison is not strong enough seriously to worry the adults. Incidentally, the same kids are besieging me at the moment, having discovered that I'm good at scratching between their incipient horns – evidently horn-growing is their version of teething troubles. They're the most charming little creatures imaginable and come in all colours from jet-black to snow-white, through nigger-brown, russet and beige with many wildly mixed piebalds. When stroked or scratched they wag their little tails frantically. A few moments ago I discovered that one of them has just consumed the entire five pages of Daphne's last, and as yet unanswered, letter but I suppose he'll survive. If some food doesn't soon appear I'll be following his example and consuming Patsy's six pages! Yet it's odd how much easier it is to bear extreme hunger than extreme thirst, which almost drives one mad. By this stage my stomach must be lined with mud, I've drunk so much of the flooded river – but though it looks like mutton broth it tastes delicious. As I wrote the last sentence the tiniest kid was getting himself on to my lap where he is now curled up happily sucking my left thumb!

We covered about thirty-five miles today through the wildest landscape I've ever seen. This Gilgit region really does something quite extraordinary to one's mind. The completely unbroken solitude and the absence of anything recalling the rest of humanity produce a unique feeling of liberation as one moves slowly through these tremendous gorges. Today the outside world and my own life – past and future – as part of that world seemed so utterly unreal that for a time I ceased to be aware of it and existed only in the present, acutely conscious of my surroundings and of physical sensation, but removed, in a dreamlike way, from myself as a person. It was a strangely relaxing experience – though in retrospect slightly eerie.

About five miles from here I got quite a scare when we came round a sharp angle of the mountainside to see, right in front of us, what looked like an impassable torrent raging down across the 'road' between huge boulders. I was about to dismount and contemplate the crisis when I realised that Rob was all set to cope. She turned left, went downstream about fifteen yards and then plunged in. The water was some twenty-five yards wide and at one stage she was actually swimming. (I'm soaked to the waist now and have nothing to change into.) Then she came out on the other side and climbed up through boulders and loose stones that I would have considered dicey even for a goat. After that she halted for a moment of her own accord and looked round as though to say 'Who's a smart horse?' so I lavished the appropriate praises and pats on her and off she jogged again. The joke is that if I'd had time to *think* about it I wouldn't have dared cross, yet we'd no alternative as it's out of the question to remain in the open after dark here because of snow-leopards and bears. (Apparently the bears are much the more dangerous of the two.) I've had my share of these nullahs ever since leaving Gilgit Town but this was by far the deepest. They begin to flow about twelve midday, when the sun has been beating for hours on the glaciers, are in full spate by 6 p.m., down to a trickle by midnight and dried up by 4 a.m. After the next few weeks they'll be finally dried up for the season, when all but the permanent glaciers have melted. It was very hot today – I should think at least 80°.

There has just been a pause to eat maize gruel out of an iron dish and drink tea with salt in it. They get salt and tea here from China (unofficially) and when one comes to think of it, it's a matter of taste and custom whether one adds sugar or salt or neither to tea. Having by choice acquired the salt habit in Pindi and district I was undismayed by this evening's brew – but I do feel guilty at eating their gruel and I can't pay them as they simply won't accept money.

Despite their filth, the people in all these little villages are truly delightful and are contributing as much as Rob and the scenery to the success of this trek. They have a simple, but easily aroused, sense of humour and I've discovered that imitating animal noises is the surest way to send a whole village into convulsions of laughter. Another way is solemnly to put my solar topee on the oldest and most respected member of the community – at this point they almost roll on the ground with mirth. They wear very distinctive and highly coloured costumes in this village and the women have quite lovely bead and silver necklaces and bracelets. As they are all Ismaili Muslims the women go unveiled. There are few traces of Mongolian blood and the majority are very fair like northern rather than southern Europeans. Their biggest worry is the colour of my face and arms: they cannot understand why I don't pull down my shirt-sleeves and shade my face from the sun!

I had expected a painful reaction to follow my sudden transference from Roz to Rob but there's a most convenient custom throughout Pakistan which has helped my muscles enormously. Since crossing the Khyber Pass I've found myself being thoroughly massaged from head to foot almost every evening, either by one of the servants of the families with whom I've stayed or, in villages, by kindly women who appear out of nowhere, knead me efficiently and disappear. I haven't yet established whether this is common form for all travellers, or is reserved for those who are self-propelled, but whatever the basis of the custom it's making my life here much less sore than it would otherwise be.

This village is at an altitude of over 10,000 feet and after dark the temperature drops sharply, so tonight I'm sleeping indoors – i.e. sharing a stinking mound of blankets with six no less stinking children. But the use of that adjective is not to be interpreted as a mark of ingratitude – I appreciate these people's hospitality even more than I do that of my wealthy hosts down-country.

GUPIS, 9 JUNE

If anyone ever asks you to drive three donkeys and a foal for twenty-four miles through the Karakoram Mountains, be *very* firm and refuse to do so – it really *is* more than flesh and blood was ever meant to endure. The position, as explained to me this morning, was that the four were being exchanged for a pony mare and foal from Gupis, but the latter was too young to travel for another fortnight whereas the donkeys were urgently required in Gupis, and a donkey foal, although looking so much frailer, is presumed tougher – therefore, would I please take the donkeys with me and save a villager the journey to Gupis? Green as I am I foresaw some of the complications and said, 'Couldn't a villager come with me, riding half the way on Rob, and when the pony foal was able to make it, couldn't a Gupis villager bring them up?' But no – it was in the bargain that the donkey village was responsible for herding both lots. So off I went at 5.45 a.m., armed with a long switch which would, in theory, enable me to steer my charges without difficulty.

Well, maybe a local on horseback could do it, but those donkeys knew they were on to a soft thing. Everyone remained happy while there was, on one side, a sheer drop of hundreds of feet into the river and, on the other side, an equally sheer wall of rock – then the brutes had no alternative but to go in a straight line. The fun started when the mountains receded in places, or the track dropped to river level and there came level stretches between river and track. Then the quartet merrily gambolled off at about ten times the rate they'd go on the road, in divers directions, through deep, yielding sand and thorny bushes, and between boulders and over streams and behind trees and around cliffs. (It's all right for you to sit back and laugh, but if *you* were galloping under a blazing sun trying to reassemble *in one place* a herd of apparently demented donkeys, you mightn't think it so amusing.) Rob was again wonderful – this is obviously a frequently recurring crisis in her life. She went after them like a sheep-dog and on the track kept reinforcing my rather half-hearted use of the switch by pushing the last donkey's rump with her nose; twenty-four miles at the pace of ambling donkeys is decidedly wearing. I passed a lovely pool, but did not dare to swim because the caravan would have been halfway to Peking by the time I came out. After twelve miles I saw that the foal couldn't possibly be driven any further without positive cruelty: from his point of view the whole idea was cruel anyway. (He was the smallest foal I've ever seen, with a mother hardly bigger than an Irish donkey foal.) So then I did what they do in Afghanistan with tiny foals and calves – tied his forefeet and hind-feet and put him across Rob in front of the saddle. I had to climb on to a rock to get him in place – he seemed amazingly heavy despite his dwarfishness – and he took a very dim view of the performance, as did his mother. (Rob was the only one to accept the situation philosophically.) By the time this was accomplished the two donkeys not involved had vanished and as I didn't feel like going into the unknown with the foal *in situ* I pursued them on foot, leaving Rob tied to a bush, the foal tied to Rob and the mother psychologically tied to the foal. A twenty-minute chase followed over burning sand and loose rocks (my biggest fear was that one of the wretches would break a leg) and then we were off again. We arrived here at 7.45 p.m., having had several pauses to dismantle the foal for feeding.

This village is a veritable metropolis – its one shop sells cloth and matches and three men from Lahore are posted here on a six months' meteorological survey – they almost wept for joy to see someone else from down-country. The area also produces *potatoes* so I'd a luxury dinner with the boys this evening – spuds and stewed clover and ghee. It would have been even more luxurious without the ghee. They make butter here by putting milk in an ill-cured sheepskin and sitting for hours rocking it to and fro on their knees. The whole family takes a turn and eventually you have butter. Then the stuff is put in another, equally ill-cured, skin and buried in the snow for two years. When resurrected the thing is allegedly a delicacy. If you want to be frightfully polite you can describe it as 'mature' – and if you survive it you'll survive anything. Sugar may be obtained by air from Pindi at 6*s.* a pound if anyone wants it. Nobody does. The people reckon to get enough from mulberries – surely the sweetest of all fruits – which are dried for winter use. Some time ago an American 'expert' came to demonstrate a better method of drying fruit, but the locals found it too expensive and have reverted to their traditional way. Incidentally, that American has become a legend in the valleys – they still giggle at the memory of him refusing to drink the spring water from the mountains without first boiling and then chlorinating it, and the kernel of the joke is that he got such violent dysentery in the end that a helicopter had to come from Gilgit to remove him.

I've come down a lot in the world today – to 7,800 feet. The Met. boys told me that the temperature in Gupis this last week has been between 80° and 88°. They have a 'Post Office' here also and once a week a runner goes to and from Gilgit (literally running in bare feet), armed with a six-foot spear against bears, wolves and leopards.

GAKUCH, 10 JUNE

The food situation has improved here since I left a few days ago – apricots are ripe now and everyone can have their fill, gratis, including cattle. These seem a rather exotic fodder for animals but transport costs are too high for fruit to be sold down-country and the people here can't eat it all. The enormous trees – like giant oaks – are laden with their crop; and in another few days plums and peaches will be just as plentiful. I notice that, though in general the people are pathetically unhealthy, most have exceptionally good teeth – possibly so much fruit?

We took it easy today, covering only twenty-two miles, during which I had three glorious swims. The barley is ripening fast now and the little fields with their grey stone walls look like patches of pure gold as one gazes down from high up on the opposite mountain. The colouring on every side here is so vivid and clear and the contrasts are so wonderfully effective in their simplicity that I just soak it all up like a sponge and hope the memory will sustain me when I get back to the hell down-country – if I ever do! The Met. boys thought the Babusar Pass would be negotiable by now on foot, though they said it definitely won't open to jeep traffic this year till mid-July. Apart from being squashed by sliding glaciers (and that would be sheer bad luck and is far less likely than being squashed by a bus in Pindi) they said the nullahs will be the chief menace. There's a PWD Rest House eight miles from the top, so I'll be sure of a night's sleep before crossing. Of course it's possible I'll have to give up at some point and return to Gilgit. (Don't worry – I won't take any foolish risks. I've often wondered what a *wise* risk is and now I know – obviously the sort I take!) I have decided to hitch-hike with Roz from Pindi to Lahore (172 miles), as we will be returning on this road in October, when the weather is more reasonable for cycling; there's no future in sweating along it for three days during the hottest fortnight of the year.

SHER QUILA RAKAPOSHI, 11 JUNE

I forgot to tell you about the pseudo-soccer match I saw in Gupis. Having delivered our herd to their destination Rob was dragging herself (and me) along the road to the Met. office when suddenly I came on the most unexpected sight – a playing field complete with twenty-two youths and a soccer ball. I know very little about soccer, but enough to realise that this is how it is *not* played. No one ever moved above trotting speed, no one ever tried to tackle anyone else, the referee never used his whistle, the ball was never headed and the two goalies sat cross-legged between the posts most of the time, looking abstracted. The real excitement from a spectator's point of view was caused by the fact that one side of the field had a sheer drop of 200 feet, so that the main object of all the players was to keep the ball from going into the ravine rather than to kick it between the posts. Of course it frequently *did* go over the edge and then followed a ten-minute interval, while the 'linesmen' stationed down there retrieved it, and during this pause everyone lay about in attitudes of utter exhaustion, as though they'd been playing their hearts out. What fascinated me was the way they avoided the ball if someone occasionally (to his own evident astonishment) kicked it hard – both teams showed more speed and agility in getting away from this dangerous missile than they did in pursuing it. The final score, curiously enough, was 0–0.

That evening, too, I had my first bottle of Punial Water, the local wine which sells at 1½*d* per quart. It's nice, yet can't be described by likening it to any other wine, as its taste is unique; but it definitely is wine and quite potent on an empty stomach. Grapes are as plentiful here as other fruits but are not cultivated in vineyards. Instead, the vines have grown to full size and are like giant fossilised serpents, often coiling from a walnut to a mulberry to a plum tree and so overwhelming the 'host trees' that it's difficult to determine their species. The wine is amber and rather cloudy and tastes faintly of that ill-cured sheepskin which plays a part in the production of most food and drink here.

We left Gakuch at 5.15 a.m., laden with apricots to 'keep me going'. I don't think that if I live to be a hundred I'll ever forget those glorious early morning starts, seeing the first shaft of sunlight come over the sharp, snowy peaks to stream down the valley, and listening to the sweet, excited bird-song and to the rush of the brooks and the whinnying of local horses greeting Rob.

We're now down again to 6,100 feet and it was damned hot by 11.30

a.m. I stopped at a tiny hamlet for four hours and met a most interesting man who spoke fluent English and gave me a lot of information about the locality. He got a government scholarship as a youth and is now trying to improve local farming methods. Aged 36, he's one of the twenty-eight children of his father's four wives. But he says that because he could not afford to feed children as he has now learnt they should be fed he refuses to marry. I thought him a very impressive character, absolutely dedicated to the task of helping his people. We sat outside his family's stone hut, in the shade of walnut and mulberry trees, beside a 'white-foam-and-green-water' torrent hurtling down from the mountain, with weeping willow and golden barley on the other side of the nullah; the glaciers on the mountains across the narrow valley look very beautiful against the deep, deep blue sky. He and I were given roughly-made wooden chairs and about twenty-two other people sat around on the ground, fascinated and uncomprehending, as we talked in English while drinking bowl after bowl of buttermilk. Some of the girls were very lovely in a Germanic sort of way, but most were so dirty and undernourished that one could only pity them.

It's just occurred to me that the inoculation I'd have needed most in this locality is the one I *didn't* have – against TB. The coughing and spitting – often of blood – are appalling and about twenty per cent of the people in these villages are clearly dying on their feet. The only consolation – a poor one – is that a case of young parents dying and leaving half a dozen children isn't the tragedy it would be in most 'civilised' communities, as the children will be as well cared for as possible by other relatives. The only essential for children *not* in short supply here is affection, and the result is an extraordinarily happy atmosphere in every family I've stayed with, despite the starvation and squalor. Each child is doted on by everyone from its tiny brothers and sisters up to its creaking great-grandparents.

I made an effort to get this family sorted out, but on discovering that the man on my left had sired three of the infants present – all aged between four and ten months – I gave up the attempt. One of his wives, aged eighteen and mother of four, looked at least forty, and the eldest wife, who was forty, had just had her sixteenth (seven dead) and looked seventy – but was very gay and cheerful. In this region wives are quite frankly bought; until recently they were exchanged for livestock, now they fetch £5 to £50 depending on their looks. If a man wants an exceptionally beautiful girl for £50, he'll pay £10 down and the rest on the instalment system. Beauty means big eyes, small mouth, curly hair, long neck, straight nose, white skin, good teeth and plenty of curves. If the beauty proves barren she will probably be divorced if she is a first wife, but another man who has already sons by his wife or wives, will buy her for her beauty alone; among Ismailis there is far less emphasis on virginity than among Sunnis or Shias. But adultery by the wife remains the crime of crimes; it is legal for the betrayed husband to kill both his wife and her lover on the spot if he catches them together. However, if the lover flees and the husband kills them apart it is murder, and he goes to gaol in Gilgit Town for eight years. I asked if murder for other motives was common but apparently it's almost unknown, so probably the corpse I found was that of a lover who got away and was killed afterwards. Theft of any kind is equally rare (possibly because no one has anything worth stealing!) and my friend couldn't tell me what the penalty is as he's never heard of a case. Girl-babies are considered bad luck and everyone concerned weeps with disappointment at their birth – which seems very odd in a society where their sale will later on bring money into the family. Boy-babies are saluted with gunfire and twenty-four hours of rejoicing, singing and dancing. Nevertheless I notice that the girl-babies receive as much kissing and cuddling from both parents and from everyone else as the boys, so the weeping must soon stop.

Leaving my hamlet, after a lunch of apricots and maize bread, I jogged along in a leisurely way towards Gulapur, where I'd intended rejoining Roz this evening. Then, about four miles from the village, a horseman came galloping towards us in a cloud of dust, pulled up and with a broad beam and a low bow handed me a visiting-card. I looked at it in some astonishment, which you'll agree is a natural reaction. Then the horseman signed that I was to follow him and he led me – by this time feeling slightly surrealistic – off the Gulapur track and over a swaying suspension bridge to a very good imitation of the Garden of Eden on the other side of the river. Finally I found myself beside a mounting-block outside the Raja's residence and there was my host greeting me as though we'd known each other for a lifetime! (He speaks adequate, though not fluent, English.)

This is quite the most fantastic set-up I've ever met. A new bungalow, very rough and ready, has just been built to replace the old stone fortress where all the other Rajas lived. Here I am installed with an oil-lamp, which is regarded in these parts as the last word in modernity (the ordinary people use the roots of the juniper bush as lamps because they burn very slowly for a long time), and with a lavatory off my room, which sounds good till you discover it is a board laid across a stream which runs through the compound. I presume our drinking water comes from the same brook and can only hope that it's taken from upstream. The place looks almost completely unfurnished, apart from about half a ton of silver polo trophies. The Raja himself is an absolute darling who reminds me of something out of a fairy tale – I suppose because life in this tiny state of 15,000 inhabitants is all so simple and crystal clear that it belongs to childhood stories rather than to adult life. He had no difficulty whatever in persuading me to stay for a few days, so I sadly said, 'goodbye, and thank you for looking after me so well', to Rob, who was then taken home by one of the Raja's henchmen. The postal runner passed on the other side of the river as I was leaving Rob so I hailed him and delivered a letter to Daphne into his leather satchel: presumably it will arrive in Ireland some day.

The Raja, who is forty-eight, has only one wife living (and one dead) which is very unenterprising of him as both his father and grandfather ran to four simultaneously. His grandfather helped define the Durand Line and was made KCIE for that and his father was an OBE, for no apparent reason except that he ruled his people well and justly. The present Raja has ten sisters and brothers and can't remember half their names.

SHER QUILA RAKAPOSHI, 12 JUNE

Life is pure bliss here – the Raja has offered me a present of a little farm under the mountains and I'm almost tempted to accept! Dinner last night consisted of stewed goat-meat and maize bread and cherries, and this morning after a breakfast of eggs and bread we set off on foot for a tour of the 'village', which is not a village in our sense of the word but about a thousand acres of fertile land with the little stone huts of the peasant farmers dotted around it and a criss-cross of artificial streams keeping the place green. The atmosphere is indeed of paradise regained – such perfect tranquillity, innocent of politics, budgets and rivalry of any kind. The Raja is accepted as father of the whole community and treats everyone as 'family' and that's that. After every harvest he checks the amount of grain in the state and decides whether any should be sold in Gilgit bazaar or not and the people accept his decision without question – that's his function as Minister for Finance. As Minister for Social Welfare he receives all families who have suffered any kind of disaster into his compound and supports them indefinitely – at the moment a hundred and twenty-four people are being maintained. As Minister for Justice he settles the disputes which the council of twelve men in each village of the state bring to his notice. This morning, while eating his breakfast, he received a deputation who reported on a dispute about a rope bridge near by. It has always been kept up by two villages, one on either side of the river, but now one village says that its people almost never use it, and that the other village should do all the repairs – so the Raja pronounced that this was fair enough and the dispute was settled in five minutes.

This morning I kept thinking of Delius' 'Walk to the Paradise Gardens' as we went through fields of golden barley being harvested by women and girls in scarlet gowns and silver and blue caps, then climbed up by very narrow paths beside sparkling streams through woods of walnut, apricot, plum, pear and peach trees to where we could look across at the pine woods on the summit of the opposite mountain and see, through binoculars, the ibex grazing – that was a *big* moment! Then we went higher still to where one of the streams forms a pool on a level, wide 'step' on the mountainside. And there, in the soft, dry sand, I saw the pug-marks of a leopard who comes here nightly to drink – another *big* moment. It looked just like an enlarged version of my cat Roarin's prints on my writing paper on a wet day! The Raja said leopards are harmless unless a man is caught out on the mountain ill or injured, when they may kill and eat him. We returned by different paths to the Residence, through groves of weeping willow and fiery blossomed pomegranate trees, past more fields of barley and green wheat, with every peasant we met stopping to kiss the Raja's right hand and discuss their problems with their 'father'. The Raja told me that three years ago he decided it would be best for the people if he abdicated and handed over the state to the Pakistan Government, but everyone rose in revolt at this idea and begged him not to – so he didn't. I can't help contrasting Punial with Swat. Of course Swat is far better off materially, but personally I prefer Punial, which is really an extension of Afghanistan. (I've come round in a semicircle so that here I'm quite near the Afghan frontier.) And though the Wali and his family are model rulers, there's no comparison between the Swat ruler-ruled relationship and that of Punial. (Admittedly the comparison is not quite fair as the population of Swat is 594,000 and the same degree of intimacy just isn't possible.) But the Walis' household lives on a plane completely different from the people's, whereas here the only real difference between the Raja's and people's standard of living is that he has meat (goat's) once a day whereas they have it occasionally. The Raja is an amazing man, with a very highly-developed sense of responsibility and a very poorly-developed sense of his own importance; he's the first person I've met since leaving Europe who is quite happy to do his own fetching and carrying despite a host of servants. He's at the people's disposal always, whether they come during his siesta or at meal-times they are never expected to wait. Every December he has to go to Pindi on business and this he hates above anything as he can't get adjusted to the crowds and noise and traffic. He says he doesn't like city people 'because they are not honest'. I know exactly what he means – not that they are dishonest in their dealings, but in their attitudes to life generally. He doesn't know much about his own family origins but thinks his people came from near Kabul in the 1860s and took this place by force – Sher Quila means 'Lion's Fort' and the area is so called because it's very difficult to conquer. He certainly looks a typical Pathan and the family are Sunnis, though all the people are Ismailis. There are two tiny mosques in the village as, of course, the sects won't worship in the same mosque unless it's unavoidable (how Christian-like can Muslims get?) and this afternoon I visited both. The Ismaili one is lavishly decorated with gaudy pictures of the old and new Aga Khan and Prince Aly Khan. The present Aga Khan came here in 1961 and the mosque is full of coloured pictures of him in local dress. The Sunni mosque is a little wooden hut in the Raja's compound – what we'd call a family chapel.

Last night while we were having dinner wonderful music (very Afghan-like) began to play near by and when I asked why, I was told that it was the traditional way of announcing that an important polo-match would be played on the following day. Afterwards we went to look at the band. One old, bearded man was playing on a sort of primitive flute and two drummers were beating with their bare hands on the tight-skin ends of earthenware pitchers, which seemed similar to Afghan instruments. Polo is the national game here and the children begin to practise as tots by running around hitting stones with polo sticks; the result is astonishingly like our national game of hurling. Of course the sticks are home-made – branches of trees cut so cleverly at intersections that they look exactly like the real thing – but the balls used in matches are orthodox, made of bamboo root and imported from East Pakistan.

At 4.30 this afternoon the band began to play again. Then, at 5, I threw in the ball and, as Michael O'Hehir would say, the game was on! What a game to watch! Never anywhere have I seen such a thrilling spectacle. Of course it was totally unlike polo as we know it; there are *no* rules in this version and every sort of attack and defence is allowed. Blood was soon streaming from over half the twelve players' heads and hands and backs but they carried on regardless. The pace was tremendously fast and the horses streaked up and down the pitch foaming with sweat. Polo sticks were broken and replaced by the minute and the ball flew all over the place like a meteor – as often in the air as on the ground. The band played non-stop in time to the thudding hoofs and wild, whirling, clashing sticks and the faster the game the faster the music, till the three musicians were in almost as much of a lather as the horses.

One thing I noticed was the complete absence of fouls as distinct from accidents. Though this was a tremendously important championship game no tempers were lost and no one deliberately went for an opponent – the injuries were as often as not received from a member of the same team during what I can only describe as one of the scrums, when the ball got stuck beside a stone wall and all twelve horses 'packed down' with every man leaning from his saddle and poking towards it through the frantic jumble of horses' legs – anything less scientific it would be difficult to imagine. The only law concerned time; after thirty minutes there was a ten-minute interval (but no change of horses – they were simply walked about by little boys while their riders mopped up each other's blood) and then the teams changed sides and I threw in the ball again and off they went. At this stage it was Sher Quila: 1 – Gulapur: 5, and the crowds sitting all around on the stone walls were silent and depressed. Then Sher Quila got going and scored four goals in rapid succession, which feat caused frenzied cheering. However, Gulapur soon came back with two, leaving it 7–5 and eight minutes to go – by now I was hoarse from yelling for Sher Quila! For those minutes the pace was incredible – the horses flashed up and down the field wheeling at each end like ballet dancers and the air was full of the noise of cracked sticks, new ones being flung out for the riders to catch in mid-air as they galloped by. With half a minute to go Sher Quila equalised, and the villagers nearly fell off the walls in their delight. At full time it was decided to play an extra ten minutes, and Sher Quila scored again, to win. I was quite exhausted by excitement and suspense as I scrambled off the wall: it took a full bottle of Punial Water to revive me! The visiting team spend the night here after these games as both men and horses are too tired to go home and I'm now being entertained by the band still playing vigorously for their benefit, on the other side of the compound.

The Raja has what I can only describe as a few toys, in which he takes a boyish delight, and one of them is a Japanese transistor radio presented to him by our mutual friend Colonel Shah. On this he listens to the 8 p.m. Pindi news every evening and the weather reports from down-country are the single depressing feature of life here; today the temperature on the plains has been 115° in the shade.

SHER QUILA RAKAPOSHI, 13 JUNE

This morning, after a 5.30 a.m. breakfast on the verandah overlooking the river, my host disappeared for a moment and then came trotting back carrying a sheaf of letters. With a shy, sheepish smile he looked rather timidly down at me and said, 'I think you are a nice woman so you won't laugh at me because I cannot read or write. But sometimes I get letters in English, so now will you read them out for me very slowly please and I will ask you to write my answer for me because I see you can do much writing every day.' So we settled down to his correspondence for the next three hours – I've rarely been so pleased by any compliment!

But it's astonishing, when you come to think of it – he and most of the villagers speak their own local language (which I won't even attempt to spell but which is a distinct language, not a dialect, though it has no alphabet) as well as Urdu and Pushto, and he also speaks Pharsi and English, yet they're all illiterate. (Pushto is known here as so many caravans have always come over the Shandur Pass from Afghanistan.) The young village schoolmaster, whose pen I have just borrowed, acts as scribe, reading and writing letters in Urdu, but he knows only a few words of English. I'm afraid his qualifications as teacher are rather limited, at least in history and geography; he thought that Ireland was one of the United States of America and he swears that the Gilgit River is the Indus, whereas in fact it's a tributary, meeting the young Indus at Bunji, about sixty miles from here.

This morning I went for a long ride on a grey stallion, around the mountain which rises right behind this valley to the north. He wasn't as restful a steed as Rob and I had no confidence in my ability to control him, but fortunately we met no interesting mares en route.

I stopped on the way back to investigate a flour-mill which must be a perfect example of the very first mill ever invented by man. It was built of the usual stones over a rapid mountain torrent. A large tree-trunk had been hollowed out to form a sloping pipe through which the water was directed to increase its force, and flowing under the little hut it revolved what looked like an aeroplane propeller. Going into the hut through a four-foot high 'door' I found an amiable, ancient and very filthy old miller superintending the processes. A stone (such as I have seen lying around villages all the way through from east Turkey) about five foot in circumference (or perhaps diameter is what I mean?), with a six-inch hole in the middle, is attached to the revolving propeller in the stream below and slowly turns on another stationary stone, grinding the grains which fall, a few at a time, in a steady stream through the (yes!) sheep-skin hanging suspended from a beam across the five-foot-high ceiling. The flour dribbles out from beneath the stone into a dirty wooden trough and that's that! Each little mill is a private concern producing just enough for one family. Usually the grandfather or great-grandfather, who is past his speed for work in the fields or on the mountains, acts as miller.

Punial is a relatively prosperous area for this part of the world and the people are never actually without food, but in most of the other villages around they spend the winter in a drunken stupor as they have plenty of wine but only enough food for one square meal a week. In August they begin to fatten a bull-calf and in December it's killed and the meat is buried in snow and used very sparingly throughout the following months. This and their dried fruits keep them from actually dying of hunger. The winters here are as cold as you'd expect and the families exist crammed thirty or forty together in little stone huts, keeping each other warm to supplement the heat of tiny wood fires and drowning their misery in the abundant Punial Water, which apparently intoxicates them much more quickly than it does me.

I got back here at 11.30 a.m., which is lunchtime, and after lunch went off again on foot to find a cool corner for my siesta, as there are so many flies in this house that it's impossible to sleep here during the day. Also it's much cooler up the mountainside among greenery and running water with a delicious little breeze blowing down from the snows. I found a delightful spot beside a whitely-foaming torrent and went asleep for an hour under a willow tree.

Some noise wakened me and I opened my eyes to see a ragged, bearded old man kneeling beside me and stretching out his hand towards my throat with a ferocious expression on his face. The thought flashed through my mind – 'Well, you were bound to be murdered sometime . . . ' and then before I could move he drew back and beamed triumphantly and showed me, crushed between his fingers, the ant which he had kindly picked off my neck! Actually, I've discovered long ago that contrary to my preconceived ideas ants *don't* usually bite. I couldn't count the number of times I've lain on a spot of ground swarming with them and they've simply continued to swarm all over me without doing any damage. However, this reminded me of the snakes, which I'd quite forgotten, so I bounded up, made my salaams to the old boy and continued up a glorious path around the lower slopes of the mountain. On the way down I came on another old boy sitting beside a stream trying to get a thorn out of his foot by prodding it with another, bigger thorn from one of the aromatic shrubs which flourish here. When he saw me he beckoned me over and signed that his eyesight was *karrab* ('bad' in Pharsi and Pushto and evidently in Urdu also) and would I please operate on the foot. A lifetime of going barefooted meant that the soles of his feet were like leather and I had to get out my knife and spend a quarter of an hour dislodging the thing. It was a brute of a thorn half an inch long but after the extraction my friend happily thrust his bleeding foot into the stream and firmly declined to come back here with me and have it dressed and disinfected – but perhaps our disinfectants would give these people blood-poisoning! I thought the whole thing enchanting: could you imagine any European peasant stopping a tourist and requesting her to attend to his revolting foot? But, of course, here one is merely another human being, if an exceedingly odd one, and it's taken for granted that one will help if necessary just as when one needs help it is unfailingly given without anyone stopping to consider inconvenience or cost.

Yesterday evening I staged a cigarette crisis: I had my last at teatime and they're unobtainable here. The Raja is a non-smoker (and non-drinker) but he produced a box of choice cigars (*very* mild compared with the quite uninhaleable Pakistani cigarettes) which I've been on ever since – they make me feel like George Sand's ghost!

After dinner tonight the Raja again urged me to accept his offer of a little farm here and settle down for life 'where Heaven and earth meets'. He had already questioned me very closely about my family and financial affairs (as do all Asians, quite uninhibitedly) and he said this evening that I'd be far better off farming in Punial rather than living on fresh air in Ireland! I thanked him very much and explained that I couldn't be happy permanently exiled from Ireland, just as he couldn't if exiled from Punial – but he wasn't convinced. As his card so clearly shows, he thinks Punial the best place in the world and he also thinks farming the only occupation fit for any self-respecting person, all other ways of earning a living being regarded as debased, if not actually immoral.

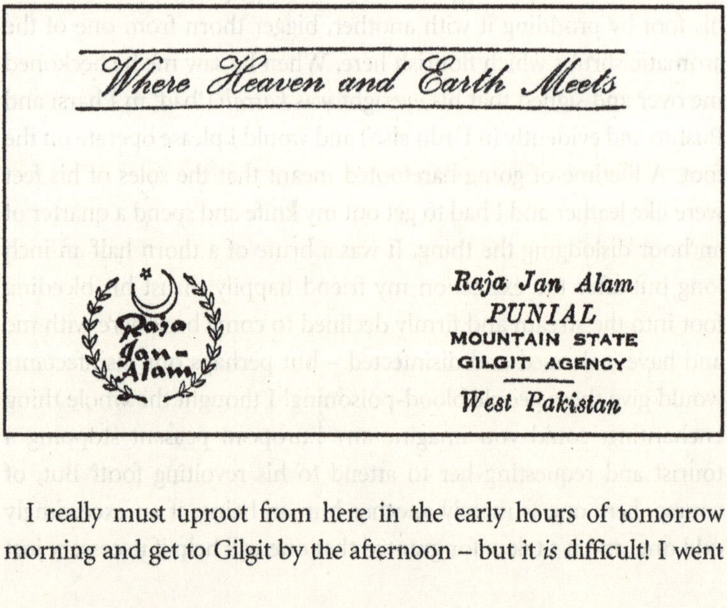
Where Heaven and Earth Meets

Raja Jan-Alam

Raja Jan Alam
PUNIAL
MOUNTAIN STATE
GILGIT AGENCY
West Pakistan

I really must uproot from here in the early hours of tomorrow morning and get to Gilgit by the afternoon – but it *is* difficult! I went for another walk before dinner, at river level this time, right down the valley; it runs due east–west, so when I was returning the last, long shadows were before me, and the few frail scraps of cloud overhead were golden, the leaves were showing silver in the westerly breeze and the air was laden with the evening scent of shrubs and herbs. I ate some wild raspberries – tiny and tart and very refreshing. I've also discovered that *un*ripe apricots are one of the best of all thirst quenchers. Now early to bed.

12

Duel with the Sun

SHER QUILA RAKAPOSHI TO BABUSAR

GILGIT, 14 JUNE

I left my Raja, who was looking disproportionately devastated by the parting, soon after 5 a.m. His grey stallion took me to Gulapur, where the locals had got adjusted to having a cycle in their midst – the teacher told me that they had crowded around Roz daily during my absence. Half the little boys of the village were demanding to be given a ride and as there are a *lot* of little boys in every Asian village, this meant that it was 8.15 before I got away.

At the hamlet which lies halfway between Gulapur and here I was waylaid by a deputation of elders and a delightful old woman ushered me into a room absolutely devoid of furniture. There we sat on a straw mat and I was given buttermilk with salt – an honour of which I was most appreciative, salt being so precious here – and a big plate of *paratis* – very greasy, but I love them if the fat is not *too* rancid – and a pot of tea with sugar in it, which is another mark of esteem. This banquet was a joint effort by the whole community; flour, ghee, tea, sugar, salt, tea-pot and china cups all came from different homes. (Normally tea-pots are never used; the leaves and milk and water and sugar or salt are put in a flat pan and boiled up together.) I really appreciated their kindness, which was obviously meant to atone for the way they had unanimously shunned me (out of sheer astonishment and fear of the unknown) when we passed through before; I will never forget that reception committee. Neither will I ever forget the number of flies in that little mud house: the air was thick with them and voices had to be raised above their buzzing. The room was packed to capacity with villagers, all sitting around beaming at me, and the girls took it in turns to sit beside me waving green willow branches to keep the flies off my person and food – a procedure which made me feel vaguely like Cleopatra!

Then, halfway between that hamlet and Gilgit, an old woman spotted me toiling uphill, dragging Roz through deep sand, so she pursued me with an apron full of the biggest and juiciest figs I've ever eaten; all in all this has been one of my better-fed days, reaching a grand climax with a four-course dinner at the mess tonight.

My first request on arrival here was for some anti-lice preparation; the brutes have been devouring me since that night when I shared verminous blankets with the children, and they have successfully put up a stiff resistance to countless applications of soap and water.

I've noticed since entering Pakistan that comparatively few people say their prayers publicly here, though the majority are Sunnis, as in Turkey and Afghanistan. At dinner tonight it became apparent that both Sunnis and Shias hate Ismailis even more than they hate each other – and that's quite a lot. They say contemptuously that Ismailis are not *real* Muslims, and accuse them of never praying to Allah and only worshipping the Aga Khan. How true all this is I wouldn't know.

The temperature here today is 101°and 112° at Pindi.

JUGLOTE, 15 JUNE

I'm often astounded by the odd conceptions people have about what constitutes beautiful scenery. Last night two United Nations surveyors, who have recently gone from Gilgit to Chilas by jeep, told me that the landscape was dreadfully dull and that I shouldn't bother to cycle but should wait for the jeep which brings supplies to Chilas every Monday. Of course I didn't believe them, knowing that the Indus Gorge couldn't possibly be dull, but when I saw how uniquely magnificent the landscape actually is I decided that they must be completely blind.

Today's run was a complete contrast to my ride up and down the Gilgit Valley, but was no less beautiful and even more desolate. During the whole forty-three miles I didn't see *one* man, goat, bird, blade of grass or any sign of life, whereas in the other valley I passed a few people and animals every day and villages were much more frequent, even if often inaccessible from my track.

This jeep road was 'cycleable' (slowly) for about thirty miles and I walked the rest through ankle-deep sand, which gave me the feeling that some invisible person was trying to pull Roz back all the time. We started at 4.30 a.m. and as I had missed my siesta yesterday I felt quite dopey by 11.30, but kept going till shade was found under a big rock. Then saying 'To hell with snakes!' I curled up on the deep, soft sand and slept soundly from 12 to 3.30. I woke to find that a strong breeze had got up, which made the air very pleasant, and after a meal of eggs and bread and apricots we set off again. The water situation was grim all day. This valley is much wider than the other and there are no streams or nullahs till you get to Juglote, while the river is always out of reach. Occasionally it's out of sight too, as the 'road' goes over sand desert with only two lines of boulders to mark the route to be followed. At other times, where the track wriggles round precipices of sheer, bare rock, it's visible 1,000 feet below, in the deep gorge it has carved through the mountains, and to be able to see and hear water you can't possibly reach is the quintessence of torture. I had to make do on six pints when I could have used at least eighteen. On arriving at the Juglote nullah I drank twelve pints just like *that* and I've drunk another six since I came to the hamlet itself. But for all its hardships I wouldn't have missed today's journey. Nanga Parbat is directly overlooking Juglote and was visible all the afternoon, thrusting up grandly from the wild array of surrounding peaks; it's definitely the second most impressive mountain I've seen, after Ararat, with Demavand a good third on my list. Lying east of the road it was a glorious spectacle at sunset, with the last golden rays pouring over the peaks to the west and being caught by the snow-laden summits of the Nanga Parbat range, whilst the Indus Gorge was already full of purple dusk and the surrounding desert was a still expanse of greyness.

The people here are reputed to be rather wild and I had trouble persuading Colonel Shah not to provide me with an escort. Finally I said, 'Where are you going to get (*a*) another bicycle and (*b*) a soldier who would ride and push it over the Babusar Pass?' He saw my point, and that was that! In fact I find the locals very kind, though admittedly they are much rougher types than in the Gilgit Valley. But I sense no danger here though I'm sleeping on a charpoy by the roadside.

My eyes are going queer again from this last week of writing by the light of juniper roots. We'll make another dawn start tomorrow, so bed now.

GONER, 16 JUNE

This is a day to go down in my personal history as having given me the toughest cycling of a lifetime, not likely ever to be surpassed, though it may be equalled tomorrow. I was up at 4 a.m. and we left Juglote at 4.30, after a meagre breakfast of dry bread and tea. Only apricots were available for my picnic lunch. I covered no more than forty-five miles between that and 5.45 p.m. but each one felt like four anywhere else and there was no time for a siesta as we were ploughing through deep sand from 8 a.m. onwards and climbing practically vertical hills, all in fierce heat. The temperature was almost up to Pindi heights because of the bare rock mountains overlooking sand-deserts devoid of plant life. What a landscape! The sheer magnitude of everything is overwhelming – the height of the mountains, the depth of the Indus gorge, the fabulous chunks of rock scattered about the desert (some are literally as big as what we in Ireland call a mountain, yet here they are simply bits of rock broken jaggedly off a nearby peak), the perfect stillness and the brutal sun; despite being half-dead by 2 p.m. it was an experience worth the exhaustion.

I'm three-quarters dead now and just waiting for some form of food before falling asleep. On yesterday's basis the traffic was hectic today – one tribesman and one jeep. The tribesman looked terrifying – armed with a spear – but actually he was very amiable and seemed thrilled to bits when I took his photo. The jeep looked no less terrifying going up a stretch of track 800 feet above the Indus on a surface that was literally loose slabs of blasted rock. All the passengers had to get out and walk up, otherwise even a jeep couldn't make this gradient. Similarly, all loads had to be removed and carried up and re-loaded at the top; it's inconceivable how even an empty vehicle can ascend these stretches: certainly the jeep is a wonderful invention.

I'm yawning so much that if no grub appears soon I'll fall asleep where I sit – anyway I'm now too tired to feel hungry. I think the heat would have finished me today but for the fact that five nullahs appeared during the last twenty miles. Not that they made much difference to the temperature, as all were in deep clefts between mountains and there was no growth around them, but I got into them fully clothed and soaked myself for about fifteen minutes from head to boots. After another fifteen minutes I was bone dry again yet these immersions kept my temperature down somewhat. The water was just pleasantly cool, not icy as in the Gilgit Valley – otherwise I daren't have plunged in when so over-heated. But as these nullahs are also from melting glaciers, this shows how hot the region is. Anyway heat shouldn't be one of my worries tomorrow as surely even in June the Babusar Pass will be cool. Beyond a doubt *I* find such heat absolutely prostrating: maybe other constitutions can take it better.

I crossed one suspension bridge today and on it was a marble plaque to the memory of seven German climbers and nine Sherpa guides who were killed while attempting Nanga Parbat on 14 June 1937. The mountain itself rises on the other side of the river and there their bodies still lie. All the Germans were under thirty years old – but perhaps they were lucky; challenging Nanga Parbat is a better way to die than fighting for Nazism.

I lost my toothbrush last week when it fell into the river. Washing my teeth is the one thing I fuss about – not that they are getting much to do these days. *Still* no sign of grub! And in this hamlet (without the Prince) there aren't even mulberries or apricots or wine: I can't imagine what the people eat. But they're very nice folk and I'm quite sure are doing their best to dig up something for me – I only hope they've not gone to the snow-line to dig up ghee!

Later. I was wakened at 10 p.m. and served with one *chapatti* of maize flour and a one-egg omelette.

CHILAS, 17 JUNE

Well, I was wrong – yesterday's effort was a cake-walk compared with today's. In fact the only enjoyable part of today's performance is this – sitting down to write about it after recovering (more or less) from the consequences.

We left Goner at 5.30 a.m. and arrived here at 4.30 p.m., having only covered twenty-eight miles, yet I came into the shade of this nullah in a state of total collapse, so decidedly at the end of my tether that I don't believe I could have kept going *one* more mile. The Tahsildar here told me that when I arrived the temperature was 114° – he didn't really have to say it! I had to walk all the way as the first twenty miles were through very deep sand, up and down very steep hills, and after that I was too dizzy from the heat to balance on Roz, even where the track was level. By 7 a.m. the sun was so hot that I was saturated through with sweat and as we only came to one nullah for wetting, cooling and refilling the water bottle, dehydration became my fear. I found shade once, under a rock, and slept very soundly from 1.40 to 2.50 p.m., although lying on sharp flints. After that the real trouble began and by 3 p.m. I was seriously worried: I had stopped sweating, which is a danger signal, and my mouth was so dry that my tongue felt like an immovable bit of stiff leather. By 3.30 I was shivering with cold, though the heat was so intense that I did not dare touch any metal part of Roz. After that I just kept going but don't remember one bit of the road – only that the green trees of Chilas were visible in the distance. I had just enough sense left, on getting to the nullah, not to drink gallons, but to lie under a willow and take mouthfuls at a time until gradually I began to sweat again and get warm. Then I rolled into the water and lay there for a few minutes with it rushing deliciously over me, after which I was able to walk another half-mile to the Tahsildar's house, where I drank gallons of buttermilk and salt followed by cups and cups of hot tea; but I couldn't look at food this evening.

Chilas is only 3,000 feet above sea level and is hellishly hot even amidst all the running brooks and dense green trees and shrubs –

because it's completely encircled by naked rock-mountains which relentlessly throw back that intolerable sun. The Tahsildar (a minor local government official) says that I must stay here tomorrow for a day's rest before going over the Babusar and I couldn't agree more! Not that the pass will be difficult after the last three days; once I get eight miles up (and I'll start at 3.30 a.m.) it will be cool, and it's heat, not gradients, that finish me off.

The horror of today's trek really was extreme with heat visibly flowing towards me in malevolent waves off the mountainsides and the dreadful desert stench of burning sand – which still persists here – nauseating me; the terrifying dehydration of mouth and nostrils and eyes until my eyelids could barely move and a sort of staring blindness came on, with the ghastly sensation of scorching air filling my lungs, and the overpowering drug-like effect of the wild thyme and sage, that grow thickly over the last few miles, being 'distilled' by the sun; and above all the despair of coming round corners and over hilltops time and time again, hoping always to see water – and never seeing it. I have often thought that death by thirst must be grimmer than most deaths and now my surmise has been confirmed. The irony of it all was that all day the vast, swirling Indus flowed beside me, inaccessible. But what a magnificent valley it is! Though I could have done without this afternoon's instalment, I wouldn't have liked to miss this morning's panoramas; the rough track soared up and up and up the sheer black and beige mountainsides till even the tremendous roar of the Indus was inaudible and it looked a mere bit of brown ribbon, coiling for miles in both directions between its colossal, but now dwarfed, cliffs. From these the desert swept flatly to the foot of gigantic peaks, some of them almost level with the track. Occasionally, on the other side of the river, there was an unexpected oasis, around a nullah, inhabited by Indus gold searchers. These are a brown-skinned people unlike the other tribes of the area and they are much despised by the local farming-folk, who consider that searching for gold is a menial occupation! (From my distance those meagre oases, as they stood out on the level 'table' of sand, reminded me of the little wooden trees I had as a child with my toy farm. I saw several of the 'gold-men' by the river's edge, perilously scooping and sieving in quest of that Indus gold which is supposed to be one of the best in Asia. Incidentally, a peculiar kind of precious stone is found around Punial and Gilgit – like an opal but better. I don't know if they belonged to ancient peoples or not but all local women have at least one in their necklaces.) Sometimes the 'gold-men' cross the river by inflating two goatskins, laying planks across them and paddling over; naturally they land about ten miles downstream because of the ferociously swift current, but they rarely have an accident.

Apart from the gold-men the only living creature I saw all day was a man who looked like John the Baptist gone to the dogs; I came on him unexpectedly and got quite a fright. He was stark naked with jet black, thick hair down to his knees, a beard to his navel, skin burned ebony by the sun and a mad-looking glint in his eye. What he lives on I can't think. I was getting out my camera when he gave a sort of insane gurgle and came towards me with hands extended, whereupon I fled – if that is the right word for scrambling through nine inches of sand up a mountainside with a bicycle! When I got to the top of the slope I looked back and saw that the apparition had forgotten me and was now sitting hunched beneath a rock engaged in the contemplation of his toes. Probably he would have been quite harmless, but I didn't feel like waiting to find out.

I notice that all the men of this village (population approximately 2,000) carry rifles just like the Afghans. They are very friendly folk, now gathered in force round the first bicycle to penetrate to Chilas; it's very funny to watch the 'bright boys' working out how a bicycle operates and then explaining the theory to their companions.

CHILAS, 18 JUNE

This morning I was told of a boy's report that when I arrived at the Chilas nullah yesterday, he was there and observed that I had the 'sun-devil' – their very graphic term for heat-delirium. Apparently I was talking loudly to myself as I reached the water; the frustrating thing is that the boy doesn't know English and I'd love to know what I was talking about. It was considerate of him to report on my condition as this signifies real heat-stroke and you have to watch your diet for a few days afterwards or acute diarrhoea is the result. No fats, eggs or meat are allowed; lots of salted lemon-juice is advised if possible (not possible here) and any fruit, oddly enough, *is* allowed. It's amazing how our instincts work; I'd had breakfast at 5.30 a.m., before this warning was delivered, but though ravenously hungry I had said 'No!' very emphatically to the eggs and had asked for apricots to eat with bread and salted tea. My other meals today have consisted of bread and apricots and gallons of skimmed milk and salt. I spent most of the day writing, sitting on a lawn beside a baby nullah under a vast plane tree. I went indoors for my siesta at 2 p.m. and was wakened at 2.40 by a frantic gale carrying fine sand which penetrated everything. But it was a wonderful relief, because when the wind died down the sky had become completely over-clouded and the temperature had dropped to 92°. A period of intense heat in this area (as in Pindi) is always followed by the temporary ease of a dust-storm. The Tahsildar thinks I should stay a few more days here but I feel fine this evening, thank God, and tomorrow Chilas will probably be unbearable again. I'd much prefer to get up to the Babusar hut and stay a few days there before going over the top, which would also help to condition my lungs for the height of the pass.

BABUSAR HUT, 19 JUNE

I'm sitting now beside a crackling fire of pine-logs with a cold gale sweeping through the surrounding forest and big, fat, damp, grey clouds drifting among the peaks and occasional splatters of rain gusting against the windows. The net result of all these delights is that I'm feeling thirty years younger, back in the climate I was born to. This reminds me of a March evening at home and I wonder what point there is in leaving here before October! It's such a strange sensation to touch things like paper and furniture and not feel them warm to the fingers and I can hardly believe that there's no sweat dripping off me on to everything. The last movement of the Choral Symphony would be *very* appropriate as background music.

I left Chilas at 3.40 a.m. in a darkness just beginning to be not total and arrived here at 12.45 p.m., having walked twenty-one miles from 3,000 to 12,000 feet – not bad going on a completely empty tummy – unless you count water! By this stage I've got adjusted to going without any breakfast (even a cup of tea), when I make early starts, though at first I found such asceticism a considerable deprivation; evidently the human mechanism can adjust to almost anything but extremes of temperature. Needless to say, my ribs are almost coming through my skin now: two and a half weeks gallivanting around Gilgit on the skin of an onion is the best way to shed superfluous fat.

Today was superb – as good as, though utterly different from, the Indus Valley. The track followed a big nullah all the way up and of course there were none of the vast landscapes of the past few days; the mountains are so close on either side that the sun didn't reach me till 9.15 – when I was too high for it to hurt – although it rose at 4.50 a.m. Also there were none of the dangers; really the Gilgit–Chilas road *is* terrifying, with those sheer drops as the narrow track goes steadily higher.

This region is quite densely populated now by the Indus Valley folk who have been moving up during the past fortnight, bringing their flocks to the summer pasturage. They have tiny 'summer residences', built of stone or wood, perched all over the mountainsides, some of the little houses being on stilts. They grow maize extensively and the terracing on these slopes is awe-inspiring. Usually the strips are too narrow and the slopes too steep for bullocks to plough so all is done by hand, even the five-year-olds helping. The whole valley floor is quite heavily wooded beside the nullah, chiefly with mulberry and walnut trees. The majority of males, from the age of twelve up, go armed, and are much addicted to murdering each other *à la* frontier tribesman, but they're amiable to me.

Three times today I had to cycle Roz down the hill I had just pushed her up to show a pop-eyed crowd of men, women and children how a cycle works; it's so easy to give them so much pleasure – they were fascinated by the performance. The men and boys always tried to push her back up the relevant bit of hill at the end of my demonstration but to their astonishment there is considerably more than meets the eye to pushing a laden cycle up a steep hill and they usually ended lying on the road with Roz mixed up with their legs and the rest of the crowd in ecstasies of laughter. They couldn't understand why I wasn't riding her up (!) and it was impossible to explain that bicycles weren't really invented for transporting people through the Himalayas, but that I'd have my reward on the other side with 120 miles of free-wheeling on a good tarred road.

I would have needed a cine-camera for the whole thing. It was comical to see the pandemonium when I first turned a corner of the road into a populated stretch of valley. From every direction they came pell-mell – down the steep mountainside from their work in the forests, across the valley from tilling their plots, wading waist-deep through the nullah, scrambling up cliffsides, leaping off the flat roofs of their little huts, deserting flocks of goats and donkeys in mid-journey, and all ending up standing inside the stone walls that line the road, staring at me in wonder and half in fear, until I smiled and said, 'Salaam Alaikum,' which they took as an invitation to jump the walls and crowd around, tinkling the bell, twirling the pedals, feeling the tyres, fiddling with the brakes, opening the saddlebag and asking where I was going to and coming from. Some of them made the Persian mistake of thinking me a boy and the rest called me Begum Sahib – a variation on the 'Memsahib' used everywhere else. They were *incredibly* dirty, making the filthy people of other areas seem clean. In Chilas I was told they never wash and I observed today that at least three-quarters of them suffer from a ghastly eye-disease which comes from dirt and has the ghoulish effect of making many of its victims look *dead* in the eyes. The stink when fifteen or twenty of them crowded round made me feel quite ill, despite the fresh mountain air. Thank God this PWD hut is here, as with the best will in the world I couldn't bring myself to stay in one of their homes, if only because the risk of disease would be too great. I was surprised to notice the great number of pock-marked faces; one would think that here they'd escape smallpox but I suppose their own dirt breeds every known disease. An odd thing was that they kept asking me to feel their pulses and those of their children; I simply can't understand this, so I must enquire as to possible reasons. Incidentally, all pulses felt seemed very weak and fast to me, but perhaps this is the altitude and normal for them; my own is racing too. They were continually inviting me into their huts for milk and *paratis* but I had to decline with an inward shudder – though with regret too because (*a*) I was hungry and (*b*) they looked so sad and disappointed! On arriving here I found that the only food suitable for my present condition was a sort of undersised broad bean about as big as a large pea with three to the pod (eaten raw). The other foods available are *paratis*, saturated in the rancidest ghee, and eggs. Quite apart from my diet I wouldn't have touched the *paratis* after that little brush with rancid ghee in Gupis. People here haven't even got the fruit on which the peasants of other Gilgit areas depend so much.

I felt the thin air today, from about 9,000 feet, and had to stop every half-mile for a few minutes to calm my heart. (I also have a theory that being undernourished does not help.) From that altitude there was a big change in scene for the pine woods begin here with gigantic trees twice the height of any other pines I've seen. I also noticed lots of holly trees and evergreen oaks – which always remind me of Castile – and there was green grass everywhere instead of arid earth. All morning the sky remained a lovely clear blue with a few pure white clouds – in welcome contrast to the brazen, colourless glare over the desert – but at midday it began to fill with grey rain or snow clouds. I'd anticipated being exhausted on arrival and going to sleep immediately, but I'm so 'toughened up' by now that I wasn't a bit tired, apart from shortness of breath, so after a fistful of raw beans I went up the mountain to collect firewood and enjoy the delicious coolness and gusts of rainy wind. From here one can see right down the twenty-mile length of the valley, which remains unclouded, to the Indus Gorge and the infinity of white peaks beyond. I don't wonder at people risking their lives to climb mountains; even getting up to 12,000 feet and standing looking down at what one has conquered is wonderfully satisfying.

This is a very adequate hut, furnished by PWD, but the summer *chowkidar* (caretaker) must have used the bedding himself as it's full of bedbugs. I have hurled it outside and I'll sleep on the floor rolled in the curtains from doors and windows, which are of thick material and easily taken down. I don't trust the charpoy – probably it has bugs in the ropes!

BABUSAR HUT, 20 JUNE

In spite of my anti-bug precautions I slept wretchedly because of sandfly bites acquired in Chilas the night after the storm. These take twenty-four hours to get troublesome and then they're hell. My face, neck, hands and arms are covered with tiny purple lumps, both itchy and sore, and I woke constantly to find myself tearing at them with my nails. It's so long since I've slept under a roof that it was disconcerting not to see the stars above me. The night sky here is a most brilliant and beautiful sight and is one of the few consolations of the hot areas. If one opens one's eyes for a moment the starlight is almost dazzling, and the Milky Way, with 'coal-sacks' and nebulae, is quite different from the same spectacle seen through an Irish atmosphere. I spent quite a lot of my first night at Chilas admiring it as the wind off the desert was like a dragon's breath – *not* conducive to sleep – yet indoors with no fans was even worse.

There were few ordinary flies in Chilas, which made up for a lot; by now I've got an obsession about them. It's not an hygienic obsession about flies on food (if they stayed on the food and kept off me I'd be quite happy) but they drive me mad with their incessant buzzing and tickling hour after hour – I suppose it's their slick 'smart-Alecness' that really infuriates. One *knows* they can't be killed but after a certain period of persecution one begins to slap frantically at them, hurting oneself in the process and leaving them totally unaffected, which makes one feel even more of a fool than usual. (There are very few here also, Allah be praised!) Personally I much prefer lice, some of which can be captured at intervals and vindictively squashed to death – very gratifying!

This morning I decided to risk eggs for breakfast, as it's almost three days since the heat-stroke, so I bought four and boiled them. Three were *very* bad and somehow that deadened my appetite for the fourth, causing me to revert to beans instead.

Opinions here vary so much about the state of the pass that I decided to go up some of the way today by a short-cut and investigate for myself. At 7.30 it was a heavenly morning with warm sun, cool breeze and cloudless sky, like a good May day in Ireland. Progress was slow, with lots of pauses to rest my pounding heart, as the short-cut is naturally a much steeper gradient than the track, but I enjoyed meandering along looking at the very lovely wild flowers in the woods and listening to the birds. Inevitably I got lost and it was 2 p.m. before I came out on the jeep track, 13,000 feet up, amid stony, barren moors. By now the sky was overclouded, thunder was crashing amidst the peaks and it was snowing lightly. (I could hardly believe that seventy-two hours ago and only twenty miles away I had been getting heat-stroke!) I didn't dare go higher because of feeling a slight nausea – caused by either altitude or starvation or both – so I walked down the six miles of track to here. There are three small glaciers completely blocking the road but on this stretch they will be very easy to negotiate on foot. Probably there are more and wider ones farther up; it was a pity I couldn't inspect the last two miles to the top for fear of over-taxing my ill-treated carcase. (I feel quite sorry for my own body these days, in a curiously detached and impersonal way; I'd like to be able to give it the feed it's certainly earned.) The delicate question now is whether to stay here another few days and get more acclimatised before pushing Roz up (good for heart) or whether to go over tomorrow and get a square meal on the other side (good for stomach). I think stomach will win because I really would be debilitated after another forty-eight hours on raw beans. (This evening my watch is repeatedly slipping down my wrist.) I have just got another three eggs – all that were available – and about a pint of milk, but the peasants are starving too, pending the delayed arrival of the camel caravans over the pass. They would share their last egg with me and are most reluctant to take money, which makes it all the more awkward. Fortunately the gradient of the track, except on the countless hairpins, is only about one in eighteen for the first six miles anyway. I don't understand why, when walking briskly down such a slope, one is completely unaffected by altitude, whereas going very slowly up one feels half dead; surely walking is in itself an exertion?

The things they can do here with pine-trunks and stones are incredible. All the way from Chilas the many bridges over the nullah are constructed of these materials only; I went under one to see how it's done but I'm not mechanically-minded enough to describe the technique. Of course this means that they cost nothing but labour, which is just as well, since they are swept away regularly every year.

Timber is one of the chief sources of cash here; it's cut high on the mountains, rolled down to the track, carried by men to the Indus, thrown in and fished out hundreds of miles downstream years later, by the contractors who have bought the trees and whose name is carved on them. The locals have a curious method of felling; they burn the trunk near the ground until it's thin enough to cut through with their tiny home-made axes. Great skill is required not to (*a*) set the whole tree on fire or (*b*) set the whole dry forest on fire. When the trees have been felled it's fascinating to see small boys steering the giant trunks down steep slopes to the track.

13

Two Wheels over Nine Glaciers

BABUSAR TO ABBOTTABAD

BASAL, 21 JUNE

For a combination of beauty, danger, excitement and hardship (of the enjoyable variety) today wins at a canter.

As I was resolutely chewing my breakfast of beans and one *chapatti* (made from about two ounces of maize flour and given me in honour of the occasion) an incoherent but kindly old man came along and told me that a pony-caravan had left the hamlet about three hours ago in a desperate attempt to cross the pass on the Mahomet-Mountain principle; they hope to collect essential stores from the camel-caravan which has now been held up at Butikundi for ten days. At the time I didn't quite grasp why the old man was telling me this – but before long I got the message!

Roz and I started out at 7 a.m. (it was rather a holiday feeling not having to be up at 4 a.m. to beat the sun) and it took me nearly two and a half hours to walk slowly up the six miles I came down yesterday in less than one and a half hours. On this stretch I passed several groups of nomads, the smoke from their little camp-fires sending an incongruously cosy smell across the bleak landscape. Equally incongruous seemed the persistent call of a cuckoo. Apart from this, the only sounds to break the distinctive silence of high places were the whistles of nomads directing their flocks and the careless melody of sheep and goat bells.

I reached the first glacier in good shape, but the sun was now high and I noted with some alarm that this great bank of melting snow had moved a few yards since yesterday. However, the pony-trail was encouragingly clear and we were soon safely over; it was at this point that the penny dropped and I saw the import of the old man's information. I stopped here to eat some of the glacier, remembering my last meal of snow in the mountains between Yugoslavia and Bulgaria. Already I was almost painfully hungry and apart from quenching my thirst the feel of the solid snow in my mouth was absurdly welcome.

For another mile the track remained clear, though so torn by the thaw that it resembled a river-bed. At this height no trees grow and the rock-strewn pastures, which in a few weeks will be a rich green, were wearily yellow after the long winter. Ahead I could now see a gigantic glacier, more than two miles wide, extending to the Top. The track disappeared beneath this about a mile to the west of where it crossed the Top and hoof-prints in the thaw-soft earth showed me that the ponies had branched off to take a direct route up, cutting all the hairpin bends which obviously lay beneath the glacier.

At this point I stopped to consider what I should do. To follow the track approximately would be much less exhausting than to take the short-cut, but it might be much more dangerous for someone ignorant of the idiosyncrasies of glaciers. So I decided to drag Roz up the direct route, not suspecting that what looked like a twenty-minute climb would take almost two hours.

By now clouds were dark and close, and a sharp wind sent gusts of little snowflakes whirling around me at intervals. I revelled in this and went bare-headed, enjoying the keenness of the air. High peaks surrounded me, cutting off the valley below, and it was a rare joy to move alone among them with the chaotic symphony of re-echoing thunder as background music.

I was now higher than I had ever been before and when I stopped at six-minute intervals to regain breath my heart-beats sounded as loud as the thunder. This suffocating sensation frightened me until I realised that the illusory feeling of repeatedly coming to the point of death was simply the mountains' way of teasing novices. By the time I was halfway up the ponies' wisdom seemed open to doubt – their trail crossed many outcrops of rock and every time I lifted Roz over one of these barriers I collapsed with exhaustion. In places the snow was so soft that I sank into it up to the knees. Elsewhere it was so hard that even the ponies' hoofs had made little impression and I kept upright only by driving my specially nailed boots into it at each step – a process which still further exhausted me. After about an hour and a half of this struggle I was at that peculiar stage when one doesn't really believe that one's objective will ever be reached, and when one's only mental awareness concerns the joy (to some incomprehensible, if not downright unnatural) of driving one's body far beyond the limits of its natural endurance. Then, having dragged Roz up another savage gradient, and over yet another litter of boulders, we suddenly found ourselves on a level plateau, about a quarter of a mile square. Sitting where I had subsided beyond the rocks, and still clutching Roz, I slowly assimilated the unlikely fact that we were on Babusar Top.

I was understandably anxious to photograph Roz at this historic point where, because of her owner's mental unsoundness, she had become the first bicycle to cross the Babusar Pass; but though I took three shots I doubt if the light was strong enough for a cheap camera. Yet, between the intermittent snowfalls, I had a clear view to east and south, where the sun was bright on a sparkle of angular peaks and on the flawless, smooth curves of the glaciers that united them.

By now the thunder had ceased and when the wind dropped the overwhelming silence of the mountains reminded me of the hush felt in a great empty Gothic cathedral at dusk – a silence which is beautiful in itself. However, I could afford no more than half an hour on the Top, for I was still fifteen miles from the head of the Kagan Valley. In my enthusiasm to get *up*, the process of getting *down* again had not been very seriously considered; possibly I was suffering from lack of vitamins to the brain, because I'd assumed that once on the south side all hazards would be left behind. This delusion was fostered during the first stage of the descent.

From the plateau I could see, about 1,000 feet below me, a vividly green valley some eight miles long and two miles wide, with a foam-white nullah flashing down its centre, and a reasonably-surfaced earth track descending at a comfortable gradient along the flank of the mountain, where snow had lain too recently for any growth to have covered the brown scree. On reaching the valley floor the track crossed the nullah and was visible running level along the base of the opposite mountains before curving away out of sight halfway down the valley. As we began to free-wheel I reflected that this was a delightful road to follow, with all the characteristics which thrill a wanderer's heart.

Half an hour later I was rapidly revising my opinion. The track's first imperfection was revealed when we arrived at the nullah, to find that where a bridge should be stood two supports, stoutly upholding nothing. I looked up and down stream with wild surmise. The ponies had not returned, therefore the ponies had forded the nullah at some point. But at what point? Unfortunately the ground here was so firm, and the bank so stony, that my diligent search for prints yielded no clues. Then, as I stood looking pathetically around me, in the faint hope of seeing some nomads, a solitary black cow (for all the world like a good little Kerry) appeared some twenty yards upstream, walking purposefully across the meadow towards the torrent. There was no other sign of life in the valley, either human or animal, and in retrospect I tend to believe that she was my guardian angel, discreetly disguised. But when I first noticed her I did not pause to speculate on her nature or origin. She was obviously going to ford the nullah for some good reason of her own, and we were going with her. I pedalled rapidly and bumpily over the grass to the point for which she was heading. There I hastily unstrapped the saddlebag, tied it to my head with a length of rope mentally and appropriately labelled 'FOR EMERGENCIES', and was ready to enter the water.

The cow, when she joined us on the bank, showed no surprise at our presence, nor did she register any alarm or despondency as I put my right arm round her neck, gripped Roz's crossbar firmly with my left hand, and accompanied her into the turmoil of icy water. It had occurred to me that if I found myself out of my depth this could become an Awkward Situation, but actually the water was never more than four feet deep, though its tremendous force would have unbalanced me had I been alone. My friend, however, was clearly used to this rôle and we crossed without difficulty, unless the agony of being two-thirds submerged in newly melted snow counts as a difficulty. I felt that there was a certain lack of civility about our abrupt parting on the opposite bank, after such a meaningful though brief association, but our ways lay in different directions and I could do nothing to express my gratitude. So I can only record here my thanks for the fairytale appearance of this little black cow.

I was now almost paralysed by the cold – soaked clothes are one thing in the desert and another thing here. After replacing the saddlebag, I couldn't tie it on, my fingers were so numb, so I had to rope it instead, before cycling over the smooth turf to the road about half a mile away. From here the track climbed steeply (which I considered frightfully bad form; having gone up *all* the way *to* the Top it should now have had the decency to go down *all* the way *from* the Top) and this was the drill for the next seven miles, switch-backing up and down or round the flanks of mountains – all snow-peaked and overlooking wonderfully green pastures with more and more of those quite indescribable flowers. The pink and yellow and red and blue and purple and gold and white blooms often grew so thickly that the meadows looked like some giant's carpet, with vast circular patterns of colour woven into the green background. (Isn't it odd how the finest flowers grow where there are fewest people to see them?)

But I had other, less aesthetic distractions on this seven-mile stretch, during which I had to cross eleven glaciers, the majority forty to fifty yards wide. Eight were 'natural', i.e. situated where they had formed in gullies over streams, and the others were from high up the mountain-sides and had slid down recently to their present positions. These were the ones which scared me, as I morbidly reckoned that there was nothing to stop them sliding still farther while Roz and I were in midstream, as you might say.

As before I followed in the steps of my thrice-blessed ponies (Allah be good to them!) but edging oneself and one's cycle across steep masses of snow and ice, where one slip would be fatal, is a slow process, and it was 4.30 by the time I'd crossed those few miles. The last two miles curved round a most beautiful lake about half a mile wide with sheer green mountains rising from the opposite side, their gullies a-glitter with glaciers. The water was a clear but dark green and one of the loveliest sights of my life was the perfect reflection of the white snow in that still depth of greenness. On my side of the slope, between road and water, was a natural rockery formed of small chunks of grey stone between which grew masses of blue and white flowers. At various points not far from the water's edge were 'icebergs' – the tops of glaciers which had slid into the lake and not yet melted. The lake is shaped as shown below, and flows away in a nullah (the infant Kagan River, of which much more later); and as I cycled towards the nullah's source I heard an odd, roaring noise in the distance. Before I'd time to diagnose it a movement caught my eye and I just saw a glacier disappearing into the water where the arrow points in my sketch. Wavelets began to lap the shore near me only minutes after, but the splash of the impact was most dramatic; it must have been a comparatively small glacier as none of it was left above the surface.

A few minutes later I came to the nullah and dismounted in disorder, confronted by the day's Chief Crisis. The bridge, which should have been where I marked it, was gone, and this time there was no question of fording as the water was some twenty feet below the road between sheer cliffs. (Here I began to feel that the day had contained enough thrills and that this was one too many.) I looked around in bewilderment, because of ponies there was no sign, yet it seemed inconceivable that they could have got through this impasse, as the road (see sketch) was overhung by a steep mountain strewn with great rough chunks of black rock. After a moment's gazing at this I suddenly, and reluctantly, registered the horrible fact that since the ponies were not visible they must have gone *over* this mountain, however far-fetched the deduction might seem. And then I still more reluctantly registered the even more horrible fact that I too must go over this mountain, and quickly too, for at 4.30 p.m. only three hours of daylight remain. (Also I knew that I would soon collapse from starvation.) So the next thing was to rediscover the ponies' trail.

To my surprise, this presented no difficulty (by now I expected everything to be difficult!) but to find it was one thing and to follow it was another. After the first few yards of carrying Roz up that gradient between those rocks my shins had been so badly banged about that I could have wept with pain, and Roz's back mudguard, severely injured while crossing the earlier nullah, was now completely torn off. Clearly this nonsense had to stop, for both our sakes, and the only alternative was to wear Roz round my neck. Thus arrayed, I proceeded upwards, still suffering from lack of oxygen, with my head sticking out of the angle between crossbar and chain and my vision obscured by the front wheel. Being in a weakened condition the ludicrous aspect of the situation struck me with special force and whenever I stopped to rest I wasted precious breath on giggling feebly at my own dottiness.

This trek lasted for about an hour and a half, of which at least half an hour was spent resting. The ponies' hoof prints were clear in the wet earth between the rocks, otherwise I would certainly have gone astray, not knowing the direction taken by the nullah. I was getting a bit desperate when I suddenly found myself crossing a level meadow free of rocks and ankle-deep in water from the thawing snows above. By now I felt so exhausted that I scarcely noticed the precipice at the edge of this meadow and almost went over on to the rocks 1,500 feet below. When I'd recovered from my escape I peered down to see seven little black figures (three ponies and four men) in the middle of a vast glacier beside the nullah. At first I couldn't understand how either men or beasts had got down there; then I realised that they must have used the glacier, which extends upwards for some 2,000 feet, bisecting the semicircular 'bite' out of the mountain, on the west side of which I was standing. But I still don't understand how even mountain ponies were induced to make that terrifying descent. And, observing the scene below, I noticed that three of the ponies had had it, and were resolutely refusing to cross the bridge of snow over the nullah. Personally, I shared their point of view.

However, our descent proved the simplest part of the whole journey. On reaching the glacier I shouted to attract the men's attention, and then pushed Roz over at the steepest point. She shot down at a rate that would have dislocated any lesser bicycle and was stopped by the bed-rolls which the men placed in her path. Next, I pushed myself over, at the least steep point, and half-rolled, half-tobogganed down – a painful progress, but one which at least required no effort. The pony-men had heard of my proposed expedition and when I arrived at their feet, in a bruised and breathless ball, I was greeted with joyful acclamation. Their leader, a very old and dignified man – who in Europe would not be allowed by his daughter to go out on a showery day – was almost in tears of relief, and ordered one of the men to carry Roz across the nullah.

We were now only a mile from Basal, and this snow bridge looked a fitting climax to the day. In two places the melting glacier had already caved in, and the pony-men had placed two planks of wood – specially carried for the purpose – across each five- or six-foot-wide crevasse. Standing on the verge, one looked down into the roaring water twelve feet below and, speaking for myself, I felt most unhappy to realise that at any moment – possibly the next moment – another wedge of glacier – possibly the wedge underfoot – would detach itself and collapse into the nullah. To add to the general feeling of insecurity the three ponies were thudding over the level snow between the crevasse and the bottom of the slope and I reflected that had they been trying they could have done no more to encourage its further disintegration.

However, the men's indifference to what I regarded as extreme peril calmed me down (I hadn't yet heard that six local men were recently drowned in a similar situation) and when Roz had been carried across the nullah I remained behind to give what help I could in persuading the ponies to venture over the planks. The unfortunate animals were lathering with fright and absolutely refusing to budge. Then I had a brainwave, which it took some time to put across in sign language, though it was simply a suggestion that if the rest of the party left the scene the three unnerved ponies might follow of their own accord. So I trotted across the boards firmly pretending that I was on O'Connell's Bridge and we all climbed the other side of the glacier to the road and made off briskly. Sure enough pathetic whinnies followed us and a moment later came the clatter of hoofs on boards and within five minutes the nervous ones had rejoined the party. This incident well illustrates the very low IQ of those men, who think that by cursing and kicking an already terrified horse they can influence him to do what he dreads. Of course they considered 'Begum Sahib' a genius for suggesting the obvious! In a way my device was cruel too – giving the poor creatures the impression that they were going to be abandoned on a glacier for ever – but at least it was short-term cruelty. The rest of this entry must wait till tomorrow as I'm too tired to finish it now.

BUTIKUNDI, 22 JUNE

To continue yesterday's entry: on leaving the narrow gorge with its snow-bridge we entered the head of the famous Kagan Valley – a very lovely sight in the light of the setting sun. Here the mountains all rise greenly to grey rock summits and on their gentle slopes graze buffalo, comically draped in heavy blankets, and huge herds of goats. Basal is what we'd call a 'townland', where the tribes-people camp during the summer when they bring up their herds, and the nearest hamlet is nineteen miles away. But there is a seasonal 'hotel' where the trans-Pass caravans stop. This consists of a tiny lean-to – not high enough for me to stand upright in – roughly built of boulders and roofed with pine-branches; there are only two walls so you can imagine the cold wind shrieking through at 14,000 feet! The proprietor, a young tribesman, sleeps outside in a goatskin tent and the fire is of dung, lit in a little hole in the ground. The fresh green leaves of a local weed carpet the floor and water comes from the young Kagan that rushes deafeningly by two yards away. I'll admit this accommodation doesn't sound luxurious, but after a day such as we'd all been through it seems positively Ritzy; it's only two miles from the top of the valley and I walked there with the pony-caravan.

On arrival we sat beside the tiny fire while tea was being made – me feeling so tired that I couldn't even attempt diary-writing. But after five tin mugs of Samson-strong tea (very sweet) I came back to life and wrote by oil-lamp for the two hours it took to cook our supper of lentils and bread. Dung is excellent fuel, just like good turf, but it's slow to cook enough for six ravenous people and the *chapattis* took what felt like weeks, each one being done separately on a flat piece of iron over the fire. (There are few bakeries in Pakistan and bread is usually made at home.) But I've been long enough in the East now to have forgotten how to feel impatient, so I enjoyed the cosy peace there in the heat while outside the blue sky faded to cold green and then was quickly black and filled with a glory of golden stars. Only the rush of the river and the deep breathing of the pony-men, who had all fallen asleep while waiting for food, broke the silence.

As we were eating, an extraordinary character came in – obviously a tribal chieftain of some sort as he was laden with gold ear-rings and bracelets and fabulous silver and stone necklaces and wore rings on every finger. He stood about six foot two in his bare feet and had the oldest face I've ever seen, yet was erect and vigorous. His long black hair and beard looked odd against the wrinkles and he had very sharp but kindly brown eyes and still excellent teeth. It goes without saying that he was filthy dirty and stank to high heaven – even more than the pony-men! He had evidently come to welcome them as the first over the pass this year and there was terrific salaaming and hand-shaking all round. On arrival he disregarded me completely but then he got used to the idea and became quite friendly. After he'd gone more strong tea completed the meal, which to me was the most wonderful I've ever eaten anywhere – despite the fact that I was sitting watching the bare-handed cook stoking the fire with dung in between kneading *chapattis.* Having taken turns puffing a post-prandial hookah the men went to sleep again and I continued writing till nearly midnight, when I curled up in my bedroll which was on hire for a shilling from the proprietor but seemed astonishingly free of inhabitants. I woke at 6.30 a.m. with an awful earache, as the cold had been intense all night and I couldn't sleep with my head covered because of the smell of the bedding. Also this evening I've a rotten sore throat and snuffles – inevitable after yesterday's wetting and freezing – but that's a small price to pay for the Babusar Pass.

We left Basal at 7.30 a.m. today, after tea and *paratis* fried in *fresh* ghee, and I took it easy, covering only the nineteen miles to this village. The Kagan Valley is so beautiful that one has to stop every hundred yards to sit and look. (Anyway, sitting and looking were about all I was good for today, as my back and shoulder muscles ache dreadfully from carrying Roz.) The Kagan River widens gradually and is a most beautiful shade of green as it races in the sunshine between great, grey boulders, bursting into violent cascades of white foam at intervals. For the first six or seven miles the road switched up and down green mountainsides and I had to cross three more glaciers (one tricky, two easy) and four rock falls brought down by the thaw. These presented difficulties as they were always at high points of the road overhanging ghastly drops. (One's 'head for heights' certainly improves in this area; six months ago I'd have shuddered even to think of cycling over loose rocks and slippery mud above such ravines.) I could see again the hoof-prints of the caravan, which had left Basal at 5 a.m., and the whole region was, by yesterday's standards, quite thickly populated with nomad herdspeople, though no dwellings were visible. I saw two magnificent eagles and the air was filled all day with lark-song. What a wonderful place this world is! Here was a valley of glorious beauty yet quite unique – different from the Ghorband or Gilgit or Indus Valleys – with its scintillating snow-peaks and regal fir trees, brilliant green meadows right up to the snowline and glistening glaciers in the gullies, waterfalls tumbling and sparkling everywhere and jewel-like wild flowers, rippling bird-songs and the faint, clean aroma of some unfamiliar herb.

We arrived here at 5 p.m. to find that some half-dozen wooden shacks make up the hamlet, plus a tea-house to cater for caravans. Coming round a bend I saw down below, in a deep hollow between the hills, the camel-caravan of fifty animals camped beside the tea-house and my pony-men busily loading up with their essentials. Then, as I came towards them, I noticed the fleecy coats and brightly-coloured turbans and marvellously-embroidered waistcoats of the cameleers – there was no doubt about *their* native land. I stopped the first one and said 'Afghanistan?' and he said 'Yes, Bulola,' and I shook hands vigorously and said 'Afghanistan very good and Bulola very good' (Bulola is the village next to Bamian), and he was as pleased by the meeting as I was, and we went off arms around shoulders, Afghan style, to have tea together. Then about fifteen other Afghans arrived and I told them where I'd been in Afghanistan and we performed the Afghan ritual of gravely admiring each other's guns and knives and they told me that I must time my return to Afghanistan to coincide with the King's birthday in October, when the national game of buzkashi is played at its best in Kabul. Again, as when coming into Afghanistan from Persia, I notice the remarkable superiority of these men in both mental and physical vigour, as compared to the peasants I've been with for the past weeks. It's possible to have quite a complicated conversation with the Afghans through signs and a few words of Pushto and English, they're so very quick on the uptake.

I'm now sitting outside one of their tents writing by firelight while supper is being cooked, having ridden with two of them to a hamlet up a tributary nullah to deliver cloth. The way was level grassland and never did I think horses could move so fast; it was a glorious sensation to gallop along the valley with the setting sun lighting up the snows ahead and my horse, having had nothing to do all day, going full stretch on the smooth turf. Fortunately I didn't want to stop him, as I don't believe I could have. I've been promised a trial ride on a camel in the morning.

NARAN, 23 JUNE

After an excellent supper of goat's meat grilled over a wood-fire, and lentils and bread, I slept soundly, rolled in snug sheepskins in a circle of Afghans around a fire which we kept up all night. I was wakened by the sun coming over the mountaintops on to our faces – such beauty to open one's eyes to! The soft, bright green of grass, the dark green of towering pines, the almost luminous green of the nearby river, the pale blue of the early sky and the pure white of glaciers between sharp, rocky peaks above smooth, sloping pastures. While the breakfast-water was boiling I was given my camel ride – very short and unsweet. (1) The camel knelt down. (2) I sat on the saddle. (3) The camel stood up. (4) The camel took one step. (5) I fell off. Fortunately this was exactly what the camel-owner had expected me to do and he caught me halfway to the ground. As these are the long-legged Arabian camels, seven to eight feet tall, this was a good thing. Actually the shorter, sturdier Bactrian variety are more common in Afghanistan itself. A camel saddle is a preposterous thing, like a wooden pouffe balanced on the hump; doubtless there are ways of *not* falling off, but my Pushto was unequal to following the owner's instructions.

After breakfast two men were going on another cloth-selling expedition to three tiny hamlets away up on the wooded slopes of a mountain and on invitation I accompanied them; we used mules for the very steep, rocky paths of the forest. Then I reluctantly left my friends at 12.15 p.m., having lunched off clover, bread and chicken; I tried to give them a present of cigarettes but of course they absolutely refused to accept it.

The weather pattern has been consistent during the past few days; it remains very sunny till about 12 p.m., then the sky quickly fills with clouds, the temperature drops and light showers freshen the air. It was delicious free-wheeling down-valley this afternoon with dense green trees all around and a grey sky overhead; except for the height of the mountains and the fury of the river, I might have been at home.

There was an amusing interlude today when I turned a corner of the track and saw a party of four unmistakably English people walking towards me. My astonishment was considerable, yet it was as nothing compared with theirs when they beheld a tattered and battered European female advancing with a bicycle from the northern wilds. Even English reserve could not withstand the shock, so they stopped to unravel the mystery and then told me that they came from Delhi and were camping on the banks of the Kagan. They thoughtfully suggested that I should stop off at their camp and ask the servants to feed me, and Mrs Haddow invited me to stay with them when I arrive in Delhi and gave me their address and telephone number on the spot. The farther one travels the more one becomes aware of the extraordinary wealth of generosity and kindness that exists in the world.

After ten miles I reached this village, to which a jeep penetrates twice weekly, and was sadly back in civilisation – if one may so describe twenty wooden huts plus a PWD rest-house with no mod cons whatever. I hadn't intended stopping here but the road was blocked by a landslide miles farther on, leaving no alternative. Naran is one of Pakistan's most famous fishing centres so enthusiasts brave what they consider the horrors of the rest-house for sport's sake, and this week a delightful Karachi family are staying here – husband, wife and five children. In conversation with them this evening I again noticed what is to me a most puzzling feature of Pakistani life. Here was a man educated, intelligent and widely-read far above the average, yet he was a travelling salesman; it's extraordinary that someone of such talent should be so wasted in a country where trained brains are at a premium.

KAGAN, 24 JUNE

The Karachi family and I started off for the 'Blue Lake' at 9 a.m. and got there at 11 a.m. after a glorious climb. (There is a jeepable road but that's miles longer.) This lake seems to be a volcanic crater, a mile wide and long, and it reflects all the snow-covered peaks that surround it on three sides. There was a cloudless blue sky above the green water when we arrived so the reflections were perfect. The surrounding glaciers are now melting but remain firm enough to be quite safe for walking so we went right round the shore; then a little breeze got up and a few clouds appeared and the beauty of the water colouring was beyond words. Just as we were leaving at 1 p.m. a party of young forestry students arrived with gallons of tea in flasks – very welcome – and I spent an hour talking with them and being photographed as one of the 'strange sights' they had encountered on their excursion. (If you could see me by this stage you'd appreciate the subtle humour of that description.)

I rejoined Roz at 4.30 after a late lunch of bread and hard-boiled eggs. It's a pity the 'reward' of free-wheeling down this valley is being marred by the temperature rising every mile. But each day different beauties surround me – I've never seen such tiny butterflies as today. They look like wild flowers taken to the wing, they're so fragile and delicately coloured.

I met another Afghan camel-caravan this evening and am staying with them tonight. It's wonderful how hospitable these people are; they saw me passing and signed to me to stop and have bread and tea with them. (They bring their own flour and make much nicer bread than the locals and drinking their green tea out of the familiar little Jap-made bowls was a pleasant change from the local brew, which is exactly as we have it in Ireland – strong and milky.) They're all delighted about the border with Pakistan being open again and are full of praise for His Imperial Majesty of Iran!

KAWAI, 25 JUNE

The Afghans and I swopped household hints last night: I told them that thyme added to their goat or chicken stew would taste delicious and they told me that the bark of the walnut tree, slightly moistened and used after every meal, was better than any toothbrush and paste. It seems extraordinary that they have never used wild thyme in cooking – they loved it in last night's stew, and I loved the walnut bark, which makes the gums tingle and leaves the teeth brilliantly white. I've been wondering for months how these people have such incredibly good teeth and this must be the explanation. No matter how filthy they may be otherwise, they are most meticulous about scouring their teeth immediately after eating.

We left Kagan at 6.30 a.m. and found the road so blocked by migrant traffic, moving up the valley to summer pastures, that it took us three hours to cover six miles. The road was all downhill, but cycling remained out of the question – one simply pushed and edged one's way through dense masses of buffaloes, cows, camels, horses, mules, donkeys, jennets, goats, sheep, kids, lambs, men, women and children. Of course, every day since crossing the Top I've been meeting these caravans, but today the migration was in full swing. Fortunately all the animals are blasé, widely-travelled creatures who take Roz in their stride. It was difficult for me, and dangerous for the riders, when a bicycle appeared suddenly in those parts where machines are almost unknown, causing horses and mules to shy and buck on the verges of precipices. (Today, *I* almost shied and went over a precipice when I saw my first machine – a jeep – since leaving Chilas a week ago!)

Recently, the government, who want to plant the high pastures with young trees, proposed to the Kochis that they should settle permanently on land in the Punjab, given to them by the State: but the tribes were so devastated by the idea that President Ayub ordered it to be dropped. For at least 3,000 years, and probably longer, these people's ancestors have been on this trek – up every June, down every October – and any other way of life would be as inhuman as caging a tiger. Actually they are quite well off by Pakistani standards, with their own meat, eggs, milk and butter, and clothing from their sheep and goats. To acquire supplies of flour, tea, sugar and salt they barter their superfluous animals. An incredible amount of silver jewellery is worn by the girls, from two years old and upwards, and by the women; some of it is very ancient and all of it is beautiful. On these long treks tiny babies are carried concealed in cloths on their mothers' backs, toddlers ride on their fathers' shoulders or on one of the animals and everything above the age of four walks sturdily, like a good Kochi. Often little girls carry top-heavy loads of pots, pans and miscellaneous household goods on their heads and sometimes little boys are in sole charge of a flock of thirty or forty animals. New-born or delicate foals or calves (except camel calves who can apparently cope with life right from scratch) are tied to some animal, other than their mother, or are carried on the men's shoulders. Puppies, hens and chickens go on the buffaloes' backs; when there's a halt one sees the fowls flying down and scratching and pecking while the humans make tea and the animals eat their fodder, and then when the signal is given to start again they fly back to their moving roosts. Each kind of animal wears a different-sounding bell and the result is quite symphonic.

It was much hotter today – uncomfortably so at midday, though it's pleasant again now. I'm stopping tonight at a *very* civilised rest-house, which just stops short of having a bathroom!

BACH, 26 JUNE

We're back to Hell today, yet we are still 4,000 feet up, so what will the true plains feel like . . . This afternoon I sadly said goodbye to the Kagan, which I had seen born from out of that high and beautiful lake; it is difficult to believe that this wide brown flow is the very same river we crossed by snow-bridge. It's quite an experience to follow a river for so long, right from the source, and to see it grow every day.

Twelve miles from Babbacot I joined the Muzzafarabad-Abbottabad road which I last cycled along exactly four weeks ago today. What a change! The countryside, then so green and lovely, is now burned brown and bone dry – you could almost hear it gasping for rain. I slept for two hours in the pine-forest but was afraid to smoke there in case the slightest spark would get amongst the tinder. I'm staying tonight at the American Presbyterian Mission Hospital here with a kindly missioner and his wife.

ABBOTTABAD, 27 JUNE

At last I'm really back to civilisation. It took me nearly two hours in the bathroom to get looking like an ordinary citizen instead of a tribeswoman, and my hostess very firmly took my shirt and pants and put them into the incinerator; they were long past being restored to cleanliness by any means known to mankind. I was dressed in Pakistani costume after the bath and then went off to the bazaar to get shorts tailored; I've suffered much in the effort not to offend Muslims but the heat is now so extreme that they'll just have to endure me in shorts. I got two yards of best khaki for 5*s.* and took them to a tailor at 6 p.m. At 9.30 p.m. the expertly-tailored garment was delivered to me here and the total cost was 10*s.* Of course I'd have looked like a vulgar picture postcard if I'd worn shorts a month ago, but having lost sixteen pounds in the last four weeks I'm relatively elegant just now.

At last the monsoon seems to be breaking here. I saw my first electric storm this evening and it was a sight of such beauty that I couldn't take my eyes off the sky for a moment. Then the rain came so forcefully that no one who hasn't witnessed such a spectacle could imagine it; yet they tell me that this is only a curtain-raiser, not the real thing! Roz has gone to hospital for a new mudguard and a brakes check; the latter were almost useless today after the fearful strain of the past weeks.

14

Running Repairs

ABBOTTABAD TO LAHORE

ABBOTTABAD, 28 JUNE

I'm staying here with the family who entertained me on my previous visit to this town. As you may remember, Farhat – one of my hostess's sisters – is a doctor, which has proved fortunate since I woke with dysentery at 2 a.m. and have spent half the day lying on my bed feeling pathetic and the other half on the hop. I'm not surprised – nor is anyone else – by this development. The recent combination of filthy food and flies and heat-stroke and over-exertion was bound to do some damage somewhere; I can only thank God that I didn't collapse until I got to this delightful family, each of whom is kindness personified and all of whom had the good sense to leave me alone today to cope with my misery in a private suite in their guest-wing.

My host is one of the wealthiest men in the area, and today I'm shamelessly revelling in the luxury of his new, palatial home on the outskirts of the town. Always, of course, there is the formidable ethical problem of such wealth as this co-existing with the poverty I've shared during these past weeks – a problem which lies at the back of one's mind and occasionally stirs uneasily. But ten years ago it would have stirred more often and more vigorously; by now it seems to me that prosperity as the West knows it today and poverty on an Eastern scale are equally harmful to the soul of Man.

This morning Farhat starkly prescribed 'starvation and sulphaguanidine tablets'. This prescription has been so successful that now my insides seem to be reintegrated and I look with disfavour on the starvation clause, having had too much of that medicine lately. But obviously Farhat knows best and I'm resigned to a plate of curds for dinner.

Today I've been reflecting on the benefits bestowed by the social anonymity of a traveller 'in the wilds'. To the peasants and tribesmen here one is merely a human being – outwardly strange but fundamentally one of them – and their spontaneous acceptance and hospitality is extended with an air of full and unselfconscious equality. In contrast, how deep is the gulf between groups of human beings in our society – go into a pub in Connemara or a café in rural Italy or even a posada in the remotest part of relatively unspoiled Spain and you find it impossible to establish the same easy *rapport.* You are at once noted as a non-peasant and are therefore someone to be envied, or admired, or despised, or kept aloof from, as individual temperaments dictate. Probably you will be treated most kindly by the peasants there, but at the deepest level you are automatically isolated because you have (they imagine) more money or more education or 'better' manners than they have. So I appreciate the chance to share the people's lives here for a time without regarding myself, or being regarded by them, as an intruder. Yet I also appreciate coming back to converse among friends who are on my own wavelength.

ABBOTTABAD, 29 JUNE

Today I wandered around the town in the sedate manner befitting my convalescent condition. In fact I felt as weak as a kitten and was good for nothing but sitting and talking, which I did at length with the Irish priests who run a big boys' college here, with the Irish nurse who has recently come out to the college as matron and who very kindly presented me with a pair of sunglasses to replace those lost crossing Babusar, and with a delightful Belfast Protestant missionary and her team of assistants, who fed me judiciously at lunchtime.

The sky was cloudless again today, after the monsoon's false start, but the air has been cooled and freshened by that storm and when I returned here at 6 p.m. we spent a very pleasant couple of hours sitting on the lawn drinking iced fruit-juices.

For this family the purdah system is in a state of flux. My hostess and her three sisters – all young women – observe it in Abbottabad, yet Farhat, who has spent some years in England, where she was accompanied by her youngest sister, obviously leads a European existence when practising her profession in Lahore. The second youngest sister is also married and lives in Mansehra, where I called to see her on my way to Bach the other day. Her husband is Assistant Commissioner there and she has a very congenial lot of in-laws with whom I spent a delightful afternoon, though I had no time to record my visit in the diary that night. The young couple joined us this evening for dinner and, observing them together, I was struck yet again by the high proportion of what are clearly happy marriages resulting from the Muslim tradition of arranged matches.

To me this has been the aspect of Eastern social life most difficult to understand – though one could argue that in a diluted form the custom was, until recently, prevalent in our own society. But since contemporary Western women expect freedom to choose their own husbands, it has taken me a long time to begin to understand the Muslim women's point of view. I have had prolonged discussions on this subject with a number of educated Muslims. The arguments which they put forward have not been entirely convincing, but the harmonious atmosphere that I have experienced in so many Muslim homes leads me to believe that their arranged marriages are just as likely to succeed as what they refer to, with faint undertones of curiosity and disapproval, as 'love marriages'.

The Muslim argument in favour of their system is simple. I've asked several women (wording my query as tactfully as possible) if they didn't feel deprived of a natural and inalienable right when someone else made for them what is the most important decision in most women's lives. To this they replied, 'No. It is our business to choose partners for our children, not for ourselves.' And each of them went on to explain, in her own way, that she considered youths and girls singularly ill-equipped to take the serious responsibility of selecting a life-partner. On the other hand parents know what's needed to make a marriage tick and continue ticking and they also know their own children – possibly better than the children know themselves at the ages of sixteen or twenty. Therefore, four parents in frank consultation are likely to arrange a more lastingly satisfactory match than two hot-blooded young things who can't see the trees for the sex. The arrangements concentrate on temperamental, social and financial suitability and leave the sexual aspect to sort itself out afterwards, with the cheerful assumption that all else being equal two healthy youngsters could hardly fail to enjoy each other physically. Indeed, the majority of women with whom I spoke on the subject assured me that the pattern of their marriages had been a steady growth of love and understanding on both sides. Personally, I can't help feeling that they miss the best of life's adventures by not falling haphazardly in love after the manner of us decadent infidels; but I do now understand the psychological mechanism of their system and can see its advantages.

I also discussed this question with a number of men here, who were emphatic that as youths they would have been terrified of the responsibility of choosing a wife; this unnatural (to us) attitude underlines the extent to which our mental and emotional processes are conditioned by our environment. Yet among a certain category of men – those who have now been educated beyond the average level of their particular social class – there is a new threat to domestic bliss. In the upper class boys and girls receive comparable educations, and intellectual affinity is therefore easily assured; but those less fortunate men, who may be the only literate members of their families, often find themselves married to women who bore them as companions because of their abruptly widened mental horizons. I've met quite a few of these victims of progress, who are usually employed as petty officials in small towns where there is an almost total lack of educated society. Inevitably they seize with tragic eagerness on the opportunity to talk to foreigners, and I sometimes wonder if, despite their inherent intelligence, they wouldn't have been happier left on an educational par with their kinsmen and neighbours. Mental loneliness is a painful thing and it seems cruel for the State to open a door invitingly and then shut it in a man's face by stationing him in a remote area. Someone, of course, has to fill those posts, but surely a man with a longer tradition of education and therefore more inward resources would fit them better than a poor devil who has simply had his appetite for learning whetted by a few student years on a scholarship.

A conspicuous feature of conversation with English-speaking Muslim men is the unabashed candour of their approach to sexual matters. This sounds as though I've been having a gay time talking pornography with a series of frustrated would-be lovers, and if one wanted to be frightfully Freudian it could be said that their penchant for talking sex with European women is a sublimation of their religion-fettered libidos. Yet none of these conversations was intended as a prelude to seduction and the odd thing is that what in a Western context might be regarded as embarrassing, if not slightly shocking subjects for discussion with a male acquaintance, are here rendered comfortably clinical by the matter-of-fact manner in which they are discussed. I find this extremely interesting. For all our Amorality or New Morality or whatever one likes to call it, we Westerners are still too dogged by Puritan obsessions to be able to call a spade a spade without inwardly pausing for everyone else inwardly to recover from the shock, which makes us look slightly immature in this respect compared with Muslims.

I'm reminded now of an incident at a dinner-party in Afghanistan where I was the only woman present; for diplomatic reasons the incident was omitted from the relevant Diary-entry and it has only now recurred to me. I was sitting in the place of honour, assimilating the pilau course and doing no harm to anyone, when the fellow-guest on my right suddenly turned to me and asked in too-good English, 'Did you ever see a man naked?' Perhaps there's a stock answer to that one but I didn't know it, and the best I could do, from amidst a mouthful of rice, was to say airily, 'Of course, Greek statues and all that.' Thereafter my neighbour could be observed silently turning over in his mind the unlimited interpretations of 'all that'. But his was an exceptional approach – though one I wouldn't have missed, however unnerving his query at the time. It certainly is a curious experience to be a woman travelling alone in Muslim countries. Most of one's time is spent in the company of men only, being treated with the respect due to a woman, but being talked to man-to-man, so that in the end one begins to feel somewhat hermaphroditic.

It's now 1.40 a.m. and for the past five minutes I've been sitting with the light off watching the weird beauty of another electric storm – a spectacle that must surely have inspired much folklore in these countries. I find it eerie enough myself and could almost believe that some demon-god is regulating the display, as vast sheets of quivering blue fill the eastern sky. Even now, with my reading lamp on again, that pallid illumination is perceptible in the room.

RAWALPINDI, 30 JUNE

This morning Farhat laid down the law on the subject of me and cycling and dysentery and heat-stroke. Her lecture ended with instructions to come here by bus and go on to Lahore by train. She herself is returning today, by air, to her hospital in Lahore and I've been invited to stop there. She will then give me another check-up and pronounce on my subsequent activities. Once upon a time I would have violently resented this situation but at the moment there's nothing I want to do less than cycle to Lahore. Thus are the mighty fallen!

The journey here seemed acutely prosaic when compared with Afghan bus expeditions. A healthy vehicle containing its legal quota of passengers left Abbottabad punctually and proceeded in an orderly fashion, arriving punctually in Pindi at 4 p.m. I was travelling along this route for the third time, and as I looked forward to the pleasure of staying with Major-General Ghawas' family, and of again meeting the Aurang Zebs, who are now down from Swat, I realised that I no longer feel like a visitor to Pakistan but like an adopted citizen. Everywhere I've made good friends, and this country, of all those so far travelled through, has become a true home from home.

Beside me in the bus sat a jubilant young man returning to his village to celebrate the birth of his first son. He told me that two perfect goat kids, of uniform colour and without blemish, would be sacrificed as part of the celebrations and their meat given to the poor of the village. (It's only one kid for a girl.) I asked him how many children he would like to have and he sighed and said not more than four but it was going to be very difficult as he and his wife were both under twenty and Allah didn't approve of contraceptives. At each stop he insisted on buying me an iced fizzy-drink – I never thought the day would dawn when I'd avidly gulp such a vile potation; temperatures of 109° in the shade have unexpected side-effects.

I received a tremendous 'welcome-back' from my friends here, and was delighted to find Colonel Shah, whom I'd already met at Peshawar, Bagdada and Swat, among those present. The evening passed in the usual way – sitting on the lawn within reach of mobile electric fans, sipping fruit-juices and talking. Social life here emphasises how nearly we Westerners have lost the art of conversation. Instead of switching on the 'telly' or dashing out to a show, how pleasant it is to sit and talk quietly about the books one has read or the people one has met or the places one has seen. And surely the individual exchange of ideas with our fellow-men is more worthwhile than mute dependence on what someone else's brain has devised for our entertainment.

The grafting of British military traditions on to the Pathan way of life has been more fortunate than most such experiments; possibly because both traditions have a certain affinity to begin with. Certainly the Pakistani army officers I've met are without exception the finest type one could be privileged to know; they seem to have evolved a code embracing the best of the two worlds which moulded them. It will be interesting to see whether this code is durable enough to be transmitted successfully to the next generation.

RAWALPINDI, 1 JULY

This morning Naseem telephoned and invited me to the President's House – where she and Aurang Zeb stay on their visits to Pindi – for dinner this evening. In honour of the occasion I then took myself off to the city's leading hairdresser and spent 5*s.* instead of the usual 1*s.* 6*d.* on a devastating hair-cut which has so transformed me that I get a shock every time I pass a mirror. Next my hostess and her three daughters passed what was for them a most enjoyable afternoon, equipping me with clothes appropriate to the Presidential Presence. Admittedly my wardrobe is unequal to that demand; at the time of writing it comprises Aurang Zeb's cast-off army slacks, my new shorts and two khaki shirts. Drastic measures were undoubtedly called for, but as Begum Ghawas and her daughters came up with garment after garment I began to wonder if they need be *quite* so drastic . . . Yet the end product was worth it all – you wouldn't have recognised me! In fact the President's household is the essence of simplicity as I knew from a previous visit, but the family's pleasure on seeing me in their national costume made the afternoon's sartorial marathon seem well worth while.

President Ayub doesn't live on the grand scale of the wealthiest Pakistanis; his domestic surroundings are more like those of the average army officer, with a comfortable but plainly furnished home where good, but not exotic, food is served. The man himself impressed me as being shrewd, honest, kind, and above all, utterly sincere. However, like many strong characters who are fighting a non-stop battle against widespread evils, he possesses a steely quality which doesn't make for easy approachability and since I'm unaccustomed to consorting with Heads of States I was myself rather more tongue-tied than usual this evening.

RAWALPINDI, 2 JULY

After breakfast Aurang Zeb called and took me to a most interesting debate of the National Assembly where I was promoted from the Distinguished Strangers' Gallery to solitary glory in the President's Box! Again I was impressed by the complete freedom of speech in the Assembly. Members may criticise as bluntly as they wish the régime in general and President Ayub in particular, and many members today were doing just that. I should think that a student of politics would be fascinated by the political scene here, which shows democracy at the crawling stage, before it has found its feet and begun to toddle.

Looking around the Assembly (which included four women members) I was struck by the complexities of trying to run a country like Pakistan as a united nation. The members ranged from near-communists through liberal Muslims to fanatically orthodox Mullahs; from white-skinned Pathans through brown-skinned Punjabis to almost black-skinned Bengalis; from wealthy hereditary princes like

Aurang Zeb through moderately well-off professional men to destitute representatives of the city slums; from men who spoke flawless Oxford English through men whose grammar and pronunciation were questionable to men who could only speak pidgin-English. And in the restaurant at the 11 a.m. interval the air was chaotic with Pushto, Urdu, Bengali, Punjabi and English, while the members (clad as variously as they spoke) sat arguing over their tea or coffee. Theoretically the unifying element here should be Islam but Pakistan's years of exposure to Western influence have brought her religion to a crisis of re-interpretation, so that it tends to disrupt at least as much as it unites, while individual citizens battle to adapt it to what they believe is best for the country, or to defend it from any change.

After so many hours in the blissful coolness of the new air-conditioned Assembly building it was quite nightmarish to step out into 108° in the shade at 1.30 p.m. Aurang Zeb took me back to the President's House where Naseem, he and I lunched together and where I had my two-hour siesta before being driven off in an air-conditioned state Chevrolet to meet an Indian journalist with whom I had an appointment. Poor Roz! I have to admit that air-conditioned Chevrolets are more suitable in present temperatures.

This Kashmir deadlock is a heart-breaking muddle and somehow all such muddles are made more muddled nowadays by the politicians' new weapon of mass-communication, which doesn't give international sores a chance to heal up but keeps re-infecting them. The Indian journalist to whom I talked this afternoon was a perfect example of just how terrifyingly irresponsible journalists can be when they want to give their public only what it wishes to read – or what its rulers wish it to read – and when objective truth is therefore utterly disregarded. Of course a certain section of the Pakistani press and radio uses exactly the same tactics of distortion and deception against India.

I had dinner with the Shahid Hamids, where the Aurang Zebs were fellow-guests. It was an enjoyable evening, but all the time I felt sad underneath, because tomorrow I leave Pindi and in a few days I leave Pakistan. At midnight the Aurang Zebs drove me home and I said *au revoir* (I hope) to the best friends I have made en route.

LAHORE, 3 JULY

What a name for a city! I'm staying in Farhat's rooms in the Lady Willingdon Hospital, which is beside the busy red-light district so I now know it only needs an 's' to make it true.

The Pakistani Railways must be a charitable organisation: they took Roz and me the 170 miles from Pindi in five hours for 3*s.* 6*d.* The third-class carriage was quite comfortable, with fans and very nice fellow-travellers who, as usual, insisted on buying me so many Pepsis that I almost blew up. They also wanted to feed me the atrocious little tid-bits which are fried and sold on every platform; a fortnight ago in Gilgit I'd have given all I possessed for one of them but today my stomach somersaulted at the very sight of those greasy balls. So then they pressed me to have some of the fly-blown sweetmeats which are also hawked at each stop, and when I persisted in refusing they looked quite hurt, and one of them went off and bought me a roast chicken, to my great embarrassment. I tried to explain that I wasn't being upstage and 'memsahibish' about their sort of food, which I normally consume *ad lib.*, and that it was merely a question of my insides not being as democratic as my principles. But no one spoke English very well so the intricacies of the situation escaped them and they simply nodded and smiled and told me that the chicken was very good and sat happily watching me unhappily eating what they wouldn't dream of affording for themselves.

With every mile we travelled south the temperature rose, the flies multiplied, the dust thickened in the air and the flat landscape became more arid. We arrived here at 3 p.m., the most intolerable hour of the day, and my first impression was of a depressing dump of a city, all stinks and stenches and not to be compared with either Peshawar or Pindi. In fact Lahore is by far the most interesting of the three from architectural and historical points of view, but at the moment I'm a bit past being interested in the Higher Things of Life: I simply registered that it was even hotter than Pindi. The only thing that cheered me up, en route from the station to the hospital, was the phraseology of a young man who told me I'd find the hospital 'on the backside of the mosque'! When I did find it Farhat gave me a real Pathan welcome, but it was of necessity brief, since the staffs of these hospitals are grossly overworked. I then went to sleep until 8 p.m. – sleep being the only effective escape from this degree of heat.

LAHORE, 4 JULY

A deliciously fat mail, collected this morning, has put me in such good humour that Farhat thinks I must be getting used to the heat. On my way through the centre of the city I passed an RAC signpost saying, 'LONDON, 6,372 MILES'; it's nice to know the exact position! I'd resolved last night to be a good little tourist today and see some of the things one ought to see here, but after a ten-mile cycle to collect the mail I only wanted to lie on my charpoy under a fan, drinking *lassee* and reading and rereading my letters. It was too hot for me even to start replies; sweat ran profusely into my eyes when I sat up and dripped merrily on to the writing pad.

Then, at about 9 p.m., Farhat roused me from my not unpleasant lethargy by offering to take me to the operating theatre, where she was about to do a Caesarean. It was a most interesting spectacle and I was tremendously impressed by the cool efficiency of her team of assistants, all recently-emancipated young women in their early twenties. (Male gynaecologists are obviously not popular in the Muslim world.) Usually only spinal anaesthetics are given here as Pakistan can't afford anything else in her public hospitals; but the skill of people like Farhat more than makes up for the shortage of drugs and modern equipment. Watching the performance I even forgot the heat – though it was intensified by my mask and gown – and when at last a little black head appeared and the baby was hauled out I felt like cheering. He was a fine healthy son who roared like a lion after one look at this world – a reaction which in the present temperature I find quite understandable.

15

Out of the Saddle

LAHORE TO DELHI

BEAS, INDIA, 5 JULY

I suppose that when one has left Ireland to cycle to India the day on which one eventually cycles across that final frontier qualifies for Red Letters. Yet this evening I'm aware of no sense of triumph, elation, excitement or anything other than loneliness for Pakistan – though you may remember that on crossing the Khyber Pass I was too stricken by the parting with Afghanistan to feel any enthusiasm for Pakistan! Now it remains to be seen if a few months in India will have a similar effect; somehow I already doubt that.

Last night Farhat pronounced me fit to cycle again, providing I never cycle between 9 a.m. and 6 p.m., never cycle too far in one day, eat masses of salt and eschew too curried curries. So this morning we set off at 4.10 a.m. to reach Amritsar before the 'medical curfew'. Already it was bright and the sweepers were busy on the streets and lots of cyclists were buzzing around, although many lazy-bones still lay fast asleep on charpoys lining the pavements; it's odd to see half the population of a city sleeping in public. By 4.45 a.m. I was passing through the cantonment area where athletes were vigorously practising cricket, tennis and volleyball. Lahore is such a huge city that it took me an hour's fast cycling to get clear of it and we didn't reach the border until 6.15 a.m. Here there were virtually no formalities to be gone through, yet it was 7.30 before I'd finished drinking the inevitable tea and talking to three delightful Customs officers about my happy days in their country. Then I plucked up courage to go, and said my last *Salaam Alaikum* (God go with you); it will be too bad if I forget myself and use that greeting on this side! I'm trying hard not to be biased, but it's the objective truth that my reception at the Indian Customs post, though very polite, was markedly cold and formal. After the warmth and apparent joy with which strangers are welcomed at every Muslim Customs post I've passed, this one left me feeling slightly forlorn.

The Punjab is the most boring terrain I've ever cycled through. My only diversion today was the bird-life; a fascinating selection of beautiful unknowns were to be seen in every direction. On crossing the frontier, the two most obvious changes are the number of women in evidence and the comparative nudity of the men. Your average Muslim wouldn't dream of showing a knee, so it was quite startling to find myself suddenly surrounded by hundreds of loin-clothed bodies.

Some ten miles from the border I stopped for a cigarette and began to learn the ABC of travelling in India. I was sitting under a tree full of tailor-birds' nests, watching waterfowl fishing in a stagnant pond, when a Hindu peasant came walking along the road carrying two brass jars of milk balanced on his shoulders. I smiled and said '*Nemuste*', but instead of returning my greeting and passing on his way *à la* Muslim, he put down his gallons, came and sat beside me and tried to squeeze my arm while making what were obviously (even in Punjabi) improper suggestions. Knowing he couldn't understand English, I said what I felt – 'Go to hell'. So he went; not to hell, but off down the road. The motto seems to be that one curbs one's natural mateyness and refrains from greeting stray Hindus – which does not make life any more pleasant. Happily, this is the Sikh State, so I have them as buffers while I readjust; many Europeans and almost all Muslims distrust the Sikhs intensely on various counts and have warned me to beware of them but so far I find them very helpful, courteous and friendly.

Amritsar, twenty-three miles from the border, is the chief city of 'Sikhdom', but because of the heat I didn't stop to explore it; on my return in the cooler weather I hope to do my duty by the Golden Temple. About three miles beyond Amritsar I was settling down to have my siesta under a wayside tree when suddenly a dust-storm began. This sounds dire but it was in fact an enormous relief, because the gale-force wind was northerly and almost cool. Taking advantage of it I pedalled on through stinging whirls of dust that reduced visibility to about twenty yards, but even this seemed a cheap price to pay for the sudden drop in the temperature. Because of the wind we covered eighty-nine miles today, reaching this little village where I'm staying with the family of the local Sikh Superintendent of the Punjab Armed Police.

Sikh boy-children and adolescents are a trifle disconcerting; a religious rule against cutting hair means that their long locks, often tied in top-knots with coloured ribbons, give the impression that the country is populated almost exclusively by girls. The good looks of the race are quite astonishing, yet somehow not altogether pleasing. Unlike the proudly handsome Afghans, whose features are made additionally impressive by the spirit within, Sikh good looks are of a conventional, rather film-star type; they are reported to have the most regrettable effects on some Western women but I can't see the remains of my virtue being undermined here! Yet they are a fine race of people, tall and well-built, in complete contrast to their weedy, vegetarian Hindu neighbours. Also, of course, they are very astute businessmen and very unscrupulous money-lenders. One of their racial characteristics is a streak of mechanical genius; I'm told that most Indian bus and truck drivers in every state are Sikhs.

So far I haven't noticed any of the dire poverty one expects in India; but then the Punjab is the country's most prosperous state – partly because of its natural resources and partly because Sikhs are in general more on the ball than Hindus. An FAO official I met today told me that their work in the Punjab is much more productive than elsewhere in India because of greater and more intelligent co-operation from the locals.

However, if the poverty of India has not yet hit me the smells of India certainly have; one of these days I'll lose my grip on the situation and be forced off Roz to vomit by the wayside. Maybe that's one reason why I've lost my appetite so completely; even after today's cycle I couldn't look at food this evening though I haven't had a bite since 4 a.m. I just drink, drink, drink – *lassee* and salt and lemon and salt and tea and salt and mango-juice and sugar – glass after glass after glass.

SIRHIND, 6 JULY

We only covered fifty-eight miles today but even that nearly killed me. At 11 a.m. I took refuge in a dak bungalow for tea and a siesta and while the tea was being made I lay on the sitting-room floor under the fan and went to sleep. A few minutes later a piercing scream wakened me: the *chowkidar*'s wife had come in and, not being used to the spectacle of Europeans slumbering on floors, had decided that I was a corpse! Actually she wasn't very far wrong; this sun acts like a sleeping-drug on me and today I felt as if I'd had an overdose. You don't realise how exhausting it is while cycling on a level road but when you stop the yawning begins and you just want to lie down where you are and go into a coma.

Really, this Punjab is the most dire thing that ever happened. The landscape is flatter than Belgium, even more overpopulated and enlivened only by thousands of cattle, the majority at a most gruesome stage of emaciation. I feel as I did during the myxomatosis epidemic at home, when I carried a hammer around in my saddlebag and killed rabbits by the score every week; but it would hardly be politic to go along on Indian roads shooting cattle. I'm all for coming to terms with other people's religious angles yet it's exceedingly difficult to have patience with this cow worship; one has to see it in action to appreciate its full brutality and stupidity. But I suppose what we describe as the Hindus' cruelty should more properly be called 'insensitivity to physical suffering', and should not be regarded as an absolute yardstick by which to measure their national character. Hindu philosophy makes no discernible attempt to achieve that natural balance between the spiritual and the material which we consciously or unconsciously inherit as part of our traditional ethic, and to a people nurtured on such a philosophy the physical sufferings of both men and animals are of far less importance than they are to us. What interests me – although such a speculation may seem naïve to the learned – is whether the Hindu chicken or the apathetic egg comes first. In other words, did Hinduism encourage a resigned acceptance of material privations of every kind because some opiate had to be given to the relevant masses, or did these masses cease to strive for a reasonable degree of material well-being because Hinduism represented it as unworthy of Man's endeavour – or, in the case of the Untouchables, as a categorical impossibility? This brings us to the caste system, of which I've obviously had no experience yet, beyond a few brief discussions. These give me the impression that the sheer impracticability of upholding it in a modern city is destroying it throughout urban societies but that it still flourishes in rural communities, though possibly in a less virulent form than previously.

Then – to continue my jaundiced list of Punjabi abominations – there's the food . . . Curries are one thing but the local messes, that taste entirely of chillies, are quite another. And they even put the dratted stuff in your lemon-drink if you don't watch it – for alleged medicinal reasons. (Of course this also applies in the Pakistani Punjab, where unfortunate Pathan immigrants, like Farhat, simply can't touch the regional dishes and have to prepare their own food.) I find it quite impossible to swallow the average meal here – though today I was ravenous and tried hard – because of the acute burning pain in my mouth and throat, however much cold water I drink between swallows. Looking at it the other way round I pity the unfortunate Indian immigrants in Europe or America, who find our food not only tasteless but positively nauseating.

The little towns and villages along my route today were just smelly conglomerations of mongrel buildings – neither Eastern nor Western – inhabited by people who were on the whole unfriendly, unhelpful and of an unintelligence surpassing even that of the Persians. However, their unfriendliness has nothing to do with me being mistaken for a British traveller; already I've observed the almost total lack of anti-British feeling, which I surmise is not unconnected with their religious teaching. Several times already I've been assured that the average Indian harbours no resentment towards Britain for two reasons, which together strike a faintly comic note. The first reason is that Britain has done so much good for India and the second reason is that their religion inculcates the suppression of resentment. (I'll leave you to sort that one out for yourselves.) As an Irishwoman, I find myself having a curiously mixed reaction to this magnanimity. On the one hand I admire it and admit we could do with a bit more of it in Ireland, but on the other hand, being of good rebel stock and *not* a Hindu, I tend to despise it, having the strong conviction that no amount of good done to a country by a conqueror can quite compensate for the loss of national freedom and the dignity that goes with it. Yet in India's case it is a very moot point whether either freedom or dignity existed throughout the subcontinent in the centuries immediately preceding the British epoch. Incidentally, on almost every occasion yesterday and today when an Indian asked my nationality and I replied 'Irish', the response was, 'Ah! de Valera's country. He is a great man!' Whereupon I grinned all over my face and said, 'Yes indeed – a very great man.' It's nice to know that on at least one point I'm going to be in harmony with the majority of Indians! It's also nice to be in a country where the word Ireland conveys something; in most places en route it was impossible to convince the average citizen that Ireland was not my mispronunciation of either Iceland or Holland. And the occasional erudite individual who had heard of it usually remarked brightly, 'Ah, yes, part of Britain', which was infinitely worse than being a mispronunciation of Holland! I've had great fun at various points along the line speaking sentences in Irish for the delectation of the locals, and my passport has been scrutinised more often as a sample of Irish script than as an official document. Which reminds me of a philologically fascinating item I acquired a few hours ago: counting up to ten in Hindi is so like counting up to ten in Irish that even I mastered it in less than three minutes!

Ever since crossing the border our way has been lined by ruined mosques, burned and bombarded in many cases and providing a terrible monument to the berserk savagery which prevailed in this area at the time of Partition. Many of their walls are now derisively plastered with crudely sexy film advertisements that no Muslim country would allow inside its frontiers. Others of these once beautiful buildings have been converted into stables or cafés or, if small, into private dwellings; it reminds one of the fate of some Russian churches. All over this region I've been conscious again of the helpless anger evoked while cycling through the First World War battlefields of Northern France, where the aura of the futile wastage of human life has not yet been dissipated by time.

Having slept today from 12 p.m. to 5 p.m. I now feel inconveniently alert at 12 a.m.! Obviously the thing to do from now on is to cycle by night.

It was only when I crossed the frontier yesterday and saw the number of tractors in use here that I registered having seen none (apart from that Persian village) since leaving Bulgaria. Splendid progress is being made in re-afforestation throughout this area and thousands of young trees are thriving by the roadside. Incidentally, this grand trunk road from Peshawar to Calcutta via Delhi is the oldest highway in India, having been built by Akbar four hundred years ago. Its metalled surface is very well kept, considering the volume of heavy traffic, but the standard of driving is appalling and I cycle in constant expectation of a premature demise. The number of cycles, both in Pakistan and here, is astronomical: even the rickshaws are tricycles, with a little covered wagon for two behind. A thing that humbles me, speaking as a moderately proficient cyclist, is the skill with which Indians contrive to pedal a cycle through a densely-thronged street with an absolutely staggering load attached to both the rider and his machine. What in Ireland would be considered a fair load for a donkey is here a fair load for a cyclist, which makes one wonder if the Indians are as weedy as they look. But then a horrifying percentage of them do die in their forties of heart diseases. It still seems odd to see women cycling all over the place – and even odder to see husbands and wives walking along the streets together or sitting chatting in eating-houses. Of course these would be less common sights in the Hindu states as Hinduism adopted the purdah system when the Muslims were the ruling power; at first it was merely a status symbol in emulation of the ladies of the Royal Court, but I'm told it's now a feature of everyday life in many village communities.

If the monsoon doesn't break soon I'll go mad; however grim the rains are they can't be as bad as this – or so I like to believe. One must have some comforting thoughts.

NEW DELHI, 7 AND 8 JULY

What a topsy-turvy life this weather drives one to! We left Sirhind at 4.20 a.m. yesterday and as the sky was still overcast I kept going till 11 a.m., by which time we'd covered sixty miles, with frequent pauses for tea-drinking, as however overcast it is the similarity to hell remains marked. In one of my tea-houses a young and very moronic police constable took me for one of the two English girls who recently disappeared en route from Delhi to Lahore.

Perhaps it's the heat souring my sweet nature, but I like the Punjab less every day. The inhabitants' chief occupation seems to be squatting watchfully beside fresh cow-pats waiting for the sun to dry them to the point where they can be picked up and kneaded into shape for use as fuel when they're fully dried. I realise that this sight should move me to pity and compassion but somehow, in my present mood, it simply adds a final touch of squalor to the whole scene.

I slept at a dak bungalow from 11.30 a.m. to 5 p.m. and then set off again, having decided to take advantage of a full moon and travel through the night. Lots of crazy traffic kept my nerves permanently taut en route as half the population were also employing my tactics. I know now why the top of every Indian bus bristles with cycles: the owners go somewhere by bus during the day and cycle back during the night. However, this national habit of nocturnal travelling means that tea- and eating-houses remain open indefinitely, so I was able to refuel at will. I notice that Indian tea is of an extraordinarily poor quality, the best being exported, and as I'm a China tea addict anyway its only useful purpose here is to convey sugar to the system. But even for this it's not very successful as sugar is scarce in the Punjab – and strictly rationed in some other states because of an artificially created shortage attributed variously to political chicanery on someone's part and to the export of sugar to America in lieu of Cuban supplies. The result is that a nasty-tasting derivative of cane-sugar is used in many tea-houses.

An odd thing happened during one pause, when a truck driver offered me £28 in rupees for my watch! It's possible that he intended to swindle me with forged notes, but more likely that the offer was genuine, imported goods being at a premium here. Had this watch not been my father's, I'd have been tempted to do a deal, and may yet sell my camera (illegally) as all the photographs taken so far are worthless.

By the way, I forgot to mention that in Amritsar, two hours after I'd crossed the frontier, Roz's lamp was stolen. This was the first theft, apart from those cigarettes in Persia, since I left home. And yesterday five one-rupee stamps were swiped off the sitting-room table in a dak bungalow while I went to the lavatory.

Last night's run was by far my most enjoyable cycle since we left the Kagan Valley; the level plain, transformed by brilliant moonlight, looked quite beautiful. We'd covered the 104 miles to Delhi by 5.30 a.m., averaging a steady fifteen miles per hour on the flat road, and it was already quite bright when we entered the city. I felt that this was not the most appropriate hour to insert myself into the Haddow household – though knowing the Haddows as I do now I've no doubt they would have taken my inopportune arrival in their stride – so I curled up on the pavement outside Old Delhi Railway Station and slept there for an hour, with my head and shoulders on Roz's back wheel, among a multitude of slumbering Indians.

We must have gone astray somewhere on the outskirts, because we should have come directly into New Delhi, and when I woke I had quite a job to find my destination on Janpath, a mysterious boulevard which I'm secretly convinced runs in sixteen different directions, though the Haddows assure me that it goes in a straight line. Anyway, I kept finding myself on sections of it which were never the right section, and in the course of my disorganised peregrinations I saw enough of New Delhi to know I'm going to like it, despite its inevitable atmosphere of being a 'half-breed' city.

The Haddows, who have lived here for over thirty years and describe themselves as being among Delhi's Ancient Monuments, are the exact antithesis to the conventional picture one has of the British in India. Mr Haddow is a dentist, and having put down roots here they elected to remain on after Partition accepting their new status with a most laudable regard for India as a nation, yet not making any crackpot attempts to lose their own national identity. It's surprising how few of the old British ruling caste have had the grace to adapt thus to changing circumstances.

NEW DELHI, 9 AND 10 JULY

I seem to have recently developed the habit of one day entering people's homes as a guest and by the next day being metamorphosed into an invalid. Yesterday morning I woke feeling slightly peculiar but went to the new Diplomatic Enclave before lunch – partly on business and partly to see its proliferation of modern architectural curiosities. Allergic as I am to most modern architecture, I must admit that some of these buildings are a joy to behold. At the wish of the Indian Government, most Diplomatic Missions to Delhi have built or are building new Embassies in a special area allotted for the purpose and I couldn't help wondering if their general attractiveness was not partly due to the absence of older buildings near by. So often it's the conflict presented by the juxtaposition of old and new structures that numbs one's appreciation of contemporary design. But I wondered too if it was really necessary to expend such vast sums of money on such sumptuous Embassies in a country as poor as India is; on the part of socialist countries especially this seems an irrational acquiescence to the present violent contrast between wealth and poverty.

As I was cycling back to the Haddows' at midday I was suddenly attacked by the most violent belly-ache I've ever suffered and during the afternoon I began to run a temperature. However, thanks to Mrs Haddow's good care it was down again by midnight and the belly-ache had also subsided, so I slept quite well. But today my temperature has been fluctuating and I've stayed in bed so I have nothing to report – a day in bed in New Delhi is like a day in bed anywhere else.

Later. This evening I've been discussing my future plans with Mrs Haddow and we agree that cycling on the plains will have to be counted out between now and November. The spirit is willing *but* . . . ! So tomorrow, with Mrs Haddow's help, I shall look for some form of voluntary work here in India to keep me happy until Roz and I can get going again.

List of Kit

CLOTHES WORN AT THE START

1 woollen vest
1 pair of woollen ankle-length underpants
1 pair of gabardine slacks
1 pair of waterproof trousers
2 heavy sweaters
1 Viyella shirt
1 gabardine wind-cheater
1 woollen balaclava helmet
1 skiing cap
1 pair of leather fur-lined gauntlets

CHANGE OF CLOTHES

1 woollen vest
1 pair of woollen ankle-length underpants
1 Viyella shirt

TOILET ARTICLES

1 bar of soap
1 face-cloth
1 hand-towel
1 toothbrush
1 tube of toothpaste

MEDICAL SUPPLIES

3 tubes of insect repellent cream
100 Chlorinate tablets (for water purification)
1 ounce of potassium permanganate (against snake bite)
1 dozen Acromycin capsules

1 tin of Elastoplast
100 Aspirin
100 Paludrin tablets (against malaria)
6 tubes of sunburn cream

BOOKS

Nehru's *History of India*
William Blake's Poems (Penguin edition)

INCIDENTALS

1 .25 automatic pistol
4 rounds of ammunition
12 Biro pens
6 notebooks
4 maps
1 cycling cape
1 camping knife
1 Thermos flask
1 mug
Passport
1 money belt
£300 in traveller's cheques

ROZ'S SPARES

1 tyre
1 inner tube
1 lamp-battery
4 links for the chain
1 brake cable
3 puncture repair outfits
1 pump connection

Total expenditure from 14 January 1963 to 8 July 1963 – £64 7*s*. 10*d*.

Index

ALSO BY DERVLA MURPHY IN SPEAKING TIGER

Where the Indus is Young: A Winter in Baltistan

'Such is the author's love of travelling and of this untouched wilderness, that the lasting impression left by this book is one of sheer joy.'
—*Colin Thubron, Sunday Telegraph*

'It is her real reverence for natural beauty that gives her writing its special quality…Dervla Murphy is a writer one should be profoundly grateful for: her books are so much more than traveller's tales.'
—*Daily Telegraph*

One winter in the mid-1970s, Dervla Murphy, her six-year-old daughter Rachel and Hallam, a hardy mule, walked into Baltistan close to Pakistan-held Kashmir—the frozen heart of the Western Himalayas. For three months they travelled along the perilous Indus Gorge and into nearby valleys, making a mockery of fear, trekking through the forbidding Karakoram mountains and lodging with the Balts, who farm one of the remotest regions on earth. Despite the hardship, Dervla never forgot the point of travel, retaining enthusiasm for her magnificent surroundings and using her sense of humour to bring out the best in her hosts, who were often locked into the melancholic mood of mid-winter.

This hair-raising, quirky and vivid account of their adventure is a classic of travel writing.

ALSO BY DERVLA MURPHY IN SPEAKING TIGER

On a Shoestring to Coorg: An Experience of Southern India

'Dervla Murphy is the best kind of traveller: observant, high-spirited, open-minded, and impervious to discomfort...[Her] keen appreciation of natural beauty makes the tiny province of Coorg appear as an earthly paradise.'
—*Sunday Telegraph*

'One of Miss Murphy's most considerable gifts is the ability to choose, get into, live in—and take us back to—places where the world is as it was and probably ever shall be. She is a connoisseur of lost Arcadias.'
—*Times Literary Supplement*

'A travel writer of rare heart and freshness.'
—*The Observer*

One of the world's great travel writers, Dervla Murphy, and her young daughter, Rachel—with little money, no taste for luxury and few concrete plans—meander their way slowly south from Bombay to the southernmost point of India, Cape Comorin, in 1973. Interested in everything they see, but only truly enchanted by people, they stay in fishermen's huts and no-star hotels, travelling in packed-out buses, on foot and by boat. But instead of pressing ever onwards, they double back to the place they liked most, the hill province of Coorg, and settle down to live there for two months. In this book, Dervla Murphy creates an extraordinarily affectionate portrait of these cardamom-scented, spiritually and agriculturally self-sufficient highlands.